hoosier hysteria

hoosier hysteria

A FATEFUL YEAR IN THE CROSSHAIRS
OF RACE IN AMERICA

MERI HENRIQUES VAHL

SHE WRITES PRESS

Published July 17, 2018
Printed in the United States of America
Print ISBN: 978-1-63152-365-6
E-ISBN: 978-1-63152-366-3
Library of Congress Control Number: 2017963319

For information, address:
She Writes Press
1563 Solano Ave #546
Berkeley, CA 94707

Interior design by Tabitha Lahr

She Writes Press is a division of SparkPoint Studio, LLC.

Names and identifying characteristics have been changed to protect the privacy of certain individuals.

For Chips and Neal, and Isabel,
and in loving memory of Mildred Holmes

prologue

"Hoosier Hysteria" is the term the people of Indiana have coined to describe their almost fanatic enthusiasm for the sport of basketball. For me, however, the expression has come to represent something entirely different: the turmoil I witnessed during the 1963–'64 school year at Indiana University.

Back then, Indiana was on the brink of a social revolution that was already sweeping through the rest of the country—a movement that questioned traditional conservative values and was therefore seen by some as a threat to the American Way of Life.

In the early 1960s, long before such global issues as ecology, the nuclear arms race, and our right to intervene in the political affairs of other nations became commonplace concerns, the subject of contention was civil rights. And although we now take it for granted, it was then a disturbing new development that college campuses all across the country were beginning to serve as lightning rods for controversy, places where conflicting philosophies met head-on, sometimes with disastrous results.

At Indiana University, the reaction to these changes was what I will always think of as Hoosier Hysteria.

chapter 1: arrival

"Are you next?"

At least, that's what I might have heard.

But I was fogbound, lost in a daydream in which I was reliving my recent and apparently miraculous escape from New York and my difficult family . . .

Arising before dawn after hours of restless tossing, then sleep-walking through my early morning routine in a weird state of hyper-exhausted excitement that lent an aura of trance-like unreality to everything I beheld.

Watching the familiar faces of my father, mother, and kid sister fade into anonymity against the gray backdrop of the Idlewild Airport terminal, and striding resolutely away toward the exit gate like a latter-day Orpheus, afraid to turn back for fear that this impossible moment might suddenly dissolve into a heart-breaking mirage.

Fidgeting through a tedious plane flight—seamless segue to the interior of a Greyhound bus, where, motion-rocked and drugged into a semi-slumber by an unsavory cocktail of human sweat mixed with diesel fumes, I endured a mind-numbing interlude as mile after mile of flat midwestern farmland scrolled past the windows with hypnotic regularity, like endlessly-repeating wallpaper.

And at last: climbing stiffly from the bus into a leafy green and limestone oasis, anticipating relief, only to be assaulted by a stupefying blast of heat and humidity. Heart-flutter of confusion as I struggled to get my bearings—standing, bewildered, amidst the steadily growing pile of trunks and boxes the driver was extracting from the bowels of his bus as pedestrians streamed by.

And somehow—eventually—finding my destination, Morrison Hall, where I joined a crowd of new arrivals, all of us packed into the lobby like a herd of restless, slow-moving cattle . . .

"ARE YOU NEXT?" the voice repeated, this time loud enough to jolt me back to the present.

Startled, I looked up.

Directly in front of me was a sturdy oak table—(*"It's the registration desk, Stupid!"* a scornful inner voice that sounded suspiciously like my mother's informed me)—and on the far side of this barrier sat three women, all of them eyeing me expectantly.

Behind me—a hasty backward glance confirmed this—stretched a disorganized line of strangers: young women accompanied by attentive escorts who must certainly be their parents. And although each face wore an identical mask of bored resignation, judging from the intense buzz of whispered conversations, there was excitement simmering just beneath the surface.

Surely I should still be back there among them, daydreaming the afternoon away.

However, all evidence seemed to indicate otherwise.

Reluctantly, I returned my attention to the ladies behind the table. "Were you speaking to me?"

"I most certainly was!" It was the oldest, the one in the middle, who answered.

She radiated dignified authority, from the iron-gray hair that was skinned back from her unsmiling face, to the square black bifocals with their long silver chain, to the masculine cut of her tweed suit, which emphasized all the harsh, bony angles of her body. Ramrod-straight posture suggested a no-nonsense personality, someone who was accustomed to having things done her way.

"I . . . I'm sorry," I blurted out, painfully aware that a blush was staining my cheeks. Criticism, however familiar, never failed to sting.

"Then don't just stand there gawking! Step forward, young lady—that's right—and speak up. Who are you and where are your parents?"

My cheeks grew even hotter. "My parents. Well actually, they ahhh . . . they ummm . . . they're not here."

"I beg your pardon!"

I tried to smile, but my mouth twisted into something that didn't feel at all right. "That's right. I came alone."

"Impossible! Our new girls are always accompanied by their parents. It's the rule." She glared at me, as if expecting my parents to suddenly materialize out of thin air at her command.

I gritted my teeth and kept my mouth shut.

"Well, where are they?" she insisted.

It was the one question I'd hoped she wouldn't ask.

And what was she going to do when she realized that I wasn't going to answer it? Would she tell me to go back home and not return unless I brought my parents?

Could she do that?

The silence stretched on.

Finally—apparently understanding that I wasn't going to respond—she turned to her companions, a frown distorting her otherwise handsome features, and gestured them into a fiercely hissed private debate that made me think of angry bees.

Freed from her intense scrutiny, I stole another furtive peek back the way I had come, licking suddenly dry lips, uncomfortably aware that I was hemmed in to the point of claustrophobia by a murmuring gaggle of teenage girls, each firmly anchored in this time and place by the weighty presence of her parents. And here I was, cast up like so much human flotsam on the distant shores of this dim Gothic vault of a room, where unfamiliar accents echoed like sirens' songs in my ears.

Despite the stifling heat, I shivered. What was to become of me?

Suddenly, as abruptly as it had begun, the women's conference ended and my interrogator's fierce gaze returned to challenge me.

She cleared her throat. "I hope you realize that this is highly irregular. Your presence here today, unchaperoned, goes against everything our school stands for." Her eyes blazed with righteous indignation. "Your parents have been extremely negligent: they are responsible for your well-being, yet they have obviously failed to provide for it. I cannot imagine what they were thinking when they permitted you to come here alone."

I knew exactly what my parents had been thinking, but it was information I would never willingly divulge—at least, not to her and certainly not under these circumstances.

"We are required to meet certain standards." My nemesis's expression grew ever more stern. "In fact, we insist upon it."

This was it: back to New York. So much for my Great Escape.

"I . . . I'm sorry," I stammered, blinking back tears. "I—"

"However," she droned on over my attempted apology, "since you've come so far and because I have the authority to do so, I have decided to go ahead and register you anyway."

A gasp of sheer relief burst from my lips, and I caught a glimpse of what might have been pity fleeting across her face.

But after this momentary sign of weakness, the woman immediately looked away, transferring her attention to the tidy stack of papers that lay on the table before her—and for the next several moments she bent over them, seemingly engrossed in the task of reorganizing them into what was, if possible, even more precise order.

When at last she looked up, it was to address me in a clipped, extremely formal tone of voice, as if she were reciting from a script. "Welcome to Indiana University, and welcome to Morrison Hall. I am Mrs. Brown, the supervisor of this dormitory."

I could feel the knots of tension in my neck and shoulders begin, ever so slightly, to ease. Apparently the worst was over.

"This"—gesturing to the pudgy little woman in a flower print dress who was seated to her right—"is my assistant, Miss Smalley."

Silver curls bobbing around her chubby face, her companion tittered a nervous hello.

"And this is Miss Bell, counselor for the freshman girls. She is here to help if you have any problems with your schoolwork or with acclimating to life at the university."

Unlike her dowdy counterpart, Miss Bell was stylishly dressed in a navy blue suit with bright red piping and a ruffled white blouse. Dark-haired and twenty-something, she wore a great deal more makeup than I thought was attractive. Her crimson lips parted in a gooey smile as she examined me with undisguised interest, and when she spoke I heard an utterly familiar yet completely unexpected nasal New Jersey twang. "Yes, do come see me any time. Feel free to chat about whatever's bothering you. I know how confusing freshman life can be."

"We hope you will come to think of Miss Bell as a substitute mother," Mrs. Brown thought fit to add.

I struggled to suppress a nervous snicker. Miss Bell was far too young to be anyone's mother, especially mine, and she was obviously a pussycat in comparison to my own contentious parent.

But I didn't tell them so. Instead, I silently exulted: *I did it! I made it here on my own, and they aren't going to send me back!* And for the first time, I admitted to myself that until that very moment I hadn't really believed that my plan to leave home could possibly succeed.

"Well, now that you know who we are," Mrs. Brown was saying, "why don't you tell us your name?"

"Oh, sure. It's Meri—Meri Henriques."

"How unusual!" Her haughty demeanor was definitely thawing. "I'm afraid you'll have to spell that for us."

As I did so, her two assistants began shuffling through a pile of documents, searching, I supposed, for whatever information the school might already possess about me.

Meanwhile, Mrs. Brown was chattering on: "A *very* unusual name. It doesn't sound American. Are you foreign, Dear? Is that why your parents aren't with you?"

Her question made my stomach seize up all over again. It wasn't her suggestion that I might be foreign—although I did sense a definite tinge of xenophobic disapproval in her voice—but rather because her curiosity was leading us back to the dreaded topic of my parents.

"I'm from New York," I hastened to say, hoping to deflect

13

her question. "Although I suspect some people might think that's a foreign country."

No one even cracked a smile in response to my rather feeble attempt at humor. But instead of letting the subject die a natural death, which was what I would certainly have preferred, I found myself blurting out, "Actually, my parents didn't come because they knew I'd be okay on my own. After all, it *is* pretty expensive, traveling all the way here, even for one person." And then I held my breath, waiting to see how Mrs. Brown would react.

"It certainly must be," she agreed, apparently willing to accept this half- or perhaps even quarter-truth.

Just then, Miss Bell saved me from making any further awkward confessions by requesting the medical forms I'd brought from home. Unfortunately, these documents were very much the worse for wear: while standing in line, I had been absentmindedly rolling and unrolling them, venting nervous energy. The resulting cylinder now resembled nothing so much as a battered, slightly soggy mailing tube.

"Sorry." Cheeks burning, I held out the mangled papers.

With an ill-concealed look of disgust, Miss Bell claimed my much-abused offering, then handed me a registration card. "Sign here." She pointed with a perfectly manicured, blood-red fingernail. "I'll explain more about this tonight, at your dorm orientation meeting."

I glanced over at the third woman, expecting some equivalent request, but the drab Miss Smalley was oblivious to our transactions; instead, she continued to paw eagerly through her own set of papers. I seemed to recall, somewhere back in the mists of my daydream-induced fog, that I might have overheard her giving the girl ahead of me a room assignment.

Meanwhile, Mrs. Brown resumed our discussion of my origins as if nothing had intervened. "New York!" she mused. "That *is* a long way to travel, especially on your own. You must be a very brave girl."

"Oh, not really," I protested. "I just knew that, one way or another, I had to get away from . . ." My voice trailed off.

This was the closest to the truth I had yet come in our brief encounter.

But Mrs. Brown continued on, unaware that I had almost blurted out an important admission about my personal history. "In fact," she was saying, "most of our girls come to us from within the state. You see, despite our university status, we like to think of ourselves as a down-home country school. Now I realize you girls from the East Coast are often surprised by this, but in fact we—"

Someone gasped.

My eyes flew to Miss Smalley, who had until now been perfectly silent. Her face was chalk-white and she stared, goggle-eyed, at a piece of paper that was clutched in her shaking hands.

"Oh, no!" she quavered. "This is dreadful!"

"Really, Miss Smalley! How many times have I warned you never to interrupt when I'm—"

"But Mrs. Brown—"

"That is enough!"

"Mrs. Brown!"

Were those actually tears in Miss Smalley's eyes?

"What is it?"

"Meri Henriques is in room 312!"

"Which is no reason to barge in on—"

"Room 312!" Miss Smalley insisted. "That means her roommate is Katherine Gates."

Slowly, like a trio of cheap wind-up dolls, all three faces swiveled in my direction. And each face wore an identical expression of disbelief and horror.

For an instant I felt nothing—and then my heart began to pound, and suddenly I was having trouble breathing. "What? Is . . . is something . . . wrong?" was all I could manage to squeak out.

No one answered; they just stared.

It was as if each of them had in a single instant been granted her own personal glimpse of the innermost circle of Dante's Inferno. Or Armageddon.

But why? Was it something I'd said?

Like a mouse in a maze, my mind raced in panicky circles, around and through our recent conversation, searching in vain for a clue—any clue—something that would explain this disastrous turn of events.

"What's wrong?" I whispered.

Still no response.

I studied their faces, sensing their fear.

Of what?

Certainly not of me!

A chill shivered down my spine.

In a frantic gestalt, my thoughts leapt to Katherine Gates: the girl who was destined to be my roommate. Somehow there had to be a connection . . . After all, I reasoned, until this latest development these women had been fairly friendly—at least, once we'd gotten past our initial awkward start.

So who was Katherine Gates?

The mere mention of her name (or was it her name in conjunction with mine?) seemed to strike terror in the hearts of these seemingly omnipotent women. Obviously she was someone important—someone they had to please.

But why? What kind of power could a mere college coed hold over three such formidable adults?

Abruptly, my anxious mind conjured up a highly improbable explanation: months earlier, when I had filled out the school's housing application, I had stated that I had no preference as to roommate—that anyone would be acceptable. Suppose Katherine was more particular? And suppose, like me, she hadn't been consulted about who her roommate would be? In that case, if she was extremely important and exceptionally fussy, these women might very well be worried, particularly if they suspected she wouldn't approve.

But why would they think that? Our conversation had only lasted a few minutes, scarcely long enough for them to have formed any kind of opinion—either positive or negative—of my personality.

Could they really have decided this quickly?

Would Katherine?

I stifled a sob.

Abruptly, as if someone had just fired off a shotgun behind their backs, the women jolted into action, all of them talking at once.

"Oh dear, what are we going to do?" Miss Smalley groaned in a barely audible whisper.

"Yes, what should we do?" Miss Bell echoed. "We can't send her up there alone. It wouldn't be right . . ." She said this even as her eyes begged Mrs. Brown to disagree.

At which point Mrs. Brown seemed to rally. Drawing herself up even straighter in her chair, she announced, "You are quite right, Miss Bell: it would be very wrong of us to make her face this alone." Improbably, she sighed. "In any case, I wouldn't like to create a situation where someone could later accuse us of having failed to do our duty, or of not having tried our best to make this work out."

What on earth were they talking about?

"Ummm . . ." I began in a shaky voice. "Excuse me, Mrs. Brown, I was wondering . . ."

Ignoring me completely, Mrs. Brown removed her spectacles and stood up. Her accomplices rose in puppet-like unison. Distaste and fatalistic resignation etched harsh lines on their faces.

"Ladies and gentlemen," Mrs. Brown said, loudly and with great dignity, "I wish to make an announcement."

In an instant the lobby was eerily quiet, and I realized with dismay that many of the people around us must have been eavesdropping on our conversation. Everywhere I looked, eyes devoured me with avid expectation.

"Please accept my apologies," Mrs. Brown was saying. "A minor problem has come up at the registration desk . . ."

A minor problem! I thought, and very nearly blurted out. What would a major problem be like, I wondered?

". . . and as a result, it seems we will have to close the desk for a short time. I'm sorry if this causes you any inconvenience."

Surreptitiously, I ran sweaty palms down the sides of my skirt. What were they going to do to me?

"And now, if you will excuse us—"

"But she hasn't finished signing in!" Miss Bell hissed.

"She can do it later." Stepping out from behind the registration desk, Mrs. Brown headed toward me with the inevitability of a boulder rolling downhill.

I backed hastily away, stumbling over the feet of the people behind me. But as I turned around to apologize, Mrs. Brown seized my wrist in a steely grip, as if she expected me to try to escape.

Nothing could have been farther from my mind.

"Miss Smalley," Mrs. Brown commanded, "take her other arm. Miss Bell, get her things."

Too shocked to resist, let alone formulate a protest, I watched in dismay as Miss Smalley scurried over to place a timid hand on my free arm, while Miss Bell picked up my bulging duffel bag and violin case.

"Did you bring anything else?" Mrs. Brown suddenly demanded of me.

"N . . . no," I managed to stammer out. "We . . . My parents sent my trunk on ahead."

"Good."

Without another word, they marched me across the lobby. Upon reaching the elevator, Mrs. Brown jabbed the UP button, while I just stood there, head down, blinking back tears.

I felt like a condemned prisoner.

My parents were right, I told myself. *I should never have come here! I WANT TO GO HOME!!!* This last thought threatened to erupt in a loud wail, but the arrival of the elevator saved me from making a fool of myself.

The women hustled me inside and, mercifully, the doors slid closed, shutting out the sea of curious eyes looking in.

No one said a word.

They're crazy—all of them! my internal soliloquy continued. *This place is run by a bunch of lunatics!*

But rather than protest my ill treatment, rather than demand answers as I might have done if I'd had even the least shred of self-confidence, I simply stood there, bracketed by my captors, passive and cowed, and desperately wishing that I was somewhere—anywhere—else.

But the next moment, I almost stopped breathing, struck by an astonishing insight, one that almost certainly explained their bizarre behavior.

They found out I'm Jewish! By sheer force of will, I managed not to babble my revelation aloud. *My mother was right: she warned me this school might have a quota!*

Months earlier, when I had filled out the school's housing application, my mother had insisted that I not answer any questions about (among other things) my religious affiliations. "None" or "no preference," she had instructed me to reply to every single personal inquiry. At the time it had seemed like a silly evasion or perhaps even paranoia, but I hadn't dared to tell her so.

Now I was no longer sure.

And since I'm already here, I continued to theorize, *it's too late for them to get rid of me—quota or not. No wonder they're angry!*

But how did they guess? I asked myself. *I don't think I look Jewish . . .* And just like that, another variation on this absurd theme popped into my mind: *Maybe they* don't *know I'm Jewish. Maybe I'm in trouble because of the way I answered their stupid questions . . . Maybe they're afraid I'm an atheist—which might be even worse than being a Jew!*

However, I lacked the nerve to inquire.

In ominous silence, the elevator ascended past the second floor.

Still, if that's the problem, my thoughts hurtled on, *how does Katherine Gates fit in? Is she some kind of religious nut—or maybe even anti-Semitic?*

The elevator creaked to a stop and the doors opened on a small, innocuous-looking lounge. We had arrived at the third floor.

"Does anyone know if Meri's trunk is here?" Mrs. Brown suddenly asked. It was the first thing anyone had said since we'd left the lobby, and I flinched at the unexpected sound of her voice.

"No, but I'll check," Miss Bell volunteered. And then she giggled: laughter that definitely verged on hysteria. "More important, I'll find out if Katherine's there."

"Be careful!" was Mrs. Brown's cryptic warning—which sent Miss Bell scurrying off down the hall like a scalded cat.

Following this exchange, the rest of us stood in silence for what must have been in reality less than a minute, although it felt like forever—until at last Miss Bell reappeared, jogging gracelessly around the corner.

"The coast is clear," she panted, and for the first time since our aborted conversation in the lobby, she actually smiled.

"Excellent." Mrs. Brown tugged on my arm, urging me forward. "Let's get this over with."

But all of a sudden, I had had enough. Every muscle in my body stiffened and I refused to budge another step. It was time to ask some long-overdue questions.

"Excuse me, Mrs. Brown," I began, determined to be polite despite all that had happened, "if you don't mind, I'd like to know what's . . ."

Her only response was to tighten her grip on my arm and drag me down the hall. From the way all three women avoided looking at or speaking to me, I might as well have been an invisible deaf-mute.

"And even though there's no sign of Katherine," Miss Bell continued, "Meri's trunk is already in the room."

"Excellent." Mrs. Brown sounded grimly satisfied. "Now no one can say we haven't done our best to try to smooth things over—and it's obviously far too late to make any changes."

We arrived in front of a varnished wooden door that was standing slightly ajar but otherwise looked no different from any of the others we had just hurried past.

Except for the number.

Room 312.

"Here we are, Dear," Mrs. Brown announced, finally deigning to acknowledge my existence. Reaching past me, she pushed the door fully open. "This is your room and, as we have already informed you, your roommate is Katherine Gates."

Before I could reply, she released me, literally shoving me across the threshold into a small, vacant room. She had surprising strength for such a skinny old lady.

I tripped over the edge of a frayed rag rug and fought to regain my balance.

"Good-bye," I heard from behind my back. "And good luck."

I whirled around to confront them, choking on a torrent of hurt, angry questions, blinded by tears.

But they were gone.

I rushed to the doorway, but the hall outside my room was eerily silent, totally devoid of any signs of life—as if what had just happened had been a figment of my imagination.

As if my three tormentors had never existed.

I started to shake.

"YOU'RE CRAZY!" I shrieked, hoping that my cries would somehow reach the ears of my vanished captors. "DO YOU HEAR ME? CRAZY!!!"

My tirade echoed down the empty corridor, past a long row of closed doors.

Abruptly I turned and stumbled back into the room.

"They're crazy!" I sobbed aloud, if only to hear the comforting sound of a familiar voice. "All of them."

The only response was silence, washing over me from the bare, impersonal walls, floating on dust motes suspended in the late-afternoon sunlight.

"Or else I am."

chapter 2: pixie

I stood alone in the center of the room, bracing myself for whatever might come next. But no one even walked past my door. Although common sense insisted that there had to be other people nearby, going about the business of moving in, just then the entire dormitory seemed deserted.

I might as well have been standing on the moon.

Where was everyone, I wondered? Didn't anyone care what happened to me?

Apparently not.

My hands wouldn't stop shaking. I clenched them into fists to deny my vulnerability. "It's not fair!" I wanted to yell, loud enough so those awful women, wherever they were, would have to listen. "Why me?"

But I didn't. Instead, with a sigh, I slumped down into a tattered beige armchair, drained and utterly defeated.

What had I done to deserve this?

My teary eyes scanned the room, barely registering its features. The walls were painted an uninspired light gray-green. Sunlight slanted in through a narrow, multi-paned window, sketching leafy patterns on one of the unmade beds. Muted voices and then—improbably—laughter drifted up from the courtyard outside.

It all seemed so ordinary!

Gnawing steadily on my fingernails, I retraced the day's events, going over the steps that had led to the debacle in the lobby. It occurred to me that if what Miss Bell had blurted out just before they had taken me upstairs was true, the women hadn't even given me a chance to register properly.

Somehow the thought was reassuring.

So it's possible they've mixed me up with someone else—a glimmer hope returned—*and everything that happened down there was just a stupid mistake.* I stood up. *Maybe I should go back downstairs and try to straighten out this mess. When those ladies realize what they've done, they'll be so embarrassed they won't know what to say. They might even let me start all over again . . .*

My stomach threatened to revolt at the thought.

On the other hand, if I take my time and unpack, they're bound to figure it out for themselves. Why, I wouldn't be surprised if they came back any minute now to apologize . . .

I glanced down at my torn and bleeding fingernails. *Disgusting,* I chided myself, echoing my mother's accusations. *Stop worrying and get busy.*

So I began to examine the room with renewed interest.

It was very small and impersonal—perhaps the pale walls and lack of decoration made it seem so—and it contained two of everything: two beds, two desks, two dressers, and two closets. Oddly, there was only one armchair: the one in which I had been sitting. The only other accessory—besides my duffel bag and violin case—was my battered green trunk, veteran of four summers at my beloved Allegheny Music Festival.

Further exploration revealed a narrow door leading into a minuscule washroom, barely large enough to turn around in, which contained a white porcelain sink, a postcard-sized mirror, and a wall-hung telephone. Passing through a second, equally narrow doorway, I discovered another room that was the mirror image of my own. There, on one of the unmade beds, was an open suitcase, but its owner was nowhere in sight. Disappointed, yet also vaguely relieved, I returned to my room.

And then I just stood there.

Short of returning to New York—which did not feel like a viable option despite all that had happened—moving in seemed like the most appropriate course of action.

But how to begin? Which part of our limited space would my absent roommate want to claim as her own? The very thought of her was enough to set off another assault on my fingernails.

I vaguely remembered overhearing the Registration ladies telling the girl ahead of me that most freshmen were assigned senior roommates to help them adjust to dorm life. I also recalled hearing something about college seniors having special privileges. Did these include the right to arrange our room—and if that was the case, would Katherine expect me to wait for her to show up?

But to do so would surely be to court disaster, for I knew that if I stood around much longer doing nothing, I would start rehashing my traumatic reception down in the lobby, or thinking about my parents, or worrying about beginning classes next week—and I didn't want to deal with any of those issues just now.

So I made a bold decision: I would sort out the room to my own satisfaction, and if Katherine didn't like it—I gave a mental shrug—well, we could always change it.

First, the beds: I assigned my absent roommate the one by the window. It was certainly the nicest corner of the room, and hopefully my generosity would go a long way toward making up for the fact that I was proceeding without her permission. Of course, she might be predisposed to dislike me no matter what I might or might not do . . .

But that was negative thinking. Time to get on with business.

Very well: Katherine would have the right-hand bed. However, that put the armchair on my side of the room. Would she think I was trying to monopolize it?

Just in case, I assigned her the larger, left-hand closet, which should have been mine.

My trunk was open and I was standing in my closet, hanging up a dress, when I heard footsteps in the hall outside and then someone entering the room.

I froze; even my stomach seemed to have turned to ice.

"Hello?" called an unfamiliar female voice. (Thank God it wasn't one of those awful Registration ladies, come back to torture me!) "Who's here?"

"I am." Backing out of the closet, I turned to greet my visitor.

A slim girl stood alone in the center of the room. Her golden skin glowed like rich amber honey, and her hair was reddish-brown. A pointy chin, a wide, generous mouth, a turned-up nose, and surprised-looking eyebrows completed the picture.

"Mischief Personified," was my first impression. Definitely someone interesting.

"Hi," I answered. And then, in all innocence: "Who are you?"

"Katherine Gates, if it's any of your business." Her scowl was fearsome. "What the hell are you doing in my room?"

I took a hasty step backwards, shocked by her hostility. No wonder the Registration ladies had been worried: Katherine was definitely not the friendly sort!

Still, politeness seemed the best approach . . .

"Hello, Katherine," I said, holding out my hand, willing it to not tremble. "I'm Meri Henriques, your roommate."

"My WHAT!?"

"Roommate. Meri Henriques." I clenched my teeth to stop my lips from quivering. "I'm glad to meet you."

Please like me, Katherine, I begged her silently.

She stared at my outstretched hand as if it was a foreign object. "Well, I'll be . . ." she breathed, apparently speaking more to herself than to me. "They finally did it."

My hand dropped back to my side. "Finally did what?"

"Did what!?" she echoed in disbelief. "Did *this*. Put us in a room together!" She was watching me with narrowed eyes, waiting to see what my response would be.

But I was mystified—as mystified by her reaction to me as I was by everything else that had happened to me that strange, disturbing day. And she must have realized it, because after a long moment she added with bitter intensity, "Well, aren't you surprised to find out that you have a Negro roommate?"

"No . . ." I hesitated. "Why? Should I be?"

For an instant her face registered disbelief, or perhaps even astonishment, and her expressive eyebrows shot up another notch. Then she did the last thing I was expecting: she burst out with a tremendous whoop of laughter and plopped down in the armchair. "Well, I'll be damned!" she repeated, shaking her head.

Just then, Miss Bell tore past our door as if her nylons were on fire. Her eyes and mouth were wide open, and her face was frozen in an expression that could only be described as "Cartoon Caricature of Horror."

I bolted for the doorway, determined to stop her. If I could just get my hands on her, I would shake her until her teeth rattled, and not let go until she'd given me a sensible explanation for this outrageous situation.

But she was gone by the time I reached the hall.

I was still standing there, feeling like a fool, searching in vain for a glimpse of my elusive quarry, when everything that had happened to me that fateful day finally caught up with me in a rush. Without warning, exhaustion, fear, and anger boiled over in an eruption of truly volcanic proportions. Doing an abrupt about-face, I turned and strode back into the room.

"That's it; I've had enough!" I barked. Balling my hands into fists, I loomed over Katherine, who was still sitting in that damn armchair, grinning like the Cheshire Cat. "What the hell is going on around here?"

Maddeningly, she began to chuckle like a teakettle that was threatening to boil over.

How dare they—first those stupid Registration ladies, and now Katherine Gates—treat me this way!

"This place is a lunatic asylum!" I shrieked, losing it completely. "Why won't anyone tell me what the hell is going on here?"

Katherine's laughter abruptly subsided. "You mean you really don't know?"

"Know *what*?" Her apparent evasion only made me angrier.

"Wow, I can hardly believe it!" She scrambled to her feet.

With a grand sweep of an arm, she announced: "Welcome to the first integrated dormitory room in the history of Indiana University."

I gaped. "You're kidding!"

"Nope."

"But this is 1963! This is America!" I protested. "It isn't possible!"

"Oh, it's possible all right."

"But I've been going to a music festival in Pennsylvania every summer for the past four years. We live on a college campus, and all the dorms are integrated. Everyone knows skin color's no big deal."

"It sure as hell is here!" Abruptly, her good humor vanished, and I wondered if we were going to have a fight after all. "This isn't Pennsylvania, and it sure as hell isn't any music festival! This is the Midwest, and pretty far south at that—which means conservative. Ultraconservative, in case you haven't heard."

"That's crazy! Why would anyone care about that stuff?"

"People care all right! Listen, the administration of this school is so conservative they're in trouble with the Federal government."

An uneasy chill shivered up my spine. "What kind of trouble?"

"Money trouble—because IU is one of the schools that gets federal funding. And you don't get the cash unless you're integrated. President Kennedy's threatened to use his executive power to cut off the school's funds if they don't change their policies."

"He can really do that?"

"You better believe it! At first the school tried to get around him by admitting the minimum number of negro students and putting us all together in a couple of funky old Quonset huts way over on the other side of campus. But that didn't wash with Kennedy. So the next semester, the school was forced to let some of us live in this dormitory, and they put six of us all together in one lousy room that was originally meant for three people."

She snorted in disgust. "And you know what President Kennedy said to that?"

By now I was so stunned that all I could do was shake my head.

"Word came down to the school administration that as far as Kennedy was concerned, nothing they'd done so far remotely resembled integration. So you can just imagine what they think of him around here . . . Anyway, I guess the school must have finally realized they'd have to give in—because here I am. And here you are . . ." She eyed me warily.

Was this it: the end of a possible friendship before it had really even begun?

"I can hardly believe it," I admitted. "Things like this can't happen."

"They happen here. All the time. Listen, didn't anyone mention the racial problems when you visited the school?"

I looked away, embarrassed, avoiding her intense gaze.

"You must have at least heard a rumor," she persisted. "What about the orientation programs—you know, the ones they give for prospective students? Those campus tours. Didn't you hear about any of this when you came to check out the school?"

"Well, I ummm . . ." I hesitated, not really wanting to admit the truth. "Actually, I didn't. Check out the school, that is. I just applied, and I was accepted. So this is the first time I've been here. I hardly know anything at all about this place."

"Well, I'll be . . ." She sank back into her armchair. "But you're supposed to visit! That's why they have visitors' days."

"I know that—but my parents wouldn't let me." Once again, to my chagrin, I could feel my cheeks burning. "As a matter of fact, they didn't want me to come here at all—not even today. They thought I should go to a local college and live at home. In fact, they're so angry I decided to come here, they said I'd have to figure out a way to get to Indiana on my own. It's a miracle I managed to get away."

"Your parents didn't bring you?"

I shook my head. "And even if they'd wanted to, they couldn't have afforded it."

"What on earth made you decide to come to IU?"

"A lot of my friends at the Music Festival are from the Midwest, and a couple of them study in the music department here. I thought I liked Midwesterners," I admitted, feeling like a fool. "And Indiana seemed a nice long way from New York. At the time it seemed like a good idea . . ."

"You mean none of your so-called friends warned you about this place?"

"Not a word."

"Some friends!"

"Yeah." I was sure she could hear the disgust in my voice.

"So I guess Indiana's turned out a little different than you expected."

"That's the understatement of the century!"

Suddenly, her face lit up with a grin.

"It isn't funny, Katherine!" I scolded, struggling to suppress a smile of my own in response to hers. "You wouldn't believe what happened downstairs when I tried to register."

"Oh, yes, I would. What a joke on Mrs. Brown and her gang: you coming here, all set to get integrated and not knowing it—and your parents staying home. Oh boy, those Registration ladies must be having fits!" She shifted in the armchair, still watching me, but with interest now rather than suspicion. "Where are you from, anyway, that you've managed to lead such a sheltered life?"

"Great Neck—it's just outside New York City."

"Well, that explains everything! My friend Rachel—you'll meet her for sure later on—she's from New York, too. And she's like you: she says she couldn't care less whether I'm green and purple or black and blue!" Her throaty chuckles seemed to percolate upward from some warm internal reservoir.

But I was far too shocked by what she'd just told me to find anything in this situation the least bit humorous.

Could her story really be true?

29

I was about to question her further, but she was already speaking.

"Hey, you know what Rachel did at the end of last semester? She told Mrs. Brown that since the dormitories were going to be integrated sooner or later, she wanted it on the record that she was requesting me as a roommate. She says I should have seen the look on Mrs. Brown's face—says she wished she'd had a camera! Of course, Mrs. Brown turned her down, but Rachel says at least she tried, and that's what counts."

Just then, Miss Bell shot past our door again, this time traveling in the opposite direction.

"What the hell's the matter with her?" I demanded, gesturing toward the now-empty doorway. "She looks like she's seen a ghost."

"Miss Bell?" If possible, Katherine looked even more mischievous. "Why, she and those Registration ladies are terrified."

"Of what?"

"They're afraid you and I are going to start tearing each other to pieces!" Her bubbly chuckles erupted, as welcome as sunshine after a thunderstorm.

I sank down on my bed. Shocked as I was, I was also relieved. None of that horrible business downstairs was my fault! And Katherine didn't hate me, I was certain of that.

What a weird place Indiana University was turning out to be, with racial problems I'd never dreamed were possible. I would later realize that my run-in at the Registration Desk was my first encounter with what I would eventually come to think of as "Hoosier Hysteria." But for now I was just beginning to work out my feelings about Katherine's revelations.

"But I have Negro friends at home," I mused aloud, more to myself than to Katherine. "At the music festival, too. So what? Everyone knows it's what you are inside that counts—not what you look like on the outside."

"That's not what they believe around here."

I glanced up, startled and rather embarrassed that she'd caught me thinking aloud. "Did they really make you live in a Quonset hut?"

"They most certainly did! And it was pretty damn grim: cold as hell in winter, and ratty as an old barn. One nasty bathroom—if that's what you call it—for every twenty people, and about as far away as possible from everything that matters on campus." Her smile was rueful. "It's funny though, after a while it sort of began to feel like home. We actually had some pretty good times there until—"

Footsteps sounded in the adjoining room, interrupting her reminiscences. "Pixie," someone called out, "is that you?"

"Sure is. Come on over, Cara."

The footsteps grew louder as the voice continued, "Pixie, you won't believe what's happened. I ran into Old Lady Brown downstairs, and she told me they're giving us white—"

The voice cut off abruptly as a slim, strikingly beautiful young black woman entered our room. Her wiry hair was cropped short in the first afro I had ever seen, and she moved with a dancer's grace. But the moment she noticed me, all traces of amusement vanished from her face, quickly replaced by guilty dread.

"It's okay, Cara," my roommate hastened to assure her. "Meri's from New York—she's like Rachel. Meri, this is Cara-lene Jones, our suitemate."

I stood up and offered my hand. I had been told by my black friends back home (and I was soon to learn this as immutable truth) that this unhesitating willingness to touch hands—this simple act of decency—was akin to a secret sign among liberal young people of the 60s; "I accept you," the gesture said. "I acknowledge you as my equal."

For a long moment, Caralene scrutinized me with golden, almond-shaped eyes—and then, apparently accepting both my peace gesture and her friend's assessment of me, she relaxed visibly, smiled, and shook my hand.

"Girl, I never thought I'd live to see this day," she admitted, turning to Katherine. "You should see those ladies down in the lobby—they're practically pissing their panties."

"I'm not surprised. Meri says they gave her a really bad time."

"I'll tell you all about it . . . later," I hastily amended.

31

Grinning, Caralene sat down on the edge of Katherine's bed. "Gosh, I wonder who my roommate's going to be?"

"It might be another freshman like Meri," Katherine suggested. "Or you might get really lucky, and it will turn out to be Rachel."

"Not much chance of that. No: mine's bound to be a freshman, too."

We were all silent for several moments, then Caralene said, "Sorry I barged in on you like that, Pixie. I didn't mean to interrupt your conversation."

"No problem. I was just telling Meri about our former lives as Quonset hut residents."

"Good old Trees." Her expression was bittersweet. "A real pretty name for a pretty awful place. You know, according to Booker T., those things were scheduled to be torn down years ago, right after the war, but instead they were 'converted' into handy dormitories when the school was forced to admit us." She sighed. "Still, I'm gonna miss old Quonset Hut Five."

A mischievous smile lit up my roommate's face. "Hey, Cara, don't pout. Isn't this place what you'd call real class?"

Caralene laughed. "Sure is—and only two people per room at that!"

"I bet you never thought you'd get to see the inside of one of these dorm rooms, either."

Which made all three of us laugh.

Now it was Miss Smalley's turn to monitor our progress. The pudgy woman went by in a hurry, puffing loudly.

We deliberately ignored her.

I turned to Katherine. "How come Caralene calls you 'Pixie'?"

"Katherine's official, but I'm Pixie to my friends."

"Okay, now you've got to tell her why," Caralene teased.

"Certainly. You see, Meri, once upon a time, when I was a little girl"—Pixie's prompt, sing-song delivery made me suspect she'd told this story many times before, and thoroughly enjoyed the telling—"one fine spring day, my daddy found me out in back of our house, sitting in my mama's flower garden under the lilac bushes. He says I was busy making something out of dirt, little pebbles, shiny pieces of glass, and flowers and stuff—this was back in North Carolina, in case I neglected to mention it—anyway, when my daddy saw me, he said, 'What are you doing under your mama's lilac bushes, Katie-Girl?' See, that's what they called me back then: 'Katie.'"

I had to smile; she was really getting into her performance, making her voice go all high and squeaky when she was quoting her younger self, and low and gravelly whenever she was speaking as her father.

"'Why, nothing, Daddy,' I told him. 'Nothing a-tall.' And my daddy said, 'Katie, your mama's gonna be mad as a hornet when she finds out you've been digging up her favorite daffodils.' But I shook my head. 'No, she's not, Daddy, 'cause I'm making her a fairy castle, and she's gonna be so proud when she finds out she's the only one in our neighborhood who has a garden full of pixies.' That really tickled my daddy. He said, 'You know, it looks to me like she already has one of those pixies sitting right in the middle of her flower bed!' And that was that: from then on, I was 'Pixie' to everyone."

Caralene laughed along with me, although I was sure she must have heard this story on numerous other occasions—and for the first time that day, I felt truly happy.

Just then, Mrs. Brown made an undignified rush past our door, with Miss Smalley close on her heels.

"Hello there, Mrs. Brown!" I sang out, giddy with relief.

Surely the worst was over. Those poor, ignorant women no longer had any power over me, and now the fear and humiliation I had experienced just a short while ago was replaced by a smug kind of pity.

"What a bunch of idiots!" I said, giggling.

"Don't you underestimate them, Meri." Caralene's lovely face was stern. "If they put their minds to it, they can make you feel like what happened today was a picnic. You wouldn't believe how much trouble they can cause."

"What kind of trouble?"

"Well, for one thing, they—"

"Yoo-hoo! Toodle-dee-doo!" trilled a cheery voice from the adjoining room. "Where are you, roommatie?"

Pixie and Caralene looked at each other in consternation.

"Hey, roommatie, it's me: Myrna May McCarthy, all the way from Fort Wayne, Indiana! I know you're here. I heard your voice. Where are you?"

"We're in here," I blurted out.

Pixie and Caralene glared at me.

"Thanks a lot, Meri!" Pixie growled under her breath.

"But we have to meet her sooner or later," I protested, stung.

"Well, if it's all the same to you, I'd prefer to make it later." Caralene stood up and headed for the hall exit.

But before she could make good her escape, a large, red-haired girl came bounding energetically out of the washroom, followed by a middle-aged white couple whose pleasant smiles evaporated the instant they set eyes upon the three of us.

chapter 3: rachel

By suppertime I had reached the erroneous but nevertheless comforting conclusion that everything that could go wrong had already done so. After all, we had heard nothing further from the ladies of the Registration Committee, and Pixie, Caralene, Myrna, and I seemed to be settling comfortably into our suite. Surely the worst was over now that Myrna's parents were gone, seemingly having resigned themselves to leaving the four of us to our collective fate.

And oh, was I glad to see the last of that duo!

The McCarthys had been outraged to discover that their precious only child had been assigned a black roommate—and to my chagrin, they hadn't been the least bit inhibited about saying so, even in front of my new friends. However, contrary to my expectations, Myrna had staunchly insisted that she was perfectly satisfied with our living arrangements as they stood.

"I will *not* change rooms!" she announced. Hands fisted on her hips, she glowered down at her parents, both of whom were several inches shorter than her and approximately half her weight. "The one I have now suits me just fine."

"You will too change!" was her mother's adamant response. "No child of mine is going to have a nigger for a roommate."

I gasped, shocked by her rudeness.

"I'm staying here!" Myrna insisted.

"Now, Myrna dear, listen to your mother," her father mumbled, meek as milquetoast. "She knows what's best."

"Stay out of this, Henry! Myrna May, stop sassing me and go get your things. We're going right back downstairs to demand a different room." Without another word, Mrs. McCarthy turned and marched back through the washroom.

"No, we won't!" Myrna shouted, close on her mother's heels, her face an apoplectic red. "I will not change rooms!"

"And I say you will!"

"WILL NOT!!!"

"Don't you use that tone of voice with me, young lady!"

"Then shut up and mind your own business!" Their conversation, if that's what you could call it, wasn't the least bit muffled by the intervening walls. "I'm a college coed now, and you can't make me do anything I don't want to, ever again!"

"Don't you shake your fist in my face!"

"DON'T TOUCH ME!"

"Put that down this instant!"

This was followed by the sound of something shattering against the opposite wall.

And so it went: a spectacular fight—even by Henriques standards.

What Pixie and Caralene thought of the McCarthys was a matter of conjecture, since both had long since fled the battlefield.

In the end, Myrna had managed to out-shout her parents; they went off shaking their heads and muttering about the ingratitude of children.

"We're Irish," Myrna told me with obvious pride as she stood unpacking the largest of her bloated suitcases. "And you know what they say about Irish tempers."

I wasn't sure I liked her, but I was willing to give her the benefit of the doubt. I suspected this had been her first chance to stage a rebellion, and I thought she'd done it with style.

***

Dinner was a disaster.

When Pixie and Caralene returned from their self-imposed exile that evening, the four of us adjourned to the cafeteria, where we picked up trays loaded with food and beverages before settling down at one of the room's many dining tables. Unfortunately, a single taste was enough to confirm what my nose had suggested: the food was vile.

"What *is* this stuff?" I demanded, poking at a pale greenish wedge that had vomitous pink goo, dotted with darker chunks, oozing down its sides. There was also a mound of grayish-white glop that looked for all the world like congealed library paste, and beside this was something that resembled a rectangle of greasy cardboard. It was little comfort that I was actually able to identify Lima beans—one of my all-time least favorite vegetables—and a slice of dry, crumbly chocolate cake.

"Salad with Russian dressing," Pixie announced around a mouthful of food, indicating the pink-coated lump. "Mashed potatoes and chicken-fried steak." Even as she spoke, she was rapidly devouring everything on her plate. By the time she finished, she was eyeing my dinner with undisguised longing.

"You want it?" I asked, pushing my tray towards her. "It's yours."

She immediately speared the thin gray slab of so-called steak, but cutting it up into bite-sized pieces and chewing it turned out to be quite a challenge, even for her.

"You hurt my feelings, Meri!" Caralene announced in a mocking little-girl whine. "I need that steak more than Pixie does."

"Why?" I couldn't suppress a shudder.

"In case you didn't notice, I haven't touched mine." Caralene pointed delicately. "So if you'd given me yours, I could have used the two of them to get my shoes re-soled."

Pixie was too busy chewing to reply.

"And if you think this stuff is bad," Caralene continued, "wait 'til you get a whiff of the Friday Night Special: frozen fish sticks with peas and tartar sauce. Yum."

To compensate for the loss of my dinner, I consumed as much milk as I could, using it to wash down the dregs of chocolate cake.

"Very nutritious!" Pixie opined.

Afterwards, we went back upstairs to finish unpacking. Myrna and I were supposed to attend a meeting for the third-floor freshmen girls later that evening, but before we had a chance to leave our suite, what turned out to be our nightly parade of visitors began to arrive.

The first was a dark-skinned young woman who came stalking into our room, bristling with annoyance that was palpable even before she'd uttered a single word. She dismissed me with a withering glance and sailed right toward Pixie.

"Girl, you know what the Three Stooges downstairs did? They gave me a goddamn white-trash roommate! No matter that she's from New York . . ."

Improbably, Pixie looked over at me and winked.

". . . she's still white-trash, far as I'm concerned, and I told those old biddies so." Our visitor's voice rose. "And they won't let me transfer back to the Trees! They say I gotta stay here in this dumb whitey dorm. Well, piss on them!"

"Calm down, Gineeva. I know you're mad, but think about it: in the long run, this might turn out to be what's best for everyone."

"Screw that!! I don't want to live here. I already told you so."

"Well, I do. And I think you'll change your mind once you've had time to think it over. By the way, this is my roommate, Meri Henriques."

Intimidated by Gineeva's angry tirade, which I somehow felt was directed at me, I had retreated into my corner of the room, where I was trying to make myself as inconspicuous as possible.

Now Gineeva shot me a look of pure, unadulterated venom. "Pixie, you always were soft on Whities," she sneered.

I remained silent, hoping she'd forget that I existed.

"What about you, Cara—you gonna stay here, too?" she

demanded of our suitemate, who had come in, attracted by the commotion.

"Sure," Caralene replied with enviable serenity. "I intend to stay here and show them they can't chase me out. And that's something you ought to consider, too, before you do any transferring."

"Fuck that! So you're gonna play Uncle Tom for them, too? I guess you-all think we should be grateful to them for giving us the chance to help integrate their lily-white dormitory. Well, screw them! I know where I belong, and it's not here!"

She headed for the door.

"Where are you going?" Pixie called after her.

"Back to the Trees!"

"But, Gineeva—"

"Don't worry, Pixie. You know Gineeva: she'll fuss and fume—and then she'll stay," Caralene announced with absolute certainty as she turned back towards her own room.

"Don't count on it," Gineeva growled after her. But her tone changed dramatically as she confronted our next visitor in the doorway. "Oh, hi there, Rachel! How you doin'?"

"Apparently better than you are."

"Ain't it the truth. Lucky me: I got integrated."

"Congratulations. I expect you'll survive."

"Yeah, 'spose I will . . . Well, see you around."

Much to my relief, Gineeva left without further ado.

"I see Gineeva's in her usual good humor," remarked the newcomer, settling into our armchair.

"Rae-chel," Pixie drawled, her voice warm with affection. "What an honor to have you visit us on our first evening of integrated bliss."

"Why, Pixie," Rachel replied with mock dignity, "the honor is all mine. It's a pleasure to find you in such luxurious surroundings." And then she giggled, an ironic and infectious sound. Her face matched the giggle: an imp with curly, light brown hair and a turned-up nose, she was the perfect Caucasian counterpart to Pixie.

"Rachel, this is my roommate, Meri Henriques," Pixie happily announced, "and she's from New York. Just like you."

I had pried myself out of my corner as soon as Gineeva exited, and now I extended my hand, smiling, as much with relief as with friendliness.

"Meri, this is Rachel Perlman, our resident intellectual and self-styled radical."

"You flatter me," our guest mumbled, sounding embarrassed. As we shook hands, she studied me with shrewd green eyes.

"What did Pixie say your name was?"

"Meri."

"No—the other part."

"Henriques."

"Yeah, I thought so." Dismissing me with a wave of her hand, she reclaimed her seat in our armchair. "You look just like him, you know," she added, apparently as an afterthought. "Dark curly hair, hazel eyes, olive skin. Spanish-looking. Even the nose is the same. All that's missing is a mustache . . . By the way, he was lousy," she finished, a complete non-sequitur if there ever was one.

"What on earth are you talking about?" I demanded.

"Your father—who else?"

"My *father*!"

"Yeah, your father: Mr. Henriques. My high school art teacher. He was lousy—and you look just like him."

Though deeply insulted by her rude summary of my father's teaching abilities—not to mention obviously far more impressed than she was by the coincidence of our meeting here, a thousand miles from home—I was unable to hold back my next question: "Why was my father a lousy teacher?"

The moment I'd uttered the words, I regretted it. For I was sure that no matter what her answer turned out to be, I wasn't going to enjoy hearing it.

Meanwhile, Pixie was watching us with keen interest, but it was obvious that she had no intention of rescuing me from this so-called friend of hers.

"Oh, he had favorites," was Rachel's airy reply. "If you did extra work, joined a committee or did special projects, he'd give you good grades. Didn't matter what your artwork looked like . . . I hated him. He was really lousy." Her eyes challenged me to refute her accusations.

I couldn't think of a single response.

For several long moments, she watched me in expectant silence, but once she realized that I wasn't going to offer an interesting rebuttal, she seemed to lose interest. To my relief, she turned back to Pixie. "Hey, guess where they put me this year?" Her face was suddenly alight with mischief. Without giving my roommate time to respond, she went on, "In one of those nice big rooms at the end of the hall—all by myself. They moved me away from the other Jewish kids. Mrs. Brown says I was driving them crazy!!" She giggled with obvious glee.

"The *other* Jewish kids?" I blurted out, apparently doomed to involve myself in this conversation, no matter how much I preferred to stay out of it.

Rachel glanced over at me. "Yeah, the Jewish Mafia. Most of them are from the South, and Mrs. Brown always sees to it that they all get rooms together, just down the hall from here— in fact, the Ghetto is right on the other side of those glass doors next to your room. Looks like they missed you, though," she added, almost as an afterthought.

"For your information, I didn't say what religion I was when I filled out my housing forms," I retorted, vexed beyond civility. "I just put 'none' for 'religious preference.'"

Her face lit up. "What a great idea! I never thought of that. It's probably why they decided to integrate you: they hoped an atheist wouldn't be too particular about her roommates."

Again that scathing laughter.

"Maybe," I admitted. By now, I hated to have to agree with her about anything.

But Rachel's mercurial attention had already shifted back to Pixie. "Hey, are you still gonna take those dumb education courses this semester—Kiddie-Lit and all that stuff?"

"Sure am," Pixie replied, seemingly unperturbed by her friend's jabs. "Just a few more classes, and I'll be all set to student teach at the local elementary school."

"Sounds great." Rachel definitely didn't mean it.

"All right then, what exotic courses have you dredged up from the bottom of this year's catalogue?"

"Good ones!" Now Rachel's enthusiasm was genuine. "The Philosophy of Kant, Chaucer's England, Medieval French, Comparative Literature, second-year Russian—"

"I think they make those courses up just for you!" Pixie chuckled. "You better watch out, Rae. With all the papers they're bound to assign, if you're not careful you're gonna get more incompletes this semester."

"You know I finished up all my old incompletes this past summer!" Rachel flared. "It takes a lot of time to research and write those papers . . . Can I help it if it takes me a bit longer than everyone else?"

"And if I know my Rachel, she got all A's," Pixie confided in a stage whisper. "I don't know how she does it: she's always late, and she always talks her teachers into giving her A's anyway. All I can say is, those must be some papers!"

Rachel actually blushed, but she was beaming. "Well, I can't let you be the only one of us who's on the honor roll, now can I?"

"Toodle-dee-doo, suitemate," Myrna warbled, emerging from the washroom. "Time for our freshman meeting."

"What is *that*?" Rachel scowled, pointing a rude finger at our hapless visitor.

"Come on, Myrna," I urged, moving quickly to intercept her, glad of any excuse to leave.

Myrna looked confused as I grabbed her arm and practically dragged her out of the room, but she didn't resist. I was relieved that I got her out of there before she could tangle with Rachel.

As we walked down the hall, I scarcely paid attention to Myrna's excited chatter. Instead, I kept shaking my head, wondering why a nice person like Pixie would choose to be friends with someone as irritating as Rachel.

———

The third floor lounge was crowded with girls, most of them already seated in chairs, on sofas, or on the floor. Many wore pajamas, bathrobes, and slippers, and nearly every head was festooned with curlers. More than a few looked tired, and I belatedly realized that I, too, was exhausted.

To state the obvious, it had been quite a day.

Now, looking around at all of those eager young faces, I was struck by an awareness of just how far from home I had actually come. There was no doubt about it: here, amidst this crowd of wholesome, blond-haired, blue-eyed, pink-skinned young women, I was definitely an alien. I was finally beginning to sense the truth of Pixie's warning: this place wasn't going to be at all like the Allegheny Music Festival. There, at least, our little racially mixed group had shared a common love of music that bound us firmly together from the moment we met. Here, there was no cement whatsoever, except for our newness and the fact that all of us were about to begin our careers as college coeds at Indiana University. I wondered if any of these strangers would ever become my friends.

Just then, the elevator chimed out a cheery *ping* and the doors slid open to reveal a smiling Miss Bell.

Suddenly, I was having trouble breathing. I attempted to make myself invisible by sidling into the farthest, darkest corner of the lounge, where I pressed my back against the wall, scarcely daring to blink.

Meanwhile, a tall, slim young woman had risen from where she had been sitting on the sofa, talking to several younger girls, and now she went over to greet Miss Bell. For the next few minutes, the two of them chatted amiably—until Miss Bell happened to glance over in my direction. Abruptly, she was no longer smiling.

My knees turned to rubber, and for an awful moment I thought she was going to summon me to her side. Instead, to my intense relief, she turned aside and called the meeting to order. When she began reading out names from an attendance sheet, my pulse dropped slowly back toward normal.

After some inane preliminary remarks, Miss Bell introduced the thin young woman, who had remained standing next to her, as Roberta Kruger, a senior and the student leader of the third floor girls—at which point Roberta took charge of the proceedings.

It was immediately obvious that she relished her role as the experienced older woman who was about to initiate us into the mysteries of college life. Heartily enthusiastic about everything, Roberta insisted that we were especially lucky to be in Morrison Hall.

"It's the best dormitory on campus—the best dorm ever! Of course," she grudgingly admitted, "there are some pretty terrific sororities you might be tempted to join later on. But for now, at least, we third floor girls of Morrison Hall are the tops!"

This pronouncement was greeted by hearty cheers.

Roberta then went on to tell us about other, more serious concerns: "Living in our dorm involves certain responsibilities. We have a reputation to uphold—which means being sure to follow the Rules. So you can't smoke in your room or invite male visitors over—they have to meet you downstairs in the lobby. And we'll be having fire drills and bed checks, both of which could happen at any time . . . And that brings us to a very important subject: whenever you leave the dorm for any reason, don't forget to sign out. I know Mrs. Brown and Miss Bell told you-all about this earlier today when you registered, but I want to remind you again because it's so important . . ."

"They never say a word about it to me!" I was tempted to interject. "I guess they had something else on their minds."

". . . and it's just as important to sign back in when you return," Roberta was saying. "Don't forget. Otherwise you'll find yourself in an awful lot of trouble."

"Do we have to sign out for everything—even for classes?" someone wanted to know.

Roberta chuckled. "Of course not. Your class schedule will be on file downstairs in the dorm office—but whenever you go anywhere else, you have to sign out."

"Be sure to include your destination," Miss Bell added, "so we'll know exactly where to find you. And if you go off campus, you must leave a phone number where you can be reached, and the name of an adult female who has agreed to be your chaperone. She has to be at least twenty-one."

While we were still digesting this interesting piece of information, Roberta began speaking again.

"Which brings us to lockout. It's at 11:00 p.m. on weekdays and Sunday nights, midnight on Friday and Saturday."

"What's lockout?" someone up front called out, and I was sure that each of us was secretly relieved that it had been someone other than ourselves who had exposed her ignorance.

"At eleven o'clock, all the dorm doors are locked from the inside," was Roberta's cheerful reply. "And if you get locked out, you have to ring the night bell so Miss Bell can let you in. Which means you're in deep doo-doo. The next day, you'll be called before the Dorm Committee—that's Mrs. Brown, Miss Bell, and Miss Smalley—and they can have you expelled from school if they think you deserve it. But usually, the first time at least, they give you some sort of punishment and another chance."

"Will we get in trouble if we're only ten minutes late?" someone asked.

"Even if you're one minute late," Miss Bell replied.

No one spoke for several moments.

"What about the guys? Do they have lockout, too?" someone finally asked.

"Of course not!" was Roberta's startled response. "They're men."

While I was still trying to puzzle out the questionable logic of her reply, Miss Bell interjected, "Don't look so glum, girls.

45

It hardly ever happens that anyone gets locked out by accident. So if you'll just be careful about getting back on time, you won't have any problems."

Roberta clapped her hands. "And now for the good stuff! Starting tomorrow night and every night for the rest of this week, we're going to have some real fun mixers . . ."

"What's a mixer?" I hissed at Myrna, who had come over to stand beside me.

She gave me a surprised look. "A dance. Don't they have them in New York?"

"Dances, yes. Mixers, no."

". . . so we've invited some real cute guys from another dorm over to meet all of you lovely ladies," Roberta was saying.

Several girls giggled.

"Which means you'll have a chance to get started dating those college men, just like you've always dreamed you would." She sighed happily.

Bored and feeling sleepier by the moment, I told myself that I was lucky just to have gotten here and past the Registration Desk; dating was something I would worry about later.

"Well, I guess that's about it for tonight," Roberta said. "Let's all go get our beauty sleep so we'll be ready for tomorrow night's mixer. Seven o'clock sharp. Don't forget."

But just as the roomful of girls began to stir, Miss Bell clutched Roberta's arm and whispered an urgent message.

"Wait, everyone!" Roberta called out. "I have one more announcement: Meri Henriques, please stay behind to see Miss Bell."

Suddenly I was wide awake, and nervous in a way that the thought of the upcoming mixer could never have inspired.

Meanwhile, the other girls were leaving, casting curious glances in my direction. Myrna waved and strolled off toward our rooms as I walked slowly over to where Miss Bell stood.

"You wanted to see me?"

"Oh, there you are, Meri! It seems there were some things we forgot to have you sign this afternoon." Her eyes didn't quite meet mine. "You know how it is: so many new students, so much paperwork, such a commotion . . ."

"Sure, Miss Bell." If that was the way she wanted to have it, I was more than happy to oblige.

I took the proffered papers, signed them without bothering to read them, and handed them back—and then I just stood there, waiting for her to either say something more or else dismiss me. To my surprise, she seemed uneasy, even more so than I was, and reluctant to continue.

"Is everything . . . er . . . you know: okay?" she finally asked.

"Sure."

"Really! Oh! Well . . . in that case . . . ummm . . . good night."

I practically ran toward the haven of my room.

Much to my relief, Rachel was just leaving. But as we passed one another, she placed a restraining hand on my arm, preventing me from escaping. "Hey, hold on a minute. I need to talk to you." Her voice dropped almost to a whisper. "In private." She drew me away from the doorway.

My stomach, which was already unsettled by my encounter with Miss Bell—and also, possibly, by dinner—did another queasy lurch.

"Okay, Rachel." I tried for a heartiness I didn't feel. "What can I do for you?"

"Not so loud," she admonished. "Listen, at the meeting: did they say anything about fire drills?"

I nodded. Why on earth did she care?

"Good." She spoke even more quietly. "I just wanted to let you know that whenever we start having them, I'll get here as quickly as I can."

"That's nice." I was afraid to ask for clarification for fear of setting off another one of her sarcastic verbal assaults. "Ummm . . . thanks."

"'Night, Rae," Pixie called from inside our room. "'Night, Meri."

"Good night, Pixie," Rachel called out. "Pleasant dreams." Her voice dropped back to a whisper. "Okay: here she goes.

Come on, Meri, you've got to see this—she does it every night."
She nudged me back toward the doorway.

Pixie was already in her pajamas, and I noticed that the blanket and upper sheet had been neatly turned down on her bed. As we stood watching, she backed halfway across the room, took a deep breath, and then launched herself forward in a flying leap. The entire bed shuddered as she hit the mattress with a resounding thump. She immediately grabbed a handful of covers, wrapped herself up in them like a chrysalis in a giant cocoon, rolled over onto her side, and closed her eyes. The next instant she was gently snoring, fast asleep.

"Amazing!" Rachel's voice was full of undisguised admiration. "Now nothing will wake her until morning. So whenever we have a fire drill, I'll come by to help you carry her downstairs. Caralene knows the routine: she answers for Pixie when they call attendance. Mrs. Brown never notices the difference." She must have registered my incredulity because she added, rather sternly, "We all do what we have to. If we left Pixie up here, she'd be in trouble with the Dorm Committee—and we can't let that happen."

Unable to think of an intelligent response, I kept my mouth firmly shut.

"Well, I'll be seeing you." Rachel turned to leave. "But don't forget: when we have our first fire drill, wait here until I come by to help you with Pixie."

Back in my room, I put on my pajamas and turned out the lights.

It had been a very strange day. I found myself wondering, as I drifted off to sleep, which would turn out to be more peculiar: Indiana University or my new friends.

chapter 4: decisions

The next morning, Pixie shook me awake.

"Get up, Meri!" Her voice was urgent. "It's seven thirty, and if we aren't in the cafeteria by a quarter to eight, they won't serve us breakfast!"

We were among the last to arrive. One whiff and I knew there had to be a better way to spend that particular half hour; from then on, I vowed, I would sleep in and pick up a carton of milk from the dispenser in the basement on the way to my first class. Caralene had been wise, I realized, to decline Pixie's invitation to join us for breakfast.

"My goodness, you certainly do drink a lot of milk!" Pixie exclaimed when I returned to our table with yet another brimful glass. "You sure you don't want any of this?" Her fork dipped toward my plate.

I shook my head, not trusting myself to speak. With a barely suppressed shudder, I watched her gobble up my serving of reconstituted scrambled eggs, greasy hash browns, and three strips of decidedly undercooked bacon.

"How can you eat that stuff?" I blurted out when she started in on the charred toast.

"Well, they don't aim to please everyone," was her breezy reply. "Myself, I never touch milk. Can't stand the color!"

Which sent Rachel and Gineeva into peals of raucous laughter, much to Pixie's delight.

After breakfast, Myrna and I walked over to the freshman orientation meeting, where each of us was handed a thick sheaf of papers: mimeographed information about the school, every department, the name and office hours of every advisor, and general course requirements for graduation. Skimming through it, I realized that it was nothing more than an abbreviated version of the school's general catalogue—therefore I was dismayed when, once the meeting had been called to order, a faculty member stood up and began reading the whole thing through to us out loud. His voice droned on and on without the slightest shade of expression—of course, I had to admit that even Lawrence Olivier would have been challenged to put some life into such a recitation.

Fidgeting in my seat, I leaned over to Myrna and grumbled, "What's going on? Do they think we're illiterate? Or do you suppose the school administration doesn't trust us to read this stuff on our own?"

She merely shrugged.

I was dozing off by the time the torture ended—at least I assumed it was over. But then a man who introduced himself as an instructor from the physical education department, stood up and began enthusing about IU's "amazing" basketball team.

"Our boys need your support, folks," he concluded. "So be sure to get out there and support them at every game—both at home and away. Let's show our rivals the true meaning of 'Hoosier Hysteria'!"

His sales pitch at an end, he said he was going to lead us in some traditional school songs. Printed lyrics were passed around, which took up even more time, and then someone up front began pounding out a tune on a battered old piano, and several hundred voices started singing—with great gusto but unfortunately quite out-of-tune—"Indy-yanner—oh, Indy-yanner . . . Indy-yanner, we're true to yooo-oo-oo! FIGHT!"

When it was over, I fled back to my room.

Pixie was out, and I was glad to have the place to myself. For a while I lay on my bed, taking mental inventory.

Now that I was here, how did I feel about nine more months at Indiana University? Could I really go through with this, or should I admit defeat, pack up, and head back home?

I could just imagine what my mother would have to say about that!

At last, with a fatalistic mental shrug, I decided that things would work out. Somehow.

Besides, I counseled myself, *it's too late to go anywhere else this semester—and you've got to admit that no matter how much of a drag that stupid orientation meeting was, it was a piece of cake compared to yesterday's fiasco!*

My stomach growled.

And so it was that a short while later I found myself walking out of my dorm, a carton of milk in one hand and my violin case in the other, heading for the Music School.

Immediately adjacent to Morrison Hall in Wells Quad, the Music School was one of the newest structures on campus and the pride of Indiana University. The moment it came into view, my spirits lifted. Surely, this was where I belonged.

However, I was arriving at the Music department armed with an agenda: explicit instructions that had been carefully spelled out by my parents before I left home. I was to sign up as either a violin or voice major, whichever I preferred and, in addition, I was to enroll in music education courses so that, at the end of four years, I would be qualified to teach elementary school. A teacher could always find a decent job, my parents, both of them teachers and survivors of the Great Depression, had assured me.

Back in New York it had seemed like a sensible, if uninspired, plan. What I hadn't taken into account—at least, not until I found myself actually walking in through the front door of the music building—was that it wasn't going to work.

I don't want to be a music teacher—or for that matter, any kind of teacher at all! I informed my amazed self. My startled Obedient Child persona stopped in her tracks. *But why?*

My immediate reaction was an emphatic, *Just look at Mom and Dad! Do they enjoy teaching one single bit?*

Well, no, but . . . my internal monologue continued.

Could you do that for the rest of your life?

In response, a shudder shook me from head to toe.

Well then, what are you going to do about it?

Which led me to yet another moment of truth: the choices I was about to make were going to affect my entire future!

And like Myrna told her parents yesterday, my inner soliloquy informed me, *no one can tell me what to do anymore. I get to make up my own mind about what's right for me.*

Propelled forward by nervous excitement and a sense of urgency, I strode through the music building, navigating its curving white halls, peering into classrooms, comforted by the familiar sights and sounds of practice studios and rehearsal halls, inspecting passing students, examining everything, questioning all.

If teaching was suddenly out, what, I wondered, was in?

Eventually, quite by accident, I found myself at the main office and decided to stop by. I needed information.

Once inside, I discovered the usual: fluorescent lights, banks of gray metal filing cabinets covering an entire wall, a notable lack of windows, a long front counter, and a big work desk with a busy secretary sitting behind it. She looked up, smiling, as I entered.

You can do this, I told myself.

"Can I help you?"

"What does a person have to do to become a music major?" I blurted out, too rattled to take time to trot out any of the conventional niceties people use to ease their way into a conversation. "Officially, I mean. I sent you some tapes and stuff in the mail, but now that I'm actually here, is there anything else I have to do?"

"What's your name?" Still smiling, she stood up and approached me. If she was trying to put me at ease, it was definitely working: her friendly manner certainly had a calming effect on my jangled nerves.

I admitted my name.

"Give me a minute to locate your file."

A brief search brought her back to the counter.

"We've got everything we need, Meri. And congratulations: the staff of the music department is delighted that you've decided to join us."

"Thanks. I've been looking forward to studying here." I hesitated. "So that's it; now I'm a music major? Is this where I sign up for classes and lessons?"

Her mouth quirked with amusement. "It's a pleasure to meet such an eager student. And I must say, looking at what you've sent us, it's unusual to find someone who's interested in two such different disciplines, violin and voice . . . But to answer your question: yes, there is an additional requirement before we can allow you to register."

"Which is?" She sounded far too cheerful to my suspicious ears.

"A mere formality—nothing at all, really. The faculty wants to hear you play or sing in person."

My mouth must have dropped open. This was definitely not in my plans. "A live audition? But I sent you a tape!"

"Well, you must admit that some unscrupulous persons might cheat . . . But don't worry," she insisted, obviously trying to reassure me, "your audition will hardly take any time at all. Why, if you're really lucky, I may be able to schedule yours for later today. That way you can get it over with right away."

"Gee, I'm not sure that I—"

"You'll do fine. Really. Now, all you have to do is decide which you're going to give up: the violin or voice."

"Give up?" I was feeling queasier by the moment.

She seemed happy to elaborate: the faculty, in its infinite wisdom, had ruled that all music students, regardless of their major, were required to have a minor in what I thought of as The Hateful Piano.

"Which means," she concluded, "that you can study either violin or voice, but not both. Otherwise you won't have time for your piano lessons."

I gaped at her, speechless.

"Personally," she went on, unaware of my rising panic, "if I were you, I'd try for voice; it's a natural with piano studies. Also, as I'm sure you're aware, the music school is famous for its opera program. The faculty is always on the lookout for talented new singers. Which could be you, if you're very lucky. In any case, auditions help the voice coaches sort students into two basic categories: those who are good enough to become opera singers, and those who aren't."

"What happens to them?" I could barely get the words out. "The others, I mean. The ones who aren't good enough?"

"We have an excellent program: we train them to be music teachers."

At that moment, if she'd asked me, confirmed opera-phobe that I was, I wouldn't have been able to tell her which fate sounded worse: music teacher, opera singer, or being boiled alive in oil!

"I . . . I've got to think about this," I said. "Consider my options. I wouldn't want to rush into anything."

She frowned. "Don't take too long to make up your mind. It's a bad idea to keep the faculty waiting. They're extremely busy, especially at this time of year."

"Is there a choir?" I asked.

Her eyebrows rose in puzzlement, yet she answered my seemingly random question. "Actually, there are several."

"Anything I can join without an audition?"

"Auditions are a must for all performance classes," she admonished, giving me a stern look. "Musicians should be able to perform on demand. However, in the case of concert chorus, the auditions are quite perfunctory. If you're interested, I can give you the room number where they're taking place."

I thanked her for her help.

"Are you sure that's all you want to do right now?" Her voice was full of concern. "Don't make the mistake of waiting too long to schedule your audition. The professors have only so much time to devote to new students."

Promising her I'd be back soon, I fled the office.

In a daze, I wandered the halls of the music building, wondering what, if anything, I would be able to salvage from the wreckage of my dreams.

"Meri Henriques? I don't believe it!"

I was so preoccupied with my grim musings that the voice barely registered and I actually flinched when someone put a hand on my arm. It took me several seconds to focus on the familiar face of a cellist who was a year older than me, and who'd played with me in my hometown symphony orchestra.

"Oh, hi, Nancy," I mumbled, unable to work up much enthusiasm.

"Why didn't you tell me you were coming here?" Her eyes sparkled with excitement. "I'm so glad to see you!"

"Gee, thanks."

"Wow, a fellow New Yorker, here in the wilds of Indiana!" She grinned. "And believe me, we need all the New Yorkers we can get—although Californians will do in a pinch."

With an effort, I responded to her warm greeting. "Nice to see you, too. Sorry I didn't let you know ahead of time that I'd be here but, to tell the truth, I didn't really know for sure myself until the very last minute." Then, before I could stop myself, out came what was really on my mind: "How do you like it here? How's the music school?"

"It's wonderful!"

"It is?"

"Hey, this place is a real-life ivory tower."

"What do you mean?"

"Well, I will admit that a lot of the local students have pretty weird ideas—although come to think of it, you probably haven't been here long enough to know it."

"What kind of weird ideas?"

"Oh, about life in general—and religion and politics in particular. And this year, everyone's making an incredible fuss about integration."

"Yeah. I found that out that the hard way."

"Hey, don't look so grim . . . See, that's what's so great about the music school: we ignore all that garbage. What matters to us is how good a musician you are, not what color your skin happens to be. And the stupid stuff that goes on in the rest of the school?" She shrugged. "Who cares? We just shut the doors of our ivory tower and ignore it."

"Actually, that might not be so easy . . ." I told her briefly about Pixie and Caralene, and my previous day's misadventure. "So you see," I concluded, "I suspect it's going to be pretty hard to ignore campus politics when I'm living right in the middle of the school's hottest issue."

She laughed. "That's how you feel right now because you just got here. But just wait: the music school faculty will keep you so busy, you won't have time to think about anything besides keeping up with your assignments. Before you know it, all that other nonsense will become background noise, and you'll be concentrating on more important things."

"I'm not so sure there are more important things."

"You're so wrong. Let me show you." And, linking her arm through mine, she took me on her own personal tour of the music school.

Not much more than an hour later, I found myself walking back out of the music building after having somehow survived a brief audition and signing up for concert chorus.

For reasons that I didn't fully understand, I felt extremely relieved.

***

Pixie was still out when I got back to our room. I put my violin case away in my closet and took out my art portfolio. Then I sat staring at it, reviewing my options.

I was a good artist—I was sure of that.

But was I good enough to justify what I was about to do?

Eventually, I picked up my portfolio and left the dorm, taking the path through the wooded area behind Morrison Hall that separated it from the art building. Upon arriving, I went directly to the office and filled out the necessary papers—and suddenly, just like that, I was an art major!

Minutes later, I was in the office of my new advisor, a well-dressed, middle-aged woman who was friendly and helpful—and who had no unsettling surprises for me. After a brief conversation, she gave me a list of the art classes I would be required to take during the next four years, pointing out the ones I should start with.

As I was about to leave her office, she stopped me. "I hope you'll enjoy your studies with us, Meri," she said. "And I wish you happiness at Indiana University. Come see me if you have any questions or problems."

"You know, until a few hours ago, I thought of myself as an artistic musician," I confessed, feeling a bit silly, "but now it turns out I'm really a musical artist."

Her good-natured laughter followed me from her office.

When I emerged outside, because I was too full of nervous energy to go straight back to my room, I decided to take a walk.

It was a crisp autumn day. The sky was intensely blue and the wind gusted, tearing red and yellow leaves off the trees. I tucked my large black portfolio under one arm and the wind caught it like a sail, sweeping me along at a trot.

The school grounds were beautiful: old, ivy-covered gray limestone buildings set in gorgeous jewel-green lawns against a backdrop of fall-colored trees.

I felt free and intensely alive, relieved to have my goals defined, with the hard work of getting to them as yet still somewhere off in the future. I told myself how lucky I was to be at Indiana instead of trapped in a dull New York City commuter college, which was where I had feared I would end up if my parents had had their way.

Pixie looked up from where she was sitting cross-legged in the middle of the floor, as I came in. "How was your day?"

"Long."

"I noticed. You missed lunch."

"Oh well, the milk machine's always open . . . What are you doing?"

"Writing my parents to tell them what's happening here."

I felt a stab of guilt. What was I going to tell my parents? How was I going to explain my sudden defection to the art department?

"Tell me about the Music School," Pixie said. "How was it? What did you do there?"

"Nothing." I heaved my portfolio onto my bed and sat down beside it. "Well . . . I did sign up for concert chorus. The truth is, I couldn't make up my mind."

"About what?"

"About whether I wanted to major in violin or voice. Because it turns out you can't do both. And they said I'd have to take piano lessons. I hate the piano!"

She chuckled. "So which did you pick?"

"Neither. I left."

"You did? Why?"

"I told you: I didn't know what else to do. They wanted me to audition. For everything. And I hate auditions! I was so frazzled! So I went and joined the Art Department instead."

Once I'd said it aloud, it didn't sound quite so irresponsible.

"Just like that? Wow, Meri, I wish I had so many talents I couldn't make up my mind which one to pick!"

"No, you don't. It's awful! But that's not all. I did something much worse: I decided not to sign up for education courses."

"How come?"

I shrugged.

"What's the problem?"

"My parents. They're both teachers and they expect me to follow in their footsteps. How am I going to tell them? They'll be so angry!"

Her smile was sympathetic. "My parents are teachers, too, and that's what they want for me. I guess they think teaching is a nice secure job."

"Mine said that, too."

"Well, try not to worry. You've done what you felt was best, and I'm sure you'll think of a way to explain it to them . . . Hey, don't frown. You figured out how to deal with the Registration ladies yesterday, didn't you?"

I kept my doubts to myself. After all, she didn't know my parents.

"My advice is to forget it for now," Pixie said, "and if you don't have anything else to do, you'd better take a look at this." She handed me a thick newspaper. "It's a schedule of all the classes they're giving this semester. You'd better start working out your schedule, right away. It isn't always all that easy to find the classes you want at the times you want."

Before I began, I went downstairs for a carton of milk. When I returned to our room, Pixie was still writing.

She's so much more obedient than I am, I thought with yet another guilty twinge. *Her parents told her to become a teacher, and that's exactly what she's doing.*

I forced myself to pick up the newspaper, and the next few minutes passed in silence. It was true, I soon realized: my schedule was going to be a problem.

"I hate this!" Pixie suddenly exclaimed, throwing down her pen.

I looked up, startled. "What's the matter?"

"Aw, my daddy, he's so smart. He knows how to spell every-thing—and obviously I don't. He always sends my letters back with all the mistakes underlined in red! He's even threatened that one of these days he's gonna give me a grade. A bad one!"

Laughing, I went back to work.

Later that same afternoon, I began my own letter home. I stuck to safe topics: my first impressions of the school, and a brief description of my strange reception by the Registration Committee and its cause. I told them about Pixie, Caralene,

Myrna, and, of course, Rachel. I also dared to mention my decision to major in art rather than music, but lacked the courage to
announce that I had no intention of taking education courses——
now, or ever.

———————

After dinner—mostly milk, in my case—Rachel came to visit
Pixie again just as I began, rather reluctantly, to get dressed for
the mixer.

She sat in our armchair like a queen on her throne, commenting at great length and with extreme rancor about the
naïveté of any freshman foolish enough to attend any social
function scheduled by the Dorm Committee.

I, meanwhile, kept dressing in angry and miserable silence,
warning myself that it would be suicidal to tell her that I felt
obligated to go.

The phone rang.

Pixie beat Caralene to it. I listened to her half of the conversation, trying to ignore Rachel's steady chatter.

"Hello? Oh, it's you, Gineeva . . . Well, I'm sorry, I didn't
mean it that way." Her face lit up. "A party? At the Trees?"

Rachel's harangue abruptly ceased.

"When?" Pixie demanded, and listened some more. "Sure
we'll come!"

She hung up. "Hey, Cara, Rachel, Meri! Gineeva says
there's going to be a party over at the Trees tomorrow night,
and we're all invited! Booker T. and the MGs are going to play.
It'll be just like old times!"

"Great!" Rachel said. "Count me in."

"Girl, are we gonna party!" Caralene whirled Pixie once
around the room, and the phone rang again.

This, I was to learn, was also a regular part of our nightly
routine.

"Hello, Lover," Pixie purred into the receiver.

Caralene went back to her room.

"It's Norman," Rachel told me in a stage whisper. "Pixie's boyfriend. He graduated last semester and joined the army. The dummy. He's stationed up north now."

"I miss you too, Sweetie," Pixie cooed. "Oh, we're not doing anything special. Just sitting around the dorm, working on our schedules and getting ready for classes next week."

Rachel giggled and Pixie shot her a warning look.

"Of course I'm not going out with anyone while you're up there. I promised. Don't you believe me?" She pouted.

Rachel put both hands over her mouth to stifle her laughter.

"Yes, Lover, I'll write every day."

"Norman wants Pixie to marry him," Rachel confided to me, still smirking. "Actually, he tried to get her to marry him this past summer, but she managed to talk him into letting her finish school first. I suspect he may end up regretting that."

Grinning like a well-fed cat, Pixie hung up.

"Rae-chel," she drawled, "you're gonna get me in trouble with Norman if you keep on like that."

And the phone rang again.

This time when Pixie answered, she only spoke briefly. "It's for you, Meri." She held out the receiver.

"Me? But I don't know anyone."

"Sure you do: Daniel Weaver."

"Who?"

She covered the receiver with one hand. "You know: my friend Daniel. You met him at dinner tonight."

Rachel snickered. "Surely you haven't forgotten, Meri; he's the guy who couldn't take his eyes off you."

I immediately realized who they meant: the aggressively intelligent young man who had lectured us interminably about his major—he was a senior in political science—all throughout dinner. I hadn't said a word because I was so embarrassed; all the while he was supposedly talking to Pixie and Rachel he'd kept staring at me, his gray eyes intense with undisguised interest.

"Oh, *that* Daniel," I mumbled, reaching for the phone.

But Pixie wasn't ready to hand it over. Her face alight with mischief, she leaned toward me and whispered, "Better watch out, Meri. He's nice—but real crazy."

Rachel guffawed.

"Thanks a lot, Pixie!" I said, as she finally relinquished the phone. "Hello, Daniel? This is Meri."

"Hi. I thought you might like to go out for a while."

"Out?"

"As in 'leave the dorm,'" he snapped back.

"You mean now?"

"Why not? You didn't say much at dinner, so I thought I'd satisfy my curiosity and ask you out for coffee."

"I can't. I mean, thanks, but I have to go to a mixer at the dorm tonight. Won't you be there?"

"Are you kidding? Mixers are dumb."

I couldn't think of an appropriate response, especially not with Rachel sitting there, watching me like a hawk.

"Then how about tomorrow night?" Daniel was asking.

I hesitated.

"Well, what do you say?"

He wasn't giving me a chance to think it through. Did I really want to go out with someone Pixie described as 'nice but crazy'?

"Come on, Meri. You're not playing hard to get, are you? That's a really stupid game."

"No! I mean, yes; I guess tomorrow is okay."

"Great! Actually, tomorrow's even better. There's a Yipsell meeting. I'll pick you up at the dorm at seven thirty."

Rather dazed by our conversation, I hung up.

"What's a Yipsell?" I wondered aloud.

"That's Y-P-S-L." Rachel's voice was full of scorn. "You know: the Young People's Socialist League."

"Oh."

"I went to one meeting, but all they did was sit around and sing stupid union songs. They're all talk and no action. Don't worry, though, we'll be thinking of you fondly tomorrow night while you're out on your wonderful Yipsell date with Daniel, and we're having fun at the Trees with Booker T." She flashed me a malicious grin.

"Oh, no!" I groaned. "I forgot."

"Poor Meri," Pixie said with a noticeable lack of sincerity. When she saw my face, she chuckled. "Don't worry, there'll be lots more parties."

"Time for our mixer, suitemate," Myrna announced, coming in from her room.

We left quickly, before Rachel had a chance to say anything more.

Rachel was right, of course.

For all her sarcasm, I had to admit that she knew about mixers—and they weren't for me!

Part of the problem was that I was extremely shy, and although I tried to pretend I didn't mind, I was secretly afraid that none of the boys would notice me.

But I needn't have worried; they noticed me, all right—and stayed carefully away. And that was the other part of the problem: I was just too different.

The most popular girl there was definitely Susan Olsen, Roberta Kruger's freshman roommate. She was tiny and pleasingly curvaceous, with blond hair, blue eyes, and a cute little nose. Once the boys recovered from their initial awkwardness, they never left her alone.

Roberta Kruger and the dorm president, a senior whose nickname was Schotzie, "warmed things up," as they described it. This consisted of leading us through some embarrassing get-acquainted games, passing out refreshments, and pairing us off for the first dances.

But the moment they stepped back to let us sort things out for ourselves, the dynamics of the room changed radically. The boys who were interested in dancing chose partners according to their own preferences—and most of them definitely preferred

Susan Olsen types—while the rest stood off to one side, discussing cars and basketball, and watching the dancers.

Inevitably, some of us were left out.

"Well, I guess we're just not Coca-Cola girls," Myrna said, sighing. By now we were standing next to the record player, on the opposite side of the room from the unattached boys.

"You have beautiful hair," I told her. What I didn't mention was that her curly red hair wasn't spectacular enough to offset the fact that she was quite overweight and rather loud.

As for myself, I suggested to Myrna that I was probably too foreign-looking to suit the tastes of the boys who were present.

"But not for everyone's taste," she commented. "Didn't I hear Rachel say you have a date tomorrow night?"

I could feel a blush coming on.

"Not bad." I heard the envy in her voice. "Especially considering that you've been here less than forty-eight hours."

"I guess so . . ."

"Well, who is it? Anyone I know?"

"Pixie's friend, Daniel Weaver. I think you met him at dinner tonight."

"That weirdo! The white guy who's a political science major?"

I was saved from having to answer by Roberta Kruger.

"Hey, you two—don't just stand there! You're supposed to be dancing. Go on, get out there and mix!"

When neither of us moved, she shook her finger at us in disapproval and stalked off.

Myrna looked at me and shrugged. "We may as well leave."

"Yeah, I guess so."

"Don't look so disappointed, Meri. After all, this way we can go upstairs and get lots of Roberta's famous beauty sleep . . . Not that it'll do either of us much good," she said with another sigh.

chapter 5: daniel

Maybe what makes him "crazy" is that he asked me out, I speculated, by now more than a little bit worried.

I was alone. Pixie, Rachel, Gineeva, and Caralene had already left for their party, bubbling over with excitement, anticipating the fun they were going to have at the Trees.

Myrna, who was apparently an eternal optimist—or else far more stoic than I was in the face of rejection—was next door, getting ready for the night's mixer.

The phone rang.

When I answered, the receptionist in the lobby announced, "Mr. Weaver is here to see Miss Henriques."

On my way downstairs, I fought off wave after wave of nervous jitters, reminding myself that it was far too late to do anything besides go through with this questionable date. I took the stairs rather than the elevator, hoping to put off the inevitable for as long as possible.

I recognized Daniel the moment I stepped from the stairwell: a rather short young man, he was lounging against the wall by the receptionist's desk with carefully studied nonchalance. He had on the same baggy beige slacks and tan shirt he'd worn at our first meeting, and his light brown hair was cropped so close I still couldn't decide whether it was straight or curly—or, for that matter, what its exact color was. He could almost have passed for one of the older boys at the previous night's mixer, for he was quite ordinary looking—ordinary, that is, until you noticed the intensely hurt and angry expression in his steel-gray eyes.

"We're going to be late," was all he said in greeting. Without another word, he turned and began walking out of the lobby. "Meeting's in town, across campus," he called back over his shoulder.

I was so taken aback by his brusque manner that it was several moments before I was able to react. Then, like a well-trained puppy, I scampered obediently after him.

Outside, he stopped beside a parked bicycle.

"Daniel—"

"No time to talk," he said. "We're in a hurry." He straddled the bike. "Get on."

I stared in disbelief.

Get on?

Me?

In a dress and nylons?

What kind of date was this, anyway? It certainly wasn't starting out the way I'd expected.

In my fantasies, the first college man I dated would be kind and courteous—and preferably tall, dark, and handsome. If I was very lucky, he would be grateful that I was willing to go out with him in the first place. And of course he would bring me flowers or, touchingly, a single rose.

"Quit standing there gawking like a dope, and get on!" Daniel snapped, startling me out of my romantic reveries.

I panicked. "W . . . wait a minute!" I sputtered. "We can't just go off like this."

"Like what? What did you expect me to do?" His voice was heavy with sarcasm. "Pick you up in a limousine?"

I knew I was blushing.

"Well?" he demanded.

"I . . . um . . . I know this sounds kind of silly"—I struggled to find the right words—"but at home, whenever I was going out, I was supposed to tell someone, and I, uh, well, I got the impression they expect us to do the same thing here."

"That's just great! You want me to wait here while you find someone to tell? How about Mrs. Brown? Or maybe you'd rather call home instead?"

He was worse than Rachel—quite possibly on a par with my mother!

How had I ever gotten myself into this mess? But since I didn't have the courage to defy him, I just shook my head. "N . . . no . . . I guess not."

"Good. Then shut up and get on. You can have the seat."

How awkward to have to hitch up my skirt and throw a leg over the bicycle frame. And how unpleasant to have to put my arms around the waist of someone I not only didn't know but by now was pretty sure I didn't even like!

I barely had time to settle myself behind him before Daniel shoved off with a sickening lurch. For the first few moments we wobbled crazily as he fought to establish his balance, and then we began picking up speed at an alarming rate. Soon we were racing across campus as fast as two people could possibly go on one small bicycle.

He rode standing on the pedals, leaning recklessly into the curves, ringing his bell, and shouting, "Get out of my way, you fucker!" at anyone unfortunate enough to cross our path.

I clutched the sides of his shirt and shut my eyes tight.

After a while, we coasted to a stop, but I waited a bit longer, until I was quite certain that we weren't going anywhere else, before I dared to open my eyes. We had stopped in what appeared to be the residential part of town, in front of a white, wood-frame house with blue shutters and a picket fence.

"Good thing that light back there was green," Daniel announced, glancing around at me. "I'm not sure I would have been able to stop for a red. My brakes are rotten."

I just sat there taking deep breaths, as if I, rather than he, had been the one who'd been pedaling.

"What's the matter with you, Meri? Are you planning on sitting there all night?"

Once I was sure that my knees would hold me up, I carefully dismounted.

Daniel leaned the bike against the fence and headed up the front walk, giving my arm a sharp tug when I failed to immediately follow. I stumbled after him in a daze.

By the time we walked in through the front door, I had recovered enough to notice that, contrary to Daniel's dire predictions, we weren't late; in fact, the meeting was just about to start.

My parents having admittedly had a fling back in the 1940s with the Communist Party (and our home having once been visited by two very straight-laced, Dragnet-cloned FBI agents who had been sent away very quickly, looking vaguely disappointed), I was more than a little curious to see what went on inside a YPSL meeting.

First there was lots of talk about current events, and then we sang union songs.

No one mentioned bombs or demonstrations.

How can an organization with such a provocative name be this dull? I wondered. Sitting on the floor beside Daniel, I decided that Rachel had a definite knack for analyzing our campus environment accurately, if rather cynically. Her assessment of last night's mixer, and now YPSL, was certainly right on the money.

I was relieved when the session ended—it had almost rivaled the freshman orientation meeting on a scale of one to ten for boredom—and I was beginning to indulge fantasies of going back to the dorm, picking up a good book, and escaping from Daniel.

Permanently.

But my dream of a swift conclusion to the evening was interrupted by Daniel himself. No sooner had we stepped out of the house than he abruptly demanded to know what I thought of the meeting.

"It was . . . ummm . . . interesting. I haven't heard some of those old union songs since I was a kid."

"You already knew them?"

"Yeah. My parents had some records, and they—"

"It's way too early to go back to the dorm," he said. "You want to try the local coffeehouse? It's right around the corner."

Beyond a doubt, I knew the answer to that question. However, under pressure and the force of his personality, I couldn't think of a polite—or comfortable—way of saying "no." I wasn't at all pleased with what finally came out of my mouth—"I guess so,"—but it was too late to take it back once it was said.

"Great!" He picked up his bike.

"But let's walk!" I hurriedly added.

As we moved through the gathering Indian summer darkness, Daniel pushing his bike and lecturing me about the meeting—who had been there and who hadn't, who was sufficiently radical and who wasn't—moment by moment, my uneasiness grew. For despite his abrasive manner, I could tell that he was attracted to me.

"You're Jewish, aren't you?" he suddenly asked, interrupting his own monologue. His eyes studied my face with disconcerting directness.

Inwardly, I cringed, wondering where this sudden change of topic was heading, but I only nodded.

"Thought so." He sounded smugly satisfied. "You remind me of a girl I knew on the kibbutz. Her name was Miriam."

"A kibbutz! In Israel?"

"They don't have them anywhere else that I'm aware of."

"What on earth were you doing on a kibbutz, Daniel? You can't be Jewish."

He chuckled. "True. But last year I decided I had to see Israel for myself—you know, really experience it, not like a tourist. I even thought I might want to live there."

"But you have to be Jewish to emigrate."

"Well, I was determined to get in anyway. So when I arrived, I just told everyone I was Jewish, and I guess the authorities decided that if I was crazy enough to pretend I was a Jew, they'd let me get away with it."

"Obviously you didn't stay."

"No. I was there for about six months, but after a while—oh, I don't know, I guess I got homesick for good old America: Mom and apple pie, and all that crap. So I came back to the States . . . And now that I'm here, I can't believe I was actually stupid enough to leave Israel."

He grinned, and I thought he looked much nicer—his self-deprecating smile softened his irritating, aggressive edge.

By this time we were standing on the sidewalk in front of a ratty old storefront.

"Well, here we are," Daniel announced, "Bloomington's one and only coffeehouse. And that's the only good movie house in town." He indicated an equally dilapidated building next door. "They show foreign films. I'm giving you the benefit of the doubt by assuming that you aren't a Doris Day/Rock Hudson fan—which is practically all they show in the other movie houses in the area."

Once I'd assured him that our artistic tastes coincided, we went inside.

The place could have been transported directly from Greenwich Village, as far as I was concerned. Old and musty, it had a somehow familiar and comfortable atmosphere, much like the Village coffeehouses I'd gravitated to over the past few years. And, as in many Village clubs, there was a small stage at the back of the room where a guitarist sat, singing folksongs.

We chose a table and ordered cappuccinos.

"That guy's from the Folksinging Club," Daniel said when he noticed where I was looking. "You like that kind of music?"

"I grew up on it."

"Me, too. Listen, the club's first meeting of the year is this coming Sunday night. I could take you..."

It was presented as a question, and I hesitated before answering, wondering if I could possibly say no without antagonizing him. Unable to face that prospect, I caved in and agreed.

Daniel smiled at me with something like relief in his eyes.

The waitress returned with our drinks.

I took a sip and almost dropped the cup.

"Daniel, this isn't cappuccino—it's hot chocolate with whipped cream!"

"Well, there *is* a hint of coffee flavoring." Once again that transfiguring grin. "You didn't expect real cappuccino did you?"

"Why not?"

"If they served honest-to-God cappuccino here, hardly anyone would drink it."

"What kind of university town is this anyway?"

"Not what you expected, huh?"

"Not at all."

"Well, in case you haven't noticed, Bloomington's at least ten years behind the rest of the country—not to mention Israel . . . No," he went on, "I knew you were different the moment I set eyes on you. You think I'd waste my time on a Midwestern freshman?"

Embarrassed by this very direct admission of interest, not to mention his arrogance, I was unable to meet his eyes. Instead, I looked down, stirred my cocoa, and decided to try to shift the conversation to safer ground.

"So, Daniel . . . Tell me about Israel. I've never known anyone who actually lived there. What was it like?"

He didn't even hesitate. "Freedom: all the freedom a person could possibly want. And a lot of hard work . . . You see, since we were near the border, we lived with the constant threat of danger: at any moment we might suddenly be fighting for our lives. But somehow it was good—it taught us to live in the moment."

Although he seemed to be speaking in clichés, I was moved by his words, and by the depth of emotion in his voice.

"I wonder if I would have liked it," I mused.

His eyes narrowed. "You might. Their morals are quite different from ours, you know. Remember I said you reminded me of a girl I knew there?"

I nodded.

"She was my lover."

He's just trying to shock and embarrass me, I told myself. And he was, at least partially, succeeding.

In a desperate attempt to change the subject yet again, I

said the first thing that popped into my head: "It sounds like you had a very interesting time in Israel, Daniel. But now that you're back home, tell me what you're studying."

Then I felt like an idiot because I already knew the answer, and he knew that I knew.

He gave me an appraising look but, to my relief, didn't challenge me. Instead, he began describing his work.

After that, things were easier.

On the way back to my dorm, we talked about Pixie, and I told him about our first meeting—was it really only two days ago?—and my run-in with the Registration ladies, which he found highly entertaining.

When we arrived back at the dorm, it was ten minutes before lockout.

The courtyard in front of Morrison Hall was inky dark beyond the harsh flood of light from the spotlights over the front entrance. Miss Bell was standing, silhouetted in the doorway, with a key ring in one hand, looking out into the night.

As we approached the steps, I realized that I'd been hearing furtive rustling noises all around us, ever since we'd entered Wells Quad. I peered about nervously, trying to penetrate the gloom.

"Daniel," I whispered, "do you hear that?"

"Yup." His matter-of-fact voice sounded overly loud in the hushed night. "Lots of activity out there tonight."

As my eyes adjusted, I saw figures on the ground, all across the courtyard. "Daniel, it's people! They're lying all over the lawn and in the bushes! What's going on?"

His laugh was short and bitter. "What do you think?"

When I didn't answer, he continued, "Remember what I said about morals being different in Israel? Well, at least the Israelis aren't hypocrites. Here everyone preaches morals, but what they really mean is: it's okay to do whatever you want—as long as you do it in the dark, where no one can catch you at it, and as long as you're done before lockout."

I frowned. "I don't believe you!"

"Ha! Hasn't anyone mentioned that the men's dorms don't have a curfew, even though the women's do? Didn't you wonder why?"

"Well, yes, but—"

"It's certainly not because the school officials care about your virtue! It's to protect themselves. They figure if a girl ends up going home pregnant, her parents won't be able to sue the school for neglect because technically their daughters have been locked in all night."

"Oh." I was too astonished to say anything more.

He stood, poised beside his bike. "Well, I'd better be going before Miss Bell decides I'm trying to steal your virginity." This time, his grin was pure malice. "So long, Meri. See you Sunday night."

Even after he'd left the quad, I could hear his voice drifting back through the nighttime darkness: "Get the fuck out of my way, assholes!"

"Shut up!" grumbled a male voice from the darkness.

"Well, I was right, wasn't I?" Pixie asked as she walked into our room at precisely two minutes past eleven.

"Right about what?"

"Daniel. He's real nice, but he's also kind of crazy."

I couldn't help smiling. "Funny: that's exactly what he said about you."

"Why, that . . . ! Well, the next time you see that no-good Daniel Weaver, you tell him he doesn't know me from Adam Orfox!"

Or maybe she'd said "Madam Orfax." Whichever it was, I had no idea how to reply.

She sat down on her bed and began taking off her shoes.

"Aren't you going to tell me about the party?" I asked.

"It was wonderful!" Her face, as she looked over at me, was radiant. "Just like old times—no, it was even better! Booker T.

and the band were super, and Jermaine Jackson came back to visit . . ."

She paused expectantly. "You know, Meri: Jermaine Jackson? The Jackson Brothers?"

I shook my head.

"Where have you been? Oh, well . . . Anyway, they're good! And did we ever party! And we'd still be partying if it wasn't for that dumb old lockout."

I took out my pajamas.

"Are you going to see Daniel again?" she suddenly asked.

"I guess so." I was sure she could hear the reluctance in my voice.

"I knew it. He's so different, he's kind of intriguing, isn't he?"

"Strange how the two of you seem to have the same opinion of each other."

"Now don't you start in on that again. Just remember what I said: he's nice but he's also kind of crazy. So watch out."

"Yup, I sure will. Thanks so much for your concern . . . Mom."

chapter 6: cards

The next night marked the beginning of what I came to think of as The Great Hearts Marathon. It was Pixie who started it, and it all came about, I later decided, because she must have been feeling a bit of a letdown after the previous night's party at the Trees—a subject that she, Caralene, and Rachel had been discussing nonstop ever since they'd returned from the festivities. However, by Saturday evening, even Pixie had run out of steam, and she began looking around for a new source of entertainment. According to her, cards were the perfect solution.

"Well, I certainly have better things to do with my time!" Rachel declared with lofty disdain—and without another word, she stalked out of our room.

I wasn't sorry to see her go.

"Cara? Myrna? Want to play cards?" Pixie called through the washroom, apparently not in the least put off by Rachel's snub.

Both girls came in.

"Sounds good to me," Caralene said eagerly. "Let's play Hearts!"

"How're we gonna do that?" Pixie countered. "We don't have enough players for a really good game."

"I'll phone Gineeva," Caralene said, her eyes alight with mischief. "She'll know exactly who to call."

While we were waiting for Caralene, Pixie started to pace. "This isn't going to work," she complained. "I can't think of anyone besides us who might be hanging around the dorm with nothing better to do on a Saturday night."

But Myrna, who had finally given up on mixers, had an idea. "Hey," she said, "what about Susan Olsen and Roberta Kruger? I think they're both staying in. Roberta doesn't date because she's engaged to a guy who lives in Tennessee, and Susan told me she was going to wash her hair and get ready for church tomorrow."

Pixie looked up. "I'm not so sure that's a good idea—"

"Meri, go ask them," Myrna said.

"But . . ."

"It'll be easy to find them," she instructed before I could state my objections. "Their room's right across the hall, on the other side of the bathroom."

"Why me?" I groaned.

"Just do it!" Myrna commanded. "We need them."

My mother had trained me well: I recognized the Voice of Authority when I heard it. And so I trotted obediently off to do Myrna's bidding, picking up a deck of cards as I left the room, not so much to make my offer look authentic as to give myself something to do besides biting my fingernails when I went over to confront the semi-strangers.

While I waited for someone to answer my knock, I shuffled Pixie's cards with nervous hands.

Susan opened the door. Her china-doll face was framed by a halo of little pink curlers that peeked out from beneath a pink cloth turban, and she was bundled up to her chin in a bulky pink chenille bathrobe.

"Hi there!" I began in as hearty a voice as I could muster. "We're about to start a game of cards over in my room and Myrna suggested—that is, we wondered if you'd like to join us."

Susan didn't react at all the way I expected—with a simple yes or no, or with some other more elaborate acceptance or refusal. Instead she just stood there, staring at my hands.

"Susan?" I tried again. "How about it? Would you like to play?"

Still no answer—just that mesmerized stare.

Was she appalled by the state of my fingernails? They were certainly a mess by anybody's standards. Or was something else going on?

In fact, it was such odd behavior that I couldn't help but wonder what she and Roberta had been doing in their room before I'd arrived. I inhaled deeply but couldn't detect any of that sweet-scented, telltale smoke.

Then, just when I'd decided that she wasn't ever going to respond, she whispered, "Are those cards? Real cards?"

"Of course they're real." Mystified, I looked down, turning the objects in question over in my hands. I held them out: a peace offering. "Here—you want to check them out?"

"NO!!!" Recoiling, she thrust both hands behind her back and gave me a look that was impossible to interpret.

"What on earth's the matter with you, Susan?"

Instead of replying, she took another step backwards, and for a moment I thought she was going to slam the door in my face. But curiosity evidently got the better of her, and she crept closer, leaning forward as if anxious for a better look.

Her reactions were so exaggerated! Suddenly, I realized what was happening: this straight-looking, blond, blue-eyed, Midwestern icon was trying to pull off some sort of outrageous comedy routine! Although I wasn't exactly sure what it was, it was definitely funny.

"Hey, you're really good!" I admired, chuckling. "Okay, I think I get it. I'm supposed to believe you're afraid of a deck of cards."

"It isn't funny!" she snapped.

"Huh?"

"Cards are the work of the Devil."

"They are?"

"Of course they are!" She sounded so serious that I began to feel embarrassed.

"How do you know?"

"My mother told me so."

She said it so straight-faced that for a moment I thought

she really meant it—but then I burst out laughing. "All right, Susan—enough is enough! I may be a bit dense, but I do know a joke when I hear one."

She stamped her foot. "I AM NOT JOKING!"

"Okay," I said. "But let me tell you how the rest of it goes, just to save you the trouble of having to go through the whole spiel. What you're going to say next is that cards are so evil they're almost as bad as evolution. Right? And then—"

"Evolution?" she spat. "Are you trying to trick me? Of course evolution's evil! What do you think I am—a Communist?"

The angry intensity of her blue eyes caused me to step back a pace. "You *are* serious!" I blurted out. And then, "I'm sorry!" My face felt so hot, I thought my skin was going to melt.

Susan just glared.

I started backing away, hands held out in front of me in a placatory gesture—but I quickly whipped them around behind my back when I realized that I was still holding those damning cards, and she was still staring daggers at them. "Well, I ummm . . . I err . . . Gee, I guess you're really not interested in playing cards after all, are you? Uh, well, so long, Susan. It's been nice talking to you . . ."

The door slammed shut with an echo that reverberated up and down the hall as I scurried back our room.

Back in the safety of our room, I told Pixie what had happened in a shaky voice.

"Oh, too bad. She's one of those," was her only comment.

At that point, Gineeva walked in, followed by an unfamiliar young woman.

"Hey, Pixie, Caralene," she said, "you-all remember Nadine, don't you? She and some of the other girls agreed to come over from the Trees."

I was amazed by how relieved I was to see some friendly—well, at least not *un*friendly—faces.

By mutual agreement, the six of us filed through our little washroom and into Caralene and Myrna's room, which was slightly bigger than ours and just as Spartan.

Moments later, two more Trees residents walked in, and after greetings were exchanged all around, everyone sat down on the floor to begin what soon turned out to be a lively Hearts marathon. Before long all of us were having such a wonderful and noisy time that I began to relax and forget about my misadventure with Susan Olsen.

"Girl," Gineeva teased Pixie, "you've really done it now: you went and got stuck with The Mag again!"

I was already learning that the Queen of Spades, which Pixie and her friends called "The Mag," was the one card *not* to get. At least, not unless you were Caralene, who never failed, once she had decided to try, to "Shoot the Moon" by collecting all of the cards and, in doing so, win the game.

Laughter filled the room. Caught up in the moment, the usually dour Gineeva even tried out a couple of catcalls.

"Hush up, Girl," Caralene hissed, "you're making too much noise! You never know who might—"

"Why, hello, girls."

My head whipped around. Miss Bell was standing in the doorway. There was a tremor in her voice that belied her hearty tone.

"I thought I'd just drop by to see how you're doing."

No one said a word.

Miss Bell tried again. "Funny thing: I was in my room when I heard a commotion over here, so I decided I'd better check and make sure all of you are . . . You know, okay."

For several moments, no one spoke. At last Pixie said, with great seriousness, "Gee, Miss Bell, thanks for your concern. Some of our friends are here from the Trees and we're all just fine."

"Oh . . . Well, it's nice to see that you girls are having so much fun." She shifted uneasily in the doorway. "So, I . . . I guess I'll be going."

And she hurried away.

Gineeva chuckled. "Girl, we got her worried! She's not sure how to take all this integrated stuff. Still thinks we might start killing each other."

In midst of the laughter, I had a sudden inspiration. "Hey, Gineeva, if you really want to worry her, the next time we play cards, you should phone the Trees and invite every single one of your friends over to join us."

Amazement, and then respect, lit up Gineeva's eyes. "Now why didn't I think of that? That's a great idea, Meri! We'll do it. Miss Bell will poop in her panties!"

"Poor Miss Bell . . ." Pixie said with mock sincerity—and we all burst out laughing again.

"Now girls, let's be serious," Caralene chided. "Time to get back to the game."

Hours into our games, our revelries were interrupted by a male voice calling from outside the open window, "Hello up there! Anyone home?"

"It's the pizza man!" Pixie exclaimed, jumping to her feet.

By then it was well past lockout, and Gineeva's friends had long since gone back to the Trees. At that time of night, the only way to get anything into or out of our dorm was by stealth or cunning. Before calling in our order to the local pizza parlor, the girls had assured me that they had solved the problem.

"Quick, Pixie, go get your stuff!" Caralene commanded as she rushed to open the window.

Pixie ran to our room and I followed her, curious.

"Where *is* that nasty old thing?" she muttered, rummaging through her rather jumbled closet.

"What are you looking for?"

"The damn basket! It's got to be here somewhere."

"What's it for?" I persisted.

"Ah, here it is! Just wait—you'll see."

Next door, Caralene was leaning out of her window, happily chatting with the delivery boy. "Good girl, Pixie!" she said when we returned. "All right everyone: it's suppertime!"

The basket, with our money inside, was lowered by a rope, and when Pixie hauled it back up, it contained a feast, or so it seemed to me: a whole pizza and several steaming-hot, foil-wrapped Strombolis (French rolls filled with meat and spicy tomato sauce).

It was the first decent meal I'd had in days.

Early Sunday morning, there was an almost tangible feeling of anticipation in the air as the bathroom across the hall from our room filled up with clouds of steam, wet bodies, and a heady mix of the perfume of various shampoos, powders, and deodorants.

Breakfast was a noisy, hurried affair, and afterwards most of the girls left for church services, talking in animated voices as they hurried past our door.

Before long, the dorm was essentially deserted.

Pixie, Rachel, and I sat in our room, keeping each other company.

"What a relief to have the place to ourselves!" Rachel remarked with her habitual sarcasm.

"Church isn't so bad, Rachel," Pixie said. "Sometimes I kind of enjoy going."

"Well, if you're truly in need of divine inspiration," Rachel said, "feel free to turn on the campus radio station and tune in the sermon of the week. Only let me know ahead of time that you're going to succumb, and I'll make sure I'm somewhere else."

The rest of the day passed quietly and Sunday evening arrived: it was time to go to the Folksinging Club meeting with Daniel.

Rachel asked if she could walk over with us.

For once, I was glad of her company. Somehow it made my "date" with Daniel seem less official.

As it turned out, although Rachel and Daniel knew each other fairly well, they maintained a cool civility. As far as I was able to determine, each of them was suspicious of the sincerity of other's devotion to the Radical Cause, and each seemed to think that the other was just a bit too soft for his or her own good. But they were in complete agreement on one subject: the University's opinion of the Folksinging Club.

"You know, the school administration is highly suspicious of the club's activities," Rachel warned me with a smirk as we entered the Student Union Building.

"Suspicious? Of what?" Like the straight man in any good comedy routine, I could always be counted upon to ask the dumb question on cue.

Daniel grinned. "Actually, they're convinced the Folksinging Club's a front for subversive activities."

"Only they can't make up their minds which ones!" Rachel added, and then she giggled. "Poor Meri—I'm afraid you're off to a really bad start."

"What do you mean?" Everything she ever said seemed calculated to make me uneasy, and this was no exception.

"Well, here you are—you haven't been at IU one whole week, and you've already gotten yourself mixed up with the worst crowd. First Yipsell, and now the Folksinging Club."

"Oh, come on, Rachel!"

"It's true," Daniel insisted, abruptly serious. "In case you haven't heard, the administration keeps track of what you join, and who you know, and where you go, and what you do there. And all of it goes onto your record—every last detail—as if you were being investigated by the Gestapo or the KGB. And you can bet on it: the school won't approve of your politics."

"Who said anything about joining Yipsell or the Folksinging Club?" I snapped, convinced they were teasing me, the gullible freshman. "All I wanted to do at Yipsell was visit one time, and tonight I want to hear some folk music."

"It doesn't matter what you want," Rachel said. "What 'They' want is to keep an eye on you."

"All right then," I demanded, irked by her smug self-assurance, "what *is* safe to join around here? What won't get me in trouble?"

Her reply was immediate: "The Young Republicans."

Both she and Daniel burst out laughing.

<hr>

In spite of Rachel and Daniel's warnings, I enjoyed the Folk-singing Club meeting so much that, before it was over, I decided to join anyway—the school administration be damned. There was obviously nothing radical about the group. *After all, how much trouble can a person get into for singing?* I asked myself.

Besides, everyone seemed extremely nice, and I was more than anxious to find a place where I felt that I belonged—someplace where I might have a chance of making friends.

The club president, a graduate student named Derek Stone, was especially intriguing. In retrospect, I suppose it was because he, too, seemed somehow different.

Unlike most men on campus, Derek had a distinctive style. Whereas they dressed conservatively, in pale button-down shirts and shapeless, unflattering wash-and-wear pants like Daniel's, Derek wore tight-fitting jeans that accentuated his long legs, and a plaid woolen shirt that hung unbuttoned over a blue work shirt. And instead of the loafers or oxfords that seemed to be regulation wear in Indiana, Derek wore cowboy boots.

I thought he was probably around twenty-five, but because his gold-rimmed glasses and his mustache hid a great deal of his face, he could have been practically any age. Tall and wiry, he moved with a restless energy, and when he spoke, I detected a trace of an unfamiliar accent.

"This year, I'm going to make it a priority to change the club's image as a perpetual loser," he said at the beginning of the meeting. "As for our concerts, my goal is to make them self-supporting, which is about the best we can hope for, since we've never succeeded in turning a profit."

Several people laughed.

"Right now, I'm negotiating with Joan Baez, who's a personal friend and would love to do a concert for such a worthy cause . . ."

People began clapping.

Derek held up a hand. "Now don't get excited—it may not work out. As those of you who've been with us in the past already know, the success—or even the existence—of this club or our concerts isn't up to us: it's up to the school authorities. And they haven't said yet whether or not they'll give us permission to have *any* concert, let alone one with Joan Baez. Also, even if they do say yes, we don't know if they'll rent us a hall that's big enough to make us some money." He shrugged. "In any event, I'm sure Joan Baez would draw a crowd, but what I'm not so sure of is the University's willingness to cooperate with us. Undoubtedly, they'd rather have us go out of business once and for all . . ."

This made me think of Daniel and Rachel's comments about the uneasy relationship between the club and the school. I had assumed they were exaggerating, but now I suspected that they might have been telling the truth. As unlikely as it seemed, there actually could be some risk involved in joining the Folksinging Club. But that was exactly what I was going to do, and I felt prepared to accept the consequences.

Derek had reached the end of his talk, saying that it was more than time to stop gabbing and get on with the music— which was, after all, what the club was really all about. He volunteered to be the first performer, and when he picked up his guitar, his nervous tension seemed to melt away. He sang well, and played very musically.

"Gee, I'd sure like to get to know him better," I muttered to myself while the next performer was making her way to the front of the room.

Much to my embarrassment, Rachel overheard me. "Who wouldn't?" she whispered back. "But you may as well forget it—

he's absolutely unapproachable. Believe me—I tried all last year, and he was strictly business. I think he's finishing a master's degree, and the rumor is that he never dates."

"Hey, what are you two gossiping about?" Daniel demanded from my other side.

"Derek Stone," I answered, aware that I was blushing.

"He doesn't sing enough protest songs," Daniel shot back. "I liked last year's president much better."

chapter 7: fall semester

Registration was an exercise in perseverance and frustration, the trial-by-fire that we all had to pass through in order to be admitted into the Inner Sanctum of university classes. Every undergraduate was assigned a time, according to his or her last name, to arrive at the gymnasium, where each department was represented by a table manned by helpers with punch cards. We waited in long lines, hoping to sign up for the classes we wanted, with the professors we wanted, at the times we wanted—a nearly impossible feat.

What chaos! I had never seen so many people packed into one place. The noise of that many voices speaking all at once was deafening, the body odor overpowering. There were 18,000 undergraduate students enrolled at Indiana University that semester, and every one of them passed through the gym that day—in fact, I was sure that most of them were there at the same time as I was! In the end, I had a raging headache and one night class, but I considered myself lucky: I had only been in the gym for four hours. If the rumors were true, some people had endured for six or seven.

Of those I knew personally, only Rachel had finished up in a little under an hour.

"That's because no one in their right mind would sign up for the classes you picked," Pixie told her with a mischievous twinkle in her eye. "I bet the only people in those classrooms will be you and the professors!"

Pixie had also gotten off fairly easily. Since she was in her final year of elementary education, her schedule was essentially predetermined.

"I promise you, Pixie, the reality of having to attend those idiotic 'Kiddie-Lit' classes will more than compensate for any agony you managed to avoid by not having to undergo much of a registration ordeal," was Rachel's scornful assessment.

Classes began. Many were excellent—among the finest I had the privilege of attending in the course of my academic career—but in the end the people, not the subject matter, were what really interested me most.

My first class at Indiana University was Zoology, and when I walked into the lecture hall at seven fifty-five that first morning, I was amazed by the sheer number of students—especially considering the hour.

Our professor, Dr. Godwin, began by outlining our highly detailed assignments, every nuance of which had to be memorized. I was disconcerted and surprised by the zealousness of my fellow students, many of whom were obviously out to impress the teacher, even on that first day—a considerable feat in a class of that size. The mystery was solved for me during my first lab session, when my lab partner told me that our class was intended for pre-med students and was also required coursework for physical therapy majors like herself. According to her, it was Dr. Godwin's job to weed out those of us who were unlikely to succeed in medical school!

I was horrified. The class had been one of the many compromises I'd been forced to make on Registration Day, and at the time, no one at the Zoology table had thought to advise me of my mistake.

The possibility of being "weeded out" filled me with terror, so immediately after lab, I rushed over to the administration building hoping to switch classes—to no avail. As a liberal arts student who had accidentally blundered into the wrong class, I was faced with the unpleasant choice of either trying to cope with the accelerated pace or dropping out. Not wanting to lose the credit, I gritted my teeth and hung on.

I had to work very hard just to keep up in that class, but one aspect I did enjoy was the lab work, especially the elaborate drawings we were required to make of the various specimens we dissected. At least, I enjoyed it once I'd recovered from the shock of entering the lab for the first time.

That fateful first day found me walking down a hall in the basement of the Life Sciences Building, checking numbers on the doors against the room number on my class card. And just as I was beginning to suspect that I might have taken a wrong turn, there it was, but—oh, horror!—etched on the door's frosted glass window, in very black letters, below the room number, were the following words:

Dr. A. Kinsey
Sex Research Lab
Authorized Personnel Only!!!

I turned and fled.

From the relative safety of the far end of the hall, I glanced furtively about, hoping that no one had noticed my odd behavior and trying to look like a casual bystander who was waiting for a friend. Surreptitiously, I rechecked the number on my punch card against the number on the door.

They matched!

Meanwhile, several more students had joined me, and it was reassuring to see that each of them reacted more or less as I had. Before long, I was standing in the midst of a small, agitated crowd.

A few minutes after lab was scheduled to begin, the door to the room in question burst open and a suspiciously (at least, to my eye) cheerful young couple came strolling out.

"Hello, over there!" the young man called out to our unhappy group. "Are you looking for the zoology lab?" He must have taken our mutual silence for assent, because he said, "Well, come on over. We were beginning to think we weren't going to have any students at all this semester!"

"Yes—don't just stand there," his female counterpart urged. "Come in!"

As we slowly shuffled forward like a herd of reluctant sheep, the male teacher jabbed his thumb at the offending words on the door. "Hey, don't let this sign scare you. It's a souvenir left over from last year. Dr. Kinsey isn't doing research here anymore. I promise."

He held the door wide open.

Peeking past him, I saw—much to my relief—lab benches and Bunsen burners, not beds and cameras. Even after I had taken a seat along the lab countertop and begun to settle in, I could still hear our instructor in the hall outside, chuckling as he reassured the late arrivals.

Every day after zoology, I walked over to the nearby English building where I had Freshman English 1A, presided over by Mr. McGregor. He was my favorite sort of teacher: a challenging one. Short and heavyset, with dark, brooding eyes and a thick thatch of wavy black hair, he could instantly silence any student—or the entire class—with a single, searing glance. He had a penetrating intelligence that drove straight to the heart of any subject, and he had little tolerance for sloppy thinking.

At our first meeting, he told us that he expected us to push ourselves to the limits of our abilities, both in class and while completing our homework assignments—the reading and writing of essays. He would grade our efforts strictly, he said, but fairly.

This seemed to upset many of my classmates, who must have been hoping for an easy course. However, Mr. McGregor was adamant: not only was he going to teach us how to write, he was also going to teach us how to think.

I enjoyed listening to the deep rumble of his voice as he paced back and forth across the room, hands clasped behind his back, shaggy eyebrows drawn together in concentration. To many of my fellow students, he probably resembled Napoleon, but to me he was a romantic figure, a modern-day counterpart to the stern and demanding Mr. Rochester of Charlotte Bronte's *Jane Eyre*.

The remainder of the morning was devoted to anthropology.

Dr. Sellers was an easy-going, extremely accessible man—an anomaly at a time when professors were traditionally aloof. He was also a fascinating lecturer. Anthropology had captured my fancy in early childhood, and I was delighted to discover that I could actually get college credit for studying it.

With each class period, Dr. Sellers always brought something new and interesting to our attention. And, as the weeks went by, an unexpected facet of his personality began to emerge: he was absolutely fearless in the face of controversy. In fact, I even suspected he actually enjoyed provoking a certain amount of it. However, the first weeks of class passed by peacefully enough. It wasn't until later in the semester that Dr. Sellers dared to take a stand against the forces of Hoosier Hysteria.

Every afternoon, after an admittedly sketchy lunch of a carton of milk from my dorm's vending machine, I walked over to the music building for concert chorus. The director was a fine musician who immediately won my heart by giving us Bach's "B-Minor Mass" to work on. No matter how discouraging the day might otherwise have been, music never failed to lift my spirits.

Afterwards, because most of my friends had classes for the

rest of the afternoon, I usually studied alone in my room. However, twice a week I fulfilled my physical education requirement by attending modern dance. And finally, three nights a week, for three hours at a stretch, there was Introduction to Drawing.

Our instructor, Mrs. Burns, was a spinsterish-looking, apparently humorless young woman who, it soon became obvious, was an even more demanding taskmaster than Dr. Godwin and Mr. McGregor combined!

In fact, she was a terror. The working conditions she imposed upon us were an education in themselves. Only an occasional cough or sniffle, or the sound of someone sharpening a pencil, broke the silence of her classroom. No one dared to so much as whisper while Mrs. Burns, somber as a nun in her black dress and crepe-soled shoes, crept noiselessly about behind our backs, stopping to peer over our shoulders at the most unexpected and inopportune moments to monitor our progress.

That first night, she told us to make a pair of dots, about two inches apart, on a piece of paper. "Now connect them freehand, with a perfectly straight line."

Upon completing the task, we waited expectantly for the next step in her arcane initiation ritual.

"Why are you just sitting there?" she snapped. "Go on."

"But you haven't said what comes next," someone dared to say.

"There is no 'next.' Just make another pair of dots and connect them. Then do it again. And again. The connecting lines must be perfectly straight, as if you had made them with a ruler. That is tonight's assignment."

Mine was not the only mouth that dropped open in disbelief.

Mrs. Burns's white-blond eyebrows drew together in a frown, but she said nothing. Instead, she adjusted her horn-rimmed glasses on her long nose and began pacing around the room, eyes riveted on the floor as if she expected to discover the answer to some fundamental cosmic question in its scuffed gray surface.

We watched her intently, fascinated and also rather apprehensive.

Abruptly, she stopped pacing and confronted us. "As you will soon discover," she said, "there is always a definite reason for every assignment I give you. It is not my policy to explain my methods. However, just this once, since it is our first meeting, I will break my own rules." Her gaze swept the room. "First of all, this exercise will teach you to have a steady hand, which is the artist's greatest asset. Secondly, it will help to develop your patience and self-control." Her blue eyes flashed. "NOW GET BUSY!" she barked.

We grabbed our pencils and launched into feverish activity.

By the time I returned to my room that night, I was seething with frustration and resentment. And I was jumpy and close to tears from the extreme effort of trying to force my hand to draw what my mind demanded.

That night I dreamed of nothing but dots and lines.

My second class with Mrs. Burns was no better: she had us draw perfectly round circles around a central dot. During the third class, we drew perfectly regular ellipses between two points.

By then I was ready to quit, convinced that she was a sadist. Piano lessons had to be easier! But I persevered, and eventually, in spite of my unhappy struggles—or perhaps because of them—I learned something about myself: I *could* make my mind control what my hand did!

Meanwhile, in between pursuing these Zen-like exercises in artistic frustration, during the brief interludes before and after class, and during short breaks, my classmates and I were becoming friends. Mrs. Burns's oppression had the effect of uniting us into a family of fellow sufferers whose closeness and loyalty would never have come about otherwise.

I understood that Mrs. Burns was not purposely cruel. Still, somewhere deep inside, I was reserving the right to rebel. By nature, I resented anyone who would so totally and unreasonably dominate me—or anyone.

And so, as the days passed, we found ourselves adjusting to the routines of the fall semester. Yet classes were merely a backdrop, the stage upon which we played out our student days. My daily experiences and friendships were somehow more real and important to me, even then. And all the while, I sensed the specter of the University, or rather the University administration, lurking behind every scene: a powerful presence, sometimes benign, sometimes hostile, but never indifferent and always watching, ready to swoop down unexpectedly at a moment's notice to alter the course of our lives.

chapter 8: just friends

"And that final scene! That was the strangest thing of all. Do you have any idea what it was supposed to mean?"

It was Saturday night, the end of our second week of classes, and Daniel and I were out on another date. The old theater next to the coffeehouse was showing Ingmar Bergman's *Seventh Seal*. He'd insisted we had to see it.

Afterwards, hiking across campus towards my dorm (my boycott against riding Daniel's bicycle was still in effect), I felt like a sleepwalker. The movie, with its eerie imagery and obscure message, was unlike anything I'd ever encountered. At first I simply trudged along, lost in thought, barely aware of my surroundings, but after a while I began talking—thinking aloud, really—in the hopes that together we might be able to decipher the film's meaning.

Daniel seemed to be as preoccupied as I was. He didn't respond to my comments.

"Daniel?"

"Huh? Did you say something?"

"You haven't been listening."

"Sorry."

"I'm trying to figure out what the movie was about. It was so confusing."

"Yeah, I guess it was."

"Well, what do you think? Was that last vision really true? What did it mean? Do you think Bergman was saying Death was actually good—or was he evil?"

Patiently, I began recapping my theories, but before I had gotten very far, Daniel interrupted.

"This is stupid! I don't give a flying fuck whether or not you understood the goddamn movie! Save your analysis for your dopey English class! They might be interested, but I'm not!"

He was angrier than I'd ever seen him, and by now I'd already witnessed several of his fiery emotional outbursts.

Daniel was an enigma: he could argue passionately for an end to what he called "our Capitalist-Imperialist government," yet he loved America enough to have been extremely homesick the entire time he'd been in Israel. If you asked his opinion, he was only too happy to tell you he hated almost everything about Indiana University—its students, the administration, and campus politics. And he was disgusted with me for what he regarded as my naive trust that the school's racial problems could be worked out without anyone having to resort to what he felt were the mandatory violent protests. Yet here he was, back in Indiana, dutifully completing his undergraduate education.

I was afraid of him: of the angry snap of his icy gray eyes whenever I dared to disagree with him, of the sarcastic words he used to cut all of my carefully thought-out arguments to shreds, and of the intensity of his loves and hates. At the same time, I was flattered that this intelligent and articulate senior was interested in me, and I actually enjoyed some of our calmer conversations.

All in all, he reminded me of an unhappy child who's only naughty because he craves attention and the comfort of his mother's arms. It wasn't just that his rages seemed childlike; I soon realized that his feelings were as easily hurt as any child's, and that he was desperate for the approval and affection of his few loyal friends.

His schedule was far busier than mine, yet he showed up at my dorm almost nightly to visit me and joke with Pixie, to whom he was obviously attached, although he spoke with scornful cynicism of their friendship. And as the days went by, I realized that he also cared for me, despite the fact that he was often rude and brusque. Yet the more frequent his visits became and the longer they lasted, the more uneasy I became, for I couldn't help but wonder what proof of my loyalty he would eventually require.

And now here he was, angry with me once again for some obscure reason. I was crushed by his summary dismissal of my speculations about the movie, and I started to stammer out a half-hearted defense.

"Forget the fucking movie!" Daniel snapped. "We have more important things to discuss."

"We do?" My stomach, which was already in some distress, suddenly acquired a flock of hyperactive butterflies.

"We certainly do!" His hand closed around my upper arm in a painful grip. "And we're not going another step until we have this out."

He steered me ungently over to a bench that was practically lost in the darkness beneath a small grove of fir trees. "Sit down!" he ordered, shoving me forward.

"What do you want to talk about?" I asked in a voice that refused to come out much above a whisper.

"Us." He dropped down beside me, closer than I liked, on the cold stone seat.

"Us?"

"Stop playing dumb, Meri! You know as well as I do that we've been seeing each other for more than two weeks now."

"I do realize that." Perhaps if I could manage to sound as coolly cynical as he was, he would calm down and stop trying to intimidate me.

"Good; I'm glad to know you keep track of something! How long did you think we could go on like this?"

"Like what?" I echoed, licking suddenly dry lips.

"'Like what?'" he mimicked. "Like *dating.*"

"I don't know . . ."

"Of course you don't, you probably haven't given it a moment's thought."

He paused, but I didn't dare to reply.

"In that case, it looks like I'll have to do the thinking for both of us. What do you want from me? Have you bothered to ask yourself?"

"W . . . want? From you?"

"Listen, in case you haven't realized it, you've been taking up an awful lot of my time."

He paused again, but this time he seemed determined to wait me out.

"I . . . I'm not sure I understand," I temporized, feeling as if I was being bulldozed into a very tight corner.

"You understand plenty!" he flared. "You and your wishy-washy, Miss Goody Two-Shoes excuses . . . You go out with a guy for two whole weeks, and then you have the nerve to sit there, pretending you don't know what he's talking about when he says that it's time to get serious!"

"Two weeks isn't very long at all!" I wanted to protest, but I wasn't brave enough.

"So it looks like one of us is going to have to take the initiative," he hurtled on. "At least I know what I want!" Before I could say another word, he pulled me to him in a rough and passionate embrace.

Shocked by the suddenness of his move, for a brief moment I was paralyzed into passivity. Then outrage kicked in, and I twisted and thrashed in his arms.

"Let go of me!" I hissed, ducking my head to avoid his greedy mouth. "What do you think you're doing?"

"What's the matter?" he jeered, struggling to retain his grip. "Is the lily-white girl afraid of a kiss? Afraid it will ruin you for life?"

I didn't bother to answer. Instead I concentrated all my energy on trying to fend him off.

We wrestled like that for several moments, neither of us gaining an advantage and both of us furious. Then, suddenly, I was on my feet, gulping for air.

"Stop it!" I panted out. "I thought we were friends."

"Friends!" he shouted, jumping up, too. "Who said anything about friends? I want to be lovers!"

"Well, I don't! And don't you ever grab me like that again!"

"You traitor! You were leading me on! In Israel no one
fooled around like that. You don't have to be in love with someone to go to bed with them. That's why they call it 'Free Love.'
Everyone knows marriage and all that monogamy bullshit is
just a pile of crap!" His voice broke in what sounded like a sob.

Without warning, he ran at me—at least, that's what I
thought he was doing—and I stumbled clumsily aside. But to my
astonishment, he rushed past me and sprinted away into the night.

I stood alone under the fir trees, sobbing and shaking,
until my anger and shock had begun to subside. Then, in a very
somber mood, I walked back to the dorm alone.

I went straight to bed, far too embarrassed to tell Pixie
what had just happened. But she must have known something
was wrong.

The next night he phoned me.

At first I was reluctant to speak to him, afraid of what he
might say. I tried to convince Pixie to tell him that I was out,
but she just gave me a quizzical look and held out the receiver.
I hoped she didn't notice that my hands were shaking when I
took it from her.

"Hello?"

"Hey, it's Daniel. I know you were probably expecting me
to come by this evening, but—"

"Well, I—"

"Listen, I've been doing some serious thinking—and I've
decided we can't go on like this."

Oh, no! Not that again! "Daniel, I—"

"You're a great kid, and I've really enjoyed our visits . . ."

Was this really Daniel Weaver, sounding for all the world
like a big brother?

". . . But to be perfectly honest, I've been spending way too much time with you. I'm having trouble keeping up with my class work, and my grades are going down the toilet. I finally have to admit that I just don't have time for a social life."

"Oh!" If that was the way he wanted to play this, I was more than happy to oblige. "Gee, I'm really sorry I interfered with your work."

"I hope your feelings aren't hurt. I know this probably sounds like a rejection, but try not to take it personally. I'll always think of you as a friend."

Friends. Wasn't that my idea? "It's okay, Daniel. I understand."

"I knew you would."

"So I guess I'll see you around."

"I guess you will . . . Say, Meri, there's another meeting of the Folksinging Club next week. I suppose you're going?"

"I was planning on it."

There were several moments of awkward silence, during which I fervently hoped that he wasn't going to ask me to go with him.

"Well, I'd better get back to work," was what he finally said.

"Okay. Good-bye—and thanks for calling."

My hands were still shaking and my heart was racing long after I'd hung up.

———

At first it was a relief to know that Daniel was no longer going to come around, confusing me with his mercurial mood swings, and upsetting me with his unwelcome desires. But as the weeks passed, I found that most of the girls around me were dating every weekend, and I wasn't doing anything at all. I began to feel lonely and neglected.

Even Pixie was leading a busy social life—particularly for someone who was supposedly engaged and therefore, at least in theory, sidelined from the school's social whirl. She was usually out several evenings a week and almost always on Friday and Saturday nights, and the majority of our phone calls—nine times out of ten from males—were for her.

Whatever it was that was taking up so much of her time, she was very cagey about it. Neither Caralene, who was her best friend, nor Rachel, who tried to keep track of everything that was going on with her friends and in the dorm, was sure about the exact nature of Pixie's social activities.

Gradually, as my first month at Indiana came to an end, I began to wonder where and how, and even if, I would ever meet another man who would be interested in dating a non-Midwestern girl.

Dating isn't all there is to college, I chided myself on more than one occasion.

Still, I was afraid that maybe "crazy" Daniel was the only male in the entire school who would be nuts enough to want to spend time with me.

If my present life at Indiana had a noticeable lack of men in it there were, at least, several interesting women. By far the most intriguing was my zoology lab partner, a young woman with the unlikely name of Shennandoah Waters.

Shennandoah was the person who had informed me, earlier in the semester, that I had accidently enrolled in a pre-med class. As a physical therapy major, zoology was just one of the many requirements she had to fulfill. She was also taking embryology—which, she confessed, was proving to be so difficult that she was afraid she might flunk.

To help her studies along she began smuggling specimens out of the lab, taking them back to her dorm room so she could examine them at her leisure. But she soon encountered an unexpected obstacle in the person of her roommate, who complained bitterly about the smelly assortment of frog corpses, formaldehyde-soaked baby sharks, and pig embryos that Shennandoah kept stashing in her desk drawer, and had even threatened to report her to their Dorm Committee if the problem continued.

Since I didn't have to live with the unsavory results of her thievery, I was in a better position than her roommate to appreciate Shennandoah's finer qualities, and before many weeks had passed, we were close friends. Yet as I got to know her better, I realized that it wasn't just our lab partnership that drew us together: it was our mutual feeling of alienation from our fellow students. Temperamentally, she was even more of a misfit than I was, although no one could have guessed it by looking at her.

Shennandoah was adorable in the classic Midwestern style—a tiny, curvaceous dynamo of energy with intense blue eyes, a cascade of waist-length blond hair, and a complexion of pink and white perfection. She blended in—and in a way I could never have hoped to achieve. However, she had one quirk of which she was particularly proud, and which, unlike stealing lab specimens, she was more than happy to publicize. She was famous—or perhaps "notorious" would be a more accurate word—throughout the school as The Girl Who Refused to Date Caucasian Men.

"But why?" I exclaimed when she first informed me of her peculiar social agenda.

"To prove a point."

"I don't understand."

"It's simple. My family's from Indianapolis, and my dad's a bigwig in local real estate, which means my parents are rich—and ultra-conservative. We live right across the street from our church and we only socialize with Methodists—anything else, especially if it involves non-whites, is practically a sin. But ever since I was a kid, I couldn't help wondering about all of those forbidden people. What made them untouchable?" She rolled her eyes. "And by the time I was old enough to date, my parents were really loading on the propaganda. I think they were almost relieved when I lost my virginity to the captain of my high school football team."

"Really!" Astonished by her open and unapologetic confession about what was usually a taboo subject, I was both embarrassed and eager for further details.

"Well, they certainly looked the other way!" Her eyes sparkled with animation and her cheeks were flushed with excitement. "Anyway, as you can probably guess, that made me even more curious. I had to find out what I was missing. So I decided that as soon as I could escape from my parents' clutches, I was going to follow their rules—only in reverse."

"What does that mean?" I prompted, becoming more intrigued by the moment.

"Well, they said: date only Methodists. So my rules are: date any man you can get your hands on, as long as he isn't a white Anglo-Saxon Protestant! Jews are okay, but Negroes, Arabs, and Asians are even better."

"Come on, Shen, don't you think you're overreacting?"

"Not at all."

"But by arbitrarily limiting yourself to certain racial types, aren't you creating a kind of reverse prejudice?"

"I'm just rearranging the rules that everyone else around here plays by."

"And you get away with it?"

"More or less. At least, my first two years at IU I dated mostly Negroes, especially the athletes. They are so sexy! Those firm muscles bulging under that fabulous brown skin!"

I had to smile; she was practically drooling.

"Then I realized how much pressure those guys must be under—not just from any white guy who saw us together but also from their own friends. And I figured if a Negro guy was brave enough to ask me out, I owed it to him to accept." Abruptly her expression sobered. "Unfortunately I've just been told, politely but quite emphatically, that none of those guys will date me anymore."

"Did they say why?"

"There's a story going around . . . See, last semester there was this Negro basketball player I was seeing—he dated lots of other white girls, too, mostly from the East Coast . . ." Her voice dropped to a whisper. "Well, no one knows for sure what happened, but this past summer they found him. He was"—she gestured vaguely at a spot below her waist—"you know . . . mutilated. The police found him in a ditch just outside of town."

"My god!" For a moment, my mind went blank with shock.

Shennandoah choked back a sob. "And he used to joke about how the white guys on the team kept warning him not to go out with any more white girls . . ."

"Oh, Shen!" I gasped, suddenly feeling queasy.

She sighed. "So I guess I understand why the rest of them are afraid."

I blinked back tears. "Did they catch whoever did it?"

She shook her head. "They probably won't. They probably don't want to."

"That's horrible!"

"That's the facts of life in Indiana." Once again she sighed.

"So now what?"

"So now I've moved on to the International House." To my surprise, her expression brightened visibly. "You should see those foreign students! They're absolutely gorgeous. Every luscious shade of brown skin imaginable!"

"But aren't those guys taking the same risk by dating you as the Negro students were?" I was unable to keep the worry from my voice.

"Maybe not—or, if they are, they haven't figured it out yet. Oh, sure, some folks still make nasty comments, but there haven't been any overt threats."

"So far . . ."

"Apparently it's not quite the same thing, in the warped minds of the local conservative community."

"Gosh, Shen, are you sure you should go through with this?" I asked nervously.

"Hey, I'm not letting any redneck bozos stop me from having a good time! And you shouldn't either. In fact, you should come with me to the International House. They'd really like you over there."

"Gee, I don't know . . ." White coeds dating foreign students? Did I really want to risk setting myself up for yet another outbreak of Hoosier Hysteria?

"Oh, come on. Those guys are great! I spend hours over there, every chance I get. They tell the best stories about their countries, and you can learn their customs and sample their cuisines. All you have to do is ask: most of those foreign guys know how to cook fantastic meals. I've even managed to pick up a few simple phrases." Her eyes gleamed. "Besides, there's this Japanese guy I have my eye on. He's a professor." She giggled. "We'll see what happens. I usually get the ones I want."

Shennandoah's single-minded pursuit of exotic men seemed to me to be an extreme example of reverse prejudice, but as I came to know her better I soon realized that although her eccentric dating strategy had started out as a way of flaunting her rebelliousness, in fact she inevitably developed a genuine affection for each of her foreign admirers.

Bemused, I watched her reaching out, greedily gathering information about a world she had never experienced. Never having been out of her home state, she was attracted by all the possibilities that had been, until now, beyond her reach.

chapter 9:

the poster committee

It was October: time for the second meeting of the Folksinging Club. I was anxious to go, but reluctant to do so alone, and nervous about what might happen during my first post-fight encounter with Daniel.

I wasn't too proud to beg.

"Come to the meeting with me, Pixie. Pleeeease."

She chuckled. "Listen, Meri, I'm not so desperate for entertainment that I'm willing to risk being seen there. Just think how that would look on my record! I might never get a teaching job. Anyway, I prefer real folk music to that nasty old stuff they sing at the club."

"They don't sing nasty stuff. And how do you know what they sing if you've never been there?"

"Rachel's given me a pretty good idea of what goes on at those meetings. Listening to Peter, Paul and Mary on my radio is plenty good enough for me, thank you very much. Now that's what I call folk music."

Out of sheer desperation, I even asked Rachel, but although she actually seemed flattered by my invitation, she said she already had something else planned for that evening.

I almost called Daniel, but common sense warned me that I would be asking for trouble.

I finally accepted the fact that if I wanted to go, it would have to be by myself. And so, with a burst of self-confidence that was unusual for me, I gathered up my courage and headed for the Student Union building.

It didn't take me long to realize how foolish my doubts had been. My lack of an escort wasn't important to anyone but me. The meeting wasn't so much a social event as a gathering of music lovers.

Daniel walked in shortly after I did. Seeing him, I felt a queasy surge of apprehension. But he merely nodded a curt hello, turned pointedly away, and went off to claim a seat on the opposite side of the room.

Relieved, I sat down in the unoccupied front row, which was about as far away from him as I could get, and also offered the attraction of being close to the action—not to mention the intriguing Derek Stone.

I wasn't alone for long. Almost immediately the seats on either side of me were taken: on my left by a young woman who introduced herself as the club secretary, and on my right by a rather portly bearded fellow with a distinctly British accent. While we were waiting for the meeting to begin, my two companions questioned me about my studies and myself. Both of them were extremely nice, and I was flattered by their interest. By the time the music started, I was enjoying myself thoroughly.

At intermission, when I stood up to stretch my legs, my British neighbor promptly rose, too.

"I say, I don't believe I've introduced myself properly." He offered his hand. "John Goodfellow."

A vivid image arose in my mind's eye: he should be sitting by the fire, dressed in a velvet lounging jacket, reading a book (Shakespeare, of course!), and smoking a pipe.

I was unable to suppress a smile, bemused by my own foolish fantasy.

He responded with a grin. "Going out for a bit of a walk round?"

I nodded.

"Mind if I join you?" he asked, reaching into the breast pocket of his brown corduroy jacket and producing—a pipe!

My smile widened.

Taking my reaction as an affirmative, he said, "Shall we be off then?"

In the hall outside, he explained that he had just been elected chairman of the club's newly formed Poster Committee. "I'm scouting about for assistants," he said. "As I seem to recall hearing you telling Secretary Betsy that you're an art major, might I interest you in joining my Poster Committee?"

"Sure. That sounds like fun."

"Jolly good! How fortunate that I met you tonight, Meri! You know, I fancy I'm something of an artist myself"—much to my amusement, he cocked his head to one side and pantomimed squinting down the length of a paintbrush and executing several bold brush strokes across an imaginary canvas—"although in my case, it's merely dabbling. Ah, well, I know that I must earn my living at something for which I'm better qualified. Which is why I'm doing graduate studies in geography, while you're working on a master's degree in art."

Honesty compelled me to admit that I wasn't a graduate student.

He chuckled. "Don't look so glum, mate. Even I was a freshman once."

At that point, someone came out to announce that the meeting was about to recommence, and John immediately asked for my phone number, promising to contact me about the Poster Committee within the next few days.

I walked back to my dorm in a warm afterglow. It was my fervent hope that John was using the Poster Committee as an excuse to get to know me better. I certainly liked him, and if he wasn't quite as fascinating as the club president, at least he seemed to be available. So, when he called first thing the next morning to ask me to "tea," I was thrilled. Surely he must be interested indeed, to have called so soon! We arranged to meet at the Student Union at three o'clock that afternoon to discuss our committee's activities and responsibilities.

—————

I was nervous all morning and had trouble concentrating on my classes. In zoology lab, Shennandoah, fed up with my absent-minded bungling, demanded to know what was wrong.

"Sorry, Shen. I guess I must've been daydreaming."

"About what?"

"Actually, I met this guy . . ."

"Tell me everything!" Her scalpel clattered to the counter-top and she rested her chin on both fists, eyeing me expectantly.

"Well . . . We met last night at the Folksinging Club."

"Go on."

"And he's a graduate student."

"That's good."

"He's British."

"A foreigner: that's even better!"

I explained about the Poster Committee, and how John had asked me to attend a meeting that afternoon. "But I got the impression that no one else will be there," I concluded. "I think he likes me."

"Great! So what's the problem?"

"The problem is, I'm afraid we're going to run out of things to talk about once we're finished with Poster Committee business. I mean, think about it, Shen: I'm just a dumb freshman and he's a teaching assistant. I'm going to bore him to death."

"Don't be silly. You're an interesting person. I'm sure you'll find plenty of things to talk about, and I'm sure John will enjoy his afternoon with you."

By the time our lab session ended, she almost had me convinced—but then it was noon, and I was even more jittery than ever. Rather than my customary stop at the milk machine, I decided to have another go at the cafeteria, hoping to kill time.

Besides, after nearly a month of semi-starvation, I was hungry enough to attempt another fling with the "food" they served.

The only vacant seat I could find was next to my neighbors, Roberta Kruger and Susan Olsen (aka The Girl Who Was Afraid of Cards). Susan was apparently still offended—her eyes flicked over me, dismissing me at a glance. But Roberta chose that moment to exercise her function as Senior Leader of the third-floor girls. In a kind, big-sisterly way, she began to draw me out about my school experiences.

I tried to answer in generalities, saying that I was happy and my classes were going well, but I suddenly found myself blurting out what was really on my mind: my insecurities about a meeting I was about to have with a certain British graduate student. By the time I'd finished my story, I felt like a fool, but I could see that both Roberta and Susan were impressed.

"Not bad!" Susan smiled at me for the first time since our run-in over cards.

"A date with a graduate student!" Roberta crowed. "Not bad at all for a freshman."

I could feel myself blushing. "Well, it isn't really a date," I said. "Actually, it's a committee meeting."

"Don't be modest," Roberta responded. "Of course it's a date! Now, tell us how you met him. Tell us all about him."

In fact, there wasn't much to tell.

"Gee, Meri, this sounds like your big chance," Roberta said when I'd reached the end of my brief recitation. "I don't blame you: I'd be nervous, too, if I was in your shoes."

"Speaking of shoes," Susan interjected, "what are you going to wear?"

Her question caught me off guard. "Wear? I haven't given it any thought."

"Well, you'd better!" Roberta scolded.

"Why can't I just wear what I have on?" I asked, feeling very foolish indeed.

Roberta glanced over at Susan and rolled her eyes. "She's got a date with a grad student, and she plans to go dressed like that!" There was no doubt whatsoever as to what she thought of my pleated plaid wool skirt and plain white cotton blouse.

"Why not?" I said, my voice quavering.

"You just can't, and that's all there is to it!" Roberta pronounced, jabbing her fork at me for emphasis. "Dating an older man is serious business. If you want to impress him, you've got to look sensational. After all, you're hoping to make him forget you're a freshman, aren't you?"

"Yes, but—"

"So what are you going to do about it?" she demanded.

"I . . . I'm not sure."

Roberta's expression underwent a dramatic transformation. She turned to Susan. "I just got the greatest idea! You and I are going to help Meri get ready for her date."

"Oh, that's really not . . ." I started to say, but they were so caught up in Roberta's excitement that my protest went unheeded.

"What on earth can we do?" Susan was asking Roberta. "Nothing short of a complete makeover would help. Besides, I'm not sure we have enough time."

"Don't be a spoil-sport, Sue. You're great with hair. You can set it and give her a sensational hairdo."

"Gosh, Roberta, I don't know . . ." She glanced over at me. "I mean, what about those curls? They're pretty wild. I think she's going to need a haircut before I'd have a prayer of styling it."

"Well, you can do that, can't you?"

"I guess so."

"Good. So you cut her hair and set it, while I take care of her clothing. I have a super new skirt and sweater set, and I'm only a little taller than Meri . . . I think."

I took advantage of her momentary hesitation to squeeze a word in. "Gee, it's awfully nice of you two to offer to help, but I don't think I can fit all of that into my schedule."

"Didn't you say you aren't meeting him until three?" Roberta demanded.

"Well yes, but I have chorus right after lunch."

"Cut class."

"I can't!"

She glared at me. "Now listen, Meri, what's more important: chorus or a date with a graduate student?"

"I, er . . ."

"Roberta's right," Susan chimed in.

"Oh . . . Okay."

"Good. Now, that's settled," Roberta said. She pushed her chair away from the table and stood up, rubbing her hands together in anticipation. "Come on, girls, let's get busy!"

Oh god, what have I gotten myself into? I wondered, but I didn't dare protest. After all, how could I disappoint them in the face of their undeniable generosity? So, after disposing of their trays and my half-eaten lunch, the three of us left the cafeteria together.

I had to admit that they went about the job in a workman-like manner.

Back in their room, Roberta quickly found a bath towel and wrapped me up like a mummy. Then Susan escorted me into their washroom, where she shoved my head under the faucet and drenched my hair with warm water.

"Hey, look, Roberta," she called out to the other room. "What a strange perm. Her hair is curly even when it's wet."

Roberta joined us over the sink.

"It's not a permanent," I protested. "My hair is naturally curly."

"Weird," Roberta said. "Can you fix it, Sue?"

"I'm not sure . . . I mean, what am I supposed to do? How do you cut hair that won't even lie down flat?"

"Come on, kid, you can figure it out," Roberta coaxed.

"Okay, okay. I'll try." She didn't sound optimistic.

"Good girl! Besides, you never know: cutting and setting it might be just the thing to straighten it out."

"Maybe we should just stop right now before—"

"You can't back out on us now, Meri," Roberta interrupted. "Don't worry—we can make it work."

With a mixture of fascination and horror, I watched in Susan's desk mirror as wet, C-shaped clippings began falling on my lap and shoulders. After a while, I closed my eyes and tried to think about something else.

"Well, that seems more or less even." Susan sounded doubtful. "Hand me the rollers, Roberta."

I forced myself to look in the mirror.

Nothing too disastrous seemed to have happened—still, it might be too early to tell. In any case, my hair was definitely a lot shorter than it had been just half an hour earlier.

Susan went on working, snipping at a stray hair or two from time to time. Having my hair rolled up in tight little bunches felt strange; "itchy and uncomfortable" was the way I would have described it, had anyone bothered to ask me.

In the midst of all the rolling and pinning, Roberta arrived on the scene carrying a tray of manicure tools and several bottles of nail polish. "Can I do this now?" she asked Susan.

"Do what?" I demanded anxiously.

"Your nails are a mess," Roberta said. "What you really need is a complete beauty salon treatment, but I'll do what I can in the short time we have. I guarantee you'll feel like a whole new person when we're done with you."

"That's what I'm afraid of!" I almost blurted out. But I kept my fears to myself.

"And once you're out from under the dryer, I'll start working on your makeup," Roberta added.

"But I never wear makeup!" I protested.

"Yeah—we noticed," Roberta said.

There's no escape, I concluded with grim fatalism. I closed my eyes to keep myself from staring at my wristwatch.

It was twenty minutes to three when they were finally done with me. All three of us stood in front of the bathroom mirror to survey their handiwork.

"She really looks great, doesn't she?" Susan asked.

Rebecca nodded. "What do you think, Meri?"

I was too stunned to answer.

A stranger looked back at me from where I should have been: a stranger with a stiffly lacquered and carefully sculpted, albeit rather frizzy, beehive hairdo. Someone else's hazel eyes peered from beneath dark fringes of mascara-laden eyelashes and heavily penciled eyebrows. Blood-red lips were in perfect, if unsubtle, harmony with fingernails and cheeks. And for the pièce de résistance: I was crammed into Roberta's too-snug, fuzzy, hot pink sweater and matching straight skirt with a kick pleat in the back. Unfortunately, there was a noticeable bulge around my waist where the skirt had been rolled up and pinned closed—Roberta, as it turned out, was both taller *and* thinner than I was.

"Well, what do you think?" Roberta repeated. She was beginning to sound anxious. "Aren't you surprised?"

I found my voice. "Oh, I'm . . . um . . . *very* surprised."

"I bet John won't recognize you," Susan said happily.

It was my greatest fear. But I thanked them as best I could, hoping I sounded sincere. After all, they had given up most of their afternoon for me.

Released from their clutches, I hurried back to my room to retrieve my purse. But then I caught sight of myself in Pixie's dresser mirror.

"Oh, god," I said out loud with a groan. "I'll die if he sees me like this!"

I crept back to my doorway and cautiously stuck my head out. I could hear Roberta and Susan's cheerful voices emanating from their room, but fortunately for my purposes their door was barely ajar.

Beating a hasty retreat into my own room, I peeled off Roberta's offending outfit and tossed it in my closet, then donned my bathrobe, grabbed a towel, washcloth, and shampoo, and scurried across hall to the women's bathroom.

The hot water felt wonderful on my skin. I scrubbed my face until it tingled, and washed and rinsed my hair until I could no longer feel any trace of hair spray. The smell of Roberta's best perfume had long-since vanished. When I felt completely clean, I turned off the shower and peered out past the shower curtain.

Not a soul in sight.

Slipping into my robe, I made a dash for my room. By the time I was dressed once again in my own comfortable clothing, it was too late to take off the nail polish, but a glance in my mirror confirmed that it and my short hair were the sole remaining survivors of my "beauty treatment." With relief, I surveyed my regular, everyday face. True, I was as dark as a Portuguese gypsy, and my hair was flyaway and unstylishly curly, but at least I was "me" again.

John would have to take me or leave me as I was.

I picked up my purse and sneaked out of the dorm by the back stairs.

———

I was still damp and somewhat out of breath by the time I arrived at the Student Union but by some miracle it was only a quarter past three.

"I'm so sorry I'm late," I told John, cheeks red.

"Couldn't bear going out without having a bit of a wash-up?" he teased, immediately putting me at ease.

It turned out that the needs of the Poster Committee were essentially nonexistent and, just as I had suspected, we were a committee of two. We sat in the Student Union lounge for a while, talking and drinking tea while John smoked his pipe and watched me with a good-natured twinkle in his eyes, until he eventually suggested taking a walk.

As we strolled along leaf-strewn paths, John described his studies and the difficulties he had had as a foreign graduate student obtaining a teaching assistantship from the University. He complained that a great deal of his time was taken up by pointless paperwork, and that his position put unexpected restrictions on his social life. He seemed convinced that the University expected him, as their employee, to avoid any personal contact with his students, which was proving to be quite difficult.

"Are you sure you understood correctly?" I asked. "What they're asking sounds impossible."

"I agree—but I'm quite sure of the rules. My boss gave me a stern lecture early on: he told me that I was too chummy with the students, said he wanted his teaching assistants to be a credit to the department, not a liability, and assured me that getting involved with my students—in any way—is strictly forbidden."

"Are you sure he didn't mean *romantically* involved?"

"I only know what he said. He said it could cost me my job."

"But how can you enjoy teaching if you can't get to know your students?"

"That's a question I've asked myself." He sighed.

"It must be very hard on you. You seem to like people."

"That I do!" he replied, exaggerating his very British accent—which, I had noticed, he often did for dramatic effect. "But me dear old boss is very strict about such matters, and my private life must remain just that . . . So don't you go takin' any geography courses, me darlin', or you won't be of any use a-tall to the Poster Committee," he concluded with a grin.

And so our acquaintance deepened into friendship.

———

In the weeks that followed, John and I regularly took long walks around campus, discussing painting, good books we had recently read, Gilbert and Sullivan operettas (which both of us loved), and our various classes.

Afterwards, when I was alone, I couldn't resist the temptation of indulging in my fireside fantasy, daydreaming about a possible future where I might be sitting opposite him in a matching armchair, knitting a sweater, while we listened to classical music on the radio.

chapter 10: troubles

All of my classes were going well that semester, with the exception of art, where I always seemed to be in trouble. Each new project we undertook possessed its own unique set of complications and pitfalls—and if there were mistakes to be made, it appeared I was destined to make them all.

At the conclusion of our torturous connect-the-dot marathon, Mrs. Burns announced that we were ready to move on to still-life drawing, a subject that I thought had interesting possibilities.

Each lesson in this new area of study was designed to teach a single aspect of rendering three-dimensional form within a two-dimensional space—for example, how to shade objects to create the illusion of depth, or how to utilize overlapping shapes to achieve the same effect. In the course of our work, we "graduated" from pencil to charcoal, and from charcoal to pen and ink. In this way, Mrs. Burns assured us, we would gain an understanding of space, form, and composition, and also develop skill in the use of several different media.

But as night followed night and week passed steadily into week, I realized that what was happening instead, was that I was becoming profoundly bored. Unconsciously, I began looking around for something more entertaining to do in class.

One fateful evening as I was attempting, without much enthusiasm, to turn a drab pile of boxes and bottles into an exciting composition, I somehow managed to drop a large chunk of charcoal into my open bottle of India ink—an almost impossible stunt if I had been purposely trying to perform it.

For a moment, I didn't react: I simply sat there, staring stupidly at the bottle. But I could imagine all too well what was happening inside: the charcoal was slowly dissolving, in the process turning itself and my expensive ink into a worthless puddle of muck.

I had to do something!

With a frantic burst of energy, I grabbed my pen and began stabbing around in the bottle, hoping to extract the charcoal before it was history. But each time I managed to spear it, I found that the charcoal, which was becoming soggier by the moment, wouldn't come back up through the bottle's narrow neck.

"If it went in, it has to come out!" I grumbled.

Finally, in desperation, I stuck my little finger as far as it would go into the bottle. Then, cautiously raising the charcoal with the pen point until it just touched my finger, I tried to apply pressure evenly from both sides, using my finger and the pen. However, coordinating the operation was extremely difficult and the charcoal immediately dropped off.

On the fourth attempt, I was luckier: I succeeded in prying out a smeary lump of ink-saturated charcoal, about half of the original piece. Taking an extra sheet of drawing paper from my portfolio, I put the charcoal down on one corner and began wiping my fingers clean on another.

Then inspiration struck: the ink-soaked charcoal made terrific fingerpaint! Soon I was happily smearing away. Funny little stick men with long tails and bowler hats danced across the page, set in motion by my gooey black fingers. I was so engrossed in my project that I forgot to keep an eye on Mrs. Burns, who was, as usual, patrolling the room. Before I realized what was happening, she'd crept up behind my desk and was peering over my shoulder.

"JESUS CHRIST!" she yelped right in my ear, causing me to shriek and drop my charcoal. "What the HELL do you think you're doing?"

The entire classroom was in an uproar. Mrs. Burns was always ladylike. She seldom spoke above a whisper, and she certainly never swore.

I cowered, red-faced, in my seat.

"This is outrageous!" She snatched up my offensive finger painting. "Miss Henriques, see me after class."

Hot with embarrassment, I returned to my still life.

Later, when I approached her, Mrs. Burns had a pile of my artwork spread out in front of her on one of the desktops.

"How do you explain this?" she asked by way of greeting. She pushed a picture toward me across the desk.

With a sinking feeling, I recognized our previous week's homework assignment, which had been to copy, as faithfully as possible, a Rembrandt etching. The one I had been given was most unappealing—a ratty-looking old man in what appeared to be a toga—and in a fit of rebelliousness, I had signed myself "Rembrandt Henriques." Unfortunately, I had forgotten to erase the damning signature before handing it in.

"I'm sorry," I mumbled.

"I don't doubt it." She gave me an appraising look over the rim of her spectacles. "Miss Henriques, your work is, on the whole, quite acceptable. But I'm afraid you must learn to take me, and this class, more seriously."

"I will, Mrs. Burns! I promise."

"We shall see."

"Is that all?" I asked hopefully.

"Not quite." Her grin was full of malice. "I'm giving you an extra homework assignment: another Rembrandt etching to copy." She held out a black-and-white print. "I'll expect you to hand it in at the beginning of our next class."

"Yes, Mrs. Burns."

I hastily collected my art supplies and turned to leave.

"And, Miss Henriques," she called after me. "This time, omit the signature."

Pixie looked up from her homework when I walked in.

"Are you okay?"

"Oh, Pixie," I said with a groan, collapsing onto my bed, "I really did it this time. I got myself in big trouble in art class tonight."

She had been sitting on the floor, but now she got up and made herself comfortable on her own bed. "Tell me what happened."

By the time I'd reached end of my recitation, she was chuckling. "Oh, well, we all make mistakes," she said. "My advice is: forget it. And in the future, be more careful with your homework. I'm sure Mrs. Burns won't hold it against you forever."

"She might."

"Don't be silly. It could have happened to anyone."

"But it didn't! It always happens to me!"

"Oh, come on now, Meri."

"It's true, Pixie—you know it is! It's because I'm different." I choked back a sob. "I try so hard to be inconspicuous, but sooner or later someone always notices, even when I don't do anything dumb. And not just in art class: it happens everywhere . . . I don't fit in!"

"Now you have some idea what it's like to be a Negro in a white man's school," she said very quietly.

That stopped me. I couldn't meet her eyes. "I guess I really haven't got much to complain about, have I?"

"Sorry. That wasn't a put-down. It just seemed like a good comparison." She was silent for a moment. "But to be perfectly honest, I have noticed: you *are* different."

I groaned.

"But I'm glad!" she cried.

"Oh, sure."

"I am. If you were like the rest of the girls, do you think I'd want to be your roommate? You think I would have stayed here?"

"I don't know."

"Well, I do! Listen, that first day, when I met you and found out that I was going to have a white freshman for a roommate, you'd better believe I was worried. I didn't think it could work out—not with anyone except Rachel. Freshman girls are usually so dumb . . . But once we started talking, with Miss Bell running past our door and all, I realized that you weren't like the others. I could tell it really didn't matter to you what color I was . . . And that's when I knew everything was going to be okay."

"Me, too." I mopped at my leaky eyes with my shirt sleeve.

She seemed to hesitate a moment before continuing, "But you know, Meri, you are awfully serious—especially for a freshman. I hope you don't think you have to act that way for my sake—because I'm older. It's fine with me if you want to cut loose once in a while. I really wouldn't mind."

"Thanks, Pixie, but that's just not me."

"Hey, everyone needs to be silly sometimes."

I hesitated, then admitted, "I've never been silly—not since I was a kid."

"What do you mean?"

Although it was a disturbing topic, I decided to try and explain my family.

"Well, my parents waited for almost twenty years before they had children, and I guess my mother resented having to share my father's attention with us. But luckily, she decided to go back to work, and my parents found a wonderful Negro lady named Mildred Holmes to take care of us. As far as my sister and I are concerned, Mildred was our real mother. She taught us so much of what I believe in . . . We used to watch Jackie Robinson on TV. She was so proud of him! She said what he was doing was important for our whole country, not just Negroes, and she taught me how to cook, sew, and iron." I was unable to suppress a bitter laugh. "Little did I know how handy that would come in when my mother got sick."

Pixie didn't say a word, just waited for me to continue.

"I was nine when she had a massive stroke, which made her even more difficult to get along with. And my parents couldn't afford to hire Mildred any more—they needed me to help my father run our household and take care of my little sister." I sat on my hands, hoping to prevent another attack on my fingernails.

"Sounds like you didn't have much of a chance to be a kid, let alone be silly," Pixie said.

I looked down.

"Hey, we don't have to talk about this if it's too upsetting," she immediately added.

"It's okay, Pixie. It's a relief to have someone to talk to."

She sat there patiently, willing to listen to whatever I felt like telling her.

"There were other problems," I finally confessed.

"What kind of problems?"

"My size—and my feet."

Her expressive eyebrows lifted in surprise. "Your feet!"

"My feet are messed up and I can't wear shoes like everyone else's: they have to be specially made. Haven't you noticed?"

"I noticed that your shoes are different, but I just assumed they were some new back-East fashion."

"You did? But 'Space Shoes' look so weird."

"Not any stranger than my saddle shoes, or some of the other things I've seen people wearing lately."

"Oh! I was so sure that everyone noticed."

"No one goes around looking at feet!" she said matter-of-factly. "And I bet if you'd quit worrying about them, no one would even suspect you have a problem."

I wasn't sure I believed her, but she had certainly given me something to think about.

"So what was that other thing you mentioned?" Pixie asked. "Something about your size."

"I'm too tall. I grew up too fast. By the time I was ten, I felt like a circus freak."

"That's ridiculous, Meri! You and I are exactly the same height. We're average."

"We are? You don't look very tall."

"Neither do you."

"Are you sure? I always feel like I'm the tallest person in every room."

"Isn't it strange how we do these things to ourselves?" she mused. "Worry about things no one else even notices?"

"Maybe you're right." I sighed. "Anyway, I was awfully

unhappy while I was growing up—but my whole world changed when I discovered the music festival."

"You mentioned that our first day here."

"I was fifteen the first time I went there. It's the only place I've ever been where I could just be myself without feeling self-conscious, or worrying about not fitting in . . . I think I already told you that almost all of the students and teachers were from the Midwest, which is what made me want to come here. The music festival proved that my life didn't have to be the way it was at home—and that I could escape from my mother." I gave Pixie a wry smile. "Unfortunately, my parents had other ideas. They wanted me to go to a local commuter college. But I kept reminding them about the IU music school's great reputation. Eventually they said I could apply, but on two conditions: I wouldn't ask to visit the school ahead of time, since they couldn't afford the airfare, and, for the same reason, I could only come here if I qualified for a scholarship, like I had at the music festival."

"Which you obviously did."

"Actually, I didn't. I was accepted on early admission—without a scholarship."

"So how'd you get around that?"

"I didn't think I could—and I could tell that my parents were relieved. They said I'd have to notify the school I wasn't coming. But I kept putting it off, hoping something would come along to save me . . . And at the last possible second, my best friend's mother called and said that her family wanted to give me a chance to go away to college."

Pixie's eyes widened. "Wow! I don't believe it!"

"All those years that my mother was sick, my friend's parents kind of adopted me. They let me stay with them whenever things got impossible at home, and they made me feel like I was part of a normal family. And since money isn't an issue, my friend's mother said they wanted to pay for my first year of college, so I could get away from home—and my mother. After this year, I'm on my own."

"Gee, I thought things like that only happened in the movies."

I gave a rueful laugh. "Believe me, so did I."

"And your parents let you accept their offer?"

"They weren't happy about it, but they finally gave in."

"And it isn't a loan?"

I shook my head.

"So that's why you don't pay monthly room and board like the rest of us. I wondered, but it didn't seem polite to ask."

"I know how lucky I am, Pixie. And I want to prove to my friend's parents that I deserve the chance they've given me. I *have* to get good grades so I'll qualify for a scholarship next year—otherwise I can't come back."

"Now I know why you study so hard."

"And why I don't have time to fool around and act like a silly freshman."

"In a way you remind me of my sister Maggie."

"Is she older or younger?"

"Two years younger—but she acts like she's the oldest." Pixie chuckled. "Sometimes I swear she thinks she's my mother. She's a nurse, and she's always fussing over me, reminding me to take my vitamins, get lots of rest, and study hard—stuff like that."

I laughed: I was sure that Pixie would offer a sister like hers quite a challenge.

"Listen, Meri." Pixie was suddenly very serious. "Can I give you some advice?"

"Okay." I hoped she couldn't hear the nervous tremor in my voice. Our whole conversation had been unsettling, and now I feared some sort of implied criticism.

I should have known better.

"It's just that studying hard and getting good grades aren't all there is to getting a scholarship at this school," she said. "They hardly ever give scholarships to out-of-state students, and when they do—well sure, they care about your grades, but they also take a real close look at your politics. You have to be careful about what you join, who you're seen with, and what you say and do. This school has spies, and they keep track of things like that."

"Come on, Pixie: spies? Rachel and Daniel said something about that, but I thought they were joking."

"It's true. So it's a real shame you went to that Yipsell meeting; that will look terrible on your record—and believe me, it's already on your record. And now you've gotten yourself mixed up with that Folksinging Club. The administration really hates them."

"But they're just a bunch of music lovers!"

"That's not how the school administration sees it. You've got a lot to learn, Meri. And you'd better watch out, because all the A's in the world won't help you once you're blacklisted."

"Gosh, Pixie, that sounds awfully melodramatic."

But I had to admit that her words echoed what John had been telling me these past few weeks. He worried constantly about the impression he was making on his boss—and through him, the school administration.

It all seemed a bit paranoid. Still, I was concerned.

"Well, thanks for the advice, Pixie," I said. "I promise I'll keep it in mind."

"I'm glad to hear it."

"And don't worry: I'm not interested in Yipsell. But I'm not about to drop out of the Folksinging Club. It's too much fun."

She shrugged. "Do what you like. But don't say I didn't warn you."

chapter 11: visitors

That night we stayed up too late talking and, as luck would have it, at 2:00 a.m. we had our first fire drill.

I awoke to the wail of a siren and the hurried shuffle of dozens of slipper-shod feet. Rachel arrived almost before I had had a chance to stagger out of bed.

By then I knew Pixie well enough to realize that it was going to be impossible to wake her. She often received phone calls—usually from men—late at night, long after both of us had gone to bed. Invariably, I was the one who got up to answer, and in the beginning I even made an attempt to get Pixie to come to the phone.

But it always turned out the same way: She would answer my request to get up quite reasonably, and then she would roll over, sinking into an even deeper slumber. Eventually, I would give up trying and simply explain to the caller that she was unavailable.

Sometimes her admirer was so grateful to hear a friendly voice in the wee hours that he would go right on talking, even though I was too sleepy to contribute much to the conversation. I would stand there in our tiny washroom, barefoot and in my nightgown, answering in monosyllabic grunts, until my befuddled mind registered a "good night" on the other end—at which time I would hang up and totter back to bed. After a while, I became so adept at answering the phone in my sleep that I often didn't have any memory of the incident until Pixie would inform me, sometimes days later, of my most recent after-hours encounter. Ironically, her friends often commented that they had enjoyed our conversation.

So when Rachel appeared the night of our first fire drill, I didn't bother asking questions, I simply did as I was told, hoisting Pixie out of bed by one arm and draping it across my shoulders while Rachel tackled her from the other side. By the time we had her on her feet, suspended between us like an enormous rag doll, Caralene had joined us, and she preceded us down the stairs. Rachel and I stumbled along, supporting Pixie, with Myrna bringing up the rear.

The air outside was bitingly cold, and suddenly I was wide awake.

"The girls in room 310 and 312 were a bit slow responding to the fire drill," Miss Bell, whose responsibility we were, said to the group disapprovingly.

She was standing several feet away from us, partially obscured by a gaggle of fiercely be-curlered, bathrobe-clad young women. I hoped she wouldn't notice Pixie, who was slumped, still unconscious, between me and Rachel.

"I'll expect you to do better next time," Miss Bell said.

"Roll call!" Mrs. Brown announced briskly from the open doorway.

We turned toward her in unison as she began reading through her list of names. Eventually, she called out, "Katherine Gates?"

"Here," Caralene drawled in her best approximation of Pixie's voice.

"Katherine Gates!" Mrs. Brown repeated, louder this time. "Where is Katherine Gates?"

"HERE!" three of us cried out simultaneously.

"That's better," Mrs. Brown said, and went on with the roll call.

Back upstairs, I was more than happy to dump Pixie, who seemed to have grown heavier during the course of our outing, back onto her bed, where she immediately grabbed a fistful of sheets and rolled over. And there she lay, smiling blissfully—or was it slyly, I wondered?—as I turned out the lights.

———

The next morning, we overslept.

I was awakened by Pixie's yelp when she opened her eyes and saw the clock. Her first class was about a quarter of a mile away in the English building—and it was about to begin. Even before I sat up in bed, she'd grabbed her clothing and toothbrush and was racing for our washroom. Minutes later she was back, tossing her pajamas on her bed and scooping up books.

"Bye, Meri," she said, as she hurried out the door.

I heard her call a greeting to someone in the hall, and then Rachel appeared in the doorway.

"My goodness, I've never seen her move that fast!" she chortled, her eyes alight with glee.

Later that morning, we heard the next chapter of the story.

Pixie sprinted across campus and into the lobby of the English building, where she decided that waiting for the elevator was a waste of time and opted instead for the main staircase, a modernistic affair composed of wide flights of marble steps with a spacious landing between each floor.

She ran up the first flight, turned the corner, proceeded upward to the second floor, rounded that corner, and panted up the next two flights to the third floor. After successfully negotiating the turn, she staggered groggily up the last long double flight to the fourth floor. But by then she was so disoriented that instead of exiting at the fourth-floor lobby, as she should have done, she turned to go up another—unfortunately nonexistent—flight of steps and ran, in slow-motion, head-first into a wall. And there she lay until the end of the class period, when her astonished classmates discovered her, smiling peacefully and snoring.

When Rachel and I escorted her back from the infirmary

just before noon, she collapsed onto her bed with a tired sigh. Her face looked very dark beneath the large white bandage that was plastered across her forehead.

"I think I'm going to have a black eye," she whispered, looking up at us with a wistful expression.

"No doubt about it," Rachel agreed. "You know, this morning, if you'd stopped long enough to ask, I would have told you to cut class."

The next day, Pixie had visitors.

In the middle of the afternoon, while we were at our desks, studying, a young woman in a crisp white medical smock strode into our room.

"Maggie!" Pixie exclaimed, jumping up so quickly that she knocked over her chair. "What are you doing here?"

She rushed to embrace the newcomer, who sidestepped her with the agility of a bullfighter and reached out and captured her wrist between her thumb and index finger, all in one smooth, practiced motion.

"Cut that out!" Pixie yelped, struggling to extricate herself from the stranger's grasp.

"You cut it out! And stop thrashing. I need to take your pulse."

"Aw, Maggie. Stop fussing and give me a hug."

"Hold still!" The young woman's eyes were riveted on her wristwatch.

"But I want to introduce you to Meri."

"Not until I'm finished."

Pixie submitted, wriggling with barely suppressed impatience.

"Now let me see that bandage," Maggie said, reaching for Pixie's head.

Pixie backed hastily away, rolling her eyes like a skittish colt. "Uh-uh. Meri, this is my sister Maggie."

"Stop trying to distract me," Maggie said, intent on cornering Pixie. "It's not going to work." But as she paused to right the

128

overturned chair, she managed to nod a friendly, if preoccupied, greeting in my general direction.

"Looks like they did a good job," she commented, peeking under the edge of the bandage. "That's a nasty lump you've got there." Her brisk tone softened as she asked with real concern, "You sure you should be up? Are you really okay?"

"Don't I look okay?" Pixie demanded. "Now stop fussing and give me a hug."

The sisters embraced.

"That's better!" Pixie released Maggie. "So why are you here?"

"Rachel called yesterday afternoon to let me know about your accident. And I called Norman and we—"

"Norman!" Pixie was already on her way out the door. "Where is he?"

"—and we decided we'd both try to get leave today, so we could see for ourselves how you are," Maggie finished with admirable composure.

"MAGGIE!" This came from out in the hall.

"Okay, okay. He's downstairs in the lobby."

Pixie dashed back into the room. "Why are you two just standing there?" She grabbed each of us by a forearm.

When we arrived in the lobby, literally dragged there by Pixie and somewhat out of breath, Norman was pacing nervously back and forth. But he stopped the moment he saw us. From where he stood, he examined Pixie carefully, a mixture of love, concern, and amusement in his dark eyes, each emotion struggling to win out over the others. Then, with a laugh, he strode across the room and engulfed her in a fierce bear hug.

I liked him immediately: he was a tall young man with a humorous grin that belied his dignified expression, and I thought he looked quite handsome in his army uniform.

Pixie introduced us, but although he responded politely, it was evident that he only had eyes for Pixie. After a few moments, Maggie suggested that we leave them alone together—but not without first making sure that Norman appreciated how extremely important it was that Pixie avoid getting over-tired.

Only after repeated promises from both parties that they wouldn't stay out too long would Maggie permit them to escape.

When we made it back upstairs, she slumped down on Pixie's bed with a sigh. "Oh, boy, am I tired!" she confessed. "I was up all night working the late shift at the hospital, and then we got in the car and drove straight down here. Bloomington sure is a long haul from Indianapolis."

"If you want to take a nap, I can study someplace else," I offered.

"Thanks, but I don't think I could sleep just now." She fixed me with an intense gaze. "Are you sure she's okay?"

It took a while to reassure her. When I succeeded, she had more questions: "How's her appetite? Is she doing her homework and getting enough sleep?"

With a barely suppressed smile, I assured Maggie that Pixie was taking good care of herself, her appetite was phenomenal, she wasn't spending too much time socializing, and she was getting plenty of rest. I even lied and said she was taking her daily dose of vitamins—I figured Maggie already had enough to worry about.

After a while, Maggie began reminiscing about Pixie as a young child, describing her as a mischievous but dearly loved little girl. She also talked about Norman, of whom she was obviously very fond.

"I sure hope he'll settle that girl down." Maggie's voice betrayed her doubts. "I know he will—unless she does something stupid."

I chuckled. She was exactly as Pixie had described her, and she could have easily convinced me, if I hadn't known better, that she, not Pixie, was the older sister.

Pixie returned a couple of hours later, glowing and happy but obviously exhausted.

Maggie stood up to leave.

"Hey, wait just a red-hot minute!" Pixie said, flopping down on her bed. "You haven't given me my present."

"What makes you think I brought you a present?"

"Because you always keep your promises. And you never forget anything. So where is it?"

"Where is what?"

"My hypodermic. The one you promised you'd bring the next time you came to see me."

"Gee, I'm not so sure that's—"

"Come on, Maggie. I know you've got it."

"I was hoping you'd forget."

"Maggie!"

"Listen, Pixie, a hypodermic needle isn't a toy. And in inexperienced hands it can be quite dangerous. You've got to be careful."

"Yeah, yeah. Sure, Maggie."

"Don't you 'sure, Maggie' me! I won't give it to you unless you promise you'll be careful."

"Okay. I'll be careful."

Maggie glared at her.

"Cross-my-heart-and-hope-to-die I'll be careful," Pixie rattled off, making the appropriate, if hurried, hand motions. "Are you satisfied? Now, where is it?"

With a sigh, Maggie reached into her shoulder bag.

"Oh, boy!" Pixie cried, bouncing off the bed.

Maggie held up a brown paper bag. "Don't go grabbing! Let me show you how to use it first."

"What on earth are you going to do with that thing?" I asked with a shudder.

"Actually, Pixie had a pretty good idea," Maggie said. "That is, it's a good idea if you know what you're doing." Then she stopped talking so she could concentrate on putting the hypodermic together. This accomplished, she took several small, translucent tubes out of the same paper bag.

"Wow!" Pixie exclaimed. "Used cartridges."

"Go get the ink," Maggie commanded.

While Pixie was rummaging through her desk drawers, she took up the explanation where Maggie had left off.

"You know how expensive the refills for cartridge pens are, Meri." Cartridge pens were the latest fad—we all had them. "Well, I figure that if I refill the refills, I can save a whole lot of money."

"That's a really good idea, Pixie."

"Yeah, but you can't do it without a hypodermic needle."

Both of us watched, transfixed, as Maggie sucked ink into the syringe. Then, with professional skill, she inserted the needle into an empty cartridge, expelling the ink.

"Okay, that's how it's done. Now you try it."

She supervised as Pixie clumsily filled another cartridge.

"Your technique's lousy, but it should improve with practice," was Maggie's critique. "Just remember: be careful! Okay?"

"Okay."

"Promise?"

But Pixie was already so engrossed in her project that she hardly noticed when Maggie said good-bye and left.

I retrieved my biology text, resigned to doing battle with Dr. Godwin's latest mega-assignment. However, from time to time, I glanced over to see how Pixie was progressing.

She was Determination Personified, sitting cross-legged on the floor amidst a scattering of cartridges and ink-blotched tissues, tongue between her teeth, scowling in fierce concentration.

I struggled through several more pages of biology text, and then . . .

"DAMN!!!"

I looked up, alarmed. "What's wrong?"

The syringe and a half-filled cartridge were lying on the floor and Pixie was wringing her left hand. "Damn!" she repeated huskily. "I just gave myself a shot of ink."

"My god! Are you okay?"

"Yeah." She snorted with disgust. Then she grinned. "Oh, well, at least the color's right; no one will ever know the difference. And don't you dare say a word about this to Maggie!"

Later that same evening, when Gineeva came by to lobby for a card game, my mind was reeling from the effort of trying to memorize the scientific jargon from that day's reading, and Pixie was the proud possessor of a drawer full of recycled ink cartridges. Both of us were glad to have an excuse for taking a break.

Cards had become a vital part of our weekly routine. Pixie, Caralene, Gineeva, and I always played, and Myrna often joined us. But no matter who was present, it had become custom—or perhaps even unwritten law—for someone to call the Trees to invite as many as possible of the resident girls to join us in our room. And, as predicted, in doing so we seldom failed to attract the attention of either Mrs. Brown or Miss Bell, who regularly came by to "check up" on us.

But there was another consequence of our actions, something I hadn't taken into account when I'd made my irreverent suggestion at the beginning of the semester: I often found that I was the only non-black card player in the room.

Pixie, Caralene, and Gineeva thought this was hilarious.

"So how does it feel to be the only whitey in a roomful of Negro women?" Gineeva demanded with a rakish grin.

"Unusual," I admitted.

"Now you know how we feel," she snapped back.

"Aw, Gineeva, give her a break," Caralene said. "She's not such a bad sort. And she does put up with you."

"Gee, thanks, Cara!" Gineeva and I both retorted in unison.

But the excitement of our card games and a prevailing spirit of camaraderie prevented me from feeling awkward for long—and after a while I realized that I had been granted a fascinating glimpse into my friends' private world, one I would never otherwise have seen. For it soon became apparent that my friends lived two separate existences: lives delineated by Black and White.

In white society, they were one sort of creature: dignified, subdued, and self-effacing, hiding their feelings behind masks of indifference—everyone, that is, but Gineeva, who was always unapologetically herself. But when these same young black women found themselves alone together in a situation where whites were no longer watching, the masks came off, and before my eyes they transformed themselves into vivid, humorous, and outrageous characters who never failed to support each other with friendship and love.

I discovered they had a secret dialect and culture all their own that they kept carefully hidden from outsiders. Always serious in public, my friends bantered and teased each other mercilessly within the privacy of their own group. They gave each other droll nicknames and irreverent, off-the-wall advice.

The first time I heard Gineeva call one of her friends a "nappy-headed nigger," I was horrified. Both Mildred and my parents had branded it into my consciousness that using that particular epithet was an unpardonable sin.

"Pixie, did you hear what Gineeva just called Nadine?" I whispered.

"It's no big deal," was her casual reply. "It's fine to call a friend that, especially if she's done something silly. Of course," she added with a grin, "you certainly couldn't get away with that."

"I wouldn't dream of using that nasty term!"

"Yeah, I know. That's why we let you in."

Yet the more I heard of my friends' banter, carried off with great panache and embellished with a lilting Southern twang, the harder it became for me to avoid imitating them. I was a born mimic, and my training as a musician and singer had only exacerbated this tendency.

In any event, the evening after Maggie and Norman's visit was a fairly quiet one by our usual standards. Only a couple of girls had come over from the Trees, and, naturally, we had decided to play Hearts.

Gineeva and Caralene were still teasing Pixie about her black eye, which was developing nicely. (Pixie hadn't told them about the ink shot, and I didn't feel it was my place to enlighten them, since the information would only provoke another round of humorous remarks at Pixie's expense.) Because of this, Gineeva was probably not paying as much attention to the card game as she should have been. Quite unintentionally, she made a considerable blunder, mistakenly taking a trick containing the dreaded Queen of Spades—and there was no chance that she was trying to Shoot the Moon.

"Girl, you got The Mag!" I blurted out, delivered in an unmistakably black Southern drawl.

Gineeva's breath hissed out like a cobra's.

There was deathly silence in the room.

I felt my face turn red as a dozen very white eyes in very black faces turned to glare at me.

I choked back bile, afraid that I was going to throw up.

Finally, utterly humiliated, I managed to stammer out, "I . . . I'm so sor . . ."

But at that moment, the horrible impasse was shattered by the unexpected sound of Pixie's irresistible chuckle: "Heh, heh, heh. Girl, will you listen to Meri," she giggled, digging her elbow into Gineeva's side. "We've corrupted her. We got her talking like one of us!"

Gineeva tried to maintain her scowl, but within seconds, to my vast relief, everyone, including Gineeva, started to laugh uproariously.

A few moments later, when the game was once again under way and I was no longer the center of attention, Pixie leaned closer. "I saved you this time," she told me in a conspiratorial whisper, "but don't you ever do that again."

"It was an accident!"

"I know it and you know it. But remember: you can only get away with calling someone 'girl' if you're one of us. I know you didn't mean anything bad by it, but coming from a white person, it's almost as insulting as 'nigger.'"

Hot with embarrassment, I resisted the temptation to try to make further excuses and explanations. And I wondered if I would ever learn the rules.

chapter 12: gathering storm

More than once during the course of that year, I had the eerie sensation that I was the human equivalent of a tape recorder. I felt as if someone had pushed my "on" button when I'd stepped onto the Indiana University campus that fateful September day, and that I was destined to go on "recording" until I had documented everything that happened to us there. I was keeping a diary, a ritual begun in childhood; in retrospect, though, the entries were sketchy and full of romantic excesses—embarrassingly so. The reality of my Indiana experience—the feelings, events, even entire conversations—all of this was indelibly etched directly onto my memory. To write it down as it unfolded would have been a near impossibility: too much was happening all around me, all the time.

My sense of being caught up in momentous events that were beyond my control was sometimes overwhelming, and was accompanied by a suspicion that for some reason I was supposed to be there to witness what was happening—a feeling that never left me as long as I remained in Indiana.

One late October day, I was walking across campus with my anthropology teacher, Dr. Sellers, and the group of students

I had come to think of as his Honor Guard (those of us who regularly escorted him to his office after every lecture—a sort of perambulating study group). It was shortly before noon, and Dr. Sellers, who was always in a good mood, was positively jovial.

"Gee, I'm really looking forward to our next class," he confided. "We're going to begin discussing one of my favorite topics: evolution."

"What's so special about evolution?" one of my fellow students asked.

"First of all, presenting the concepts effectively is a really interesting challenge. Also, evolution is the most controversial thing I teach—at least in this neck of the woods—and if everything goes according to norm, that usually means trouble."

There was a sudden flutter in the pit of my stomach that had nothing at all to do with the approaching lunch hour. On the other hand, I couldn't help but notice that there was definitely an anticipatory gleam in Dr. Seller's eye.

"What kind of trouble?" someone else wanted to know, and I thought she sounded as uneasy as I felt.

By now Dr. Sellers was practically beaming. "Political trouble. I can always count on a few hotheads storming out of my classroom and heading straight over to President Stahr's office, demanding that he fire me."

He said it so matter-of-factly that I was astonished. "Just for teaching evolution?" I blurted out.

"You bet your life."

"Aren't you afraid of losing your job?" one of the young men asked.

"Hey, how can they fire me when all I'm doing is teaching what I've been hired to teach?" He chuckled. "Oh, I guess I was surprised and even alarmed the first time it happened, but by now I'm used to it. I think I'd be surprised if it *didn't* happen. So I decided, *What the heck: I've got tenure, and if there's going to be a ruckus anyway, why not give those folks something to remember me by?*"

"What are you going to do?" someone asked.

"Just you wait and see. I've worked up a real barn-burner of a slide lecture. Be sure you come to our next class."

I wouldn't have missed it for anything.

⸻

An expectant hush fell over the auditorium as Dr. Sellers began: "Today, every educated person accepts the fact of evolution"—that single statement brought grumbles from the audience—"and we certainly aren't here to argue about whether or not evolution occurred, since it obviously did."

The muttering grew louder, and I felt my shoulders tense as I recalled Susan Olsen's reaction to Pixie's deck of cards and my flippant mention of evolution. *Is this going to be another demonstration of Hoosier Hysteria?* I wondered as I glanced uneasily around at my classmates.

How far was Dr. Sellers prepared to push these people?

"What we *are* here to do is examine the evidence," Dr. Sellers said. He asked the projectionist to dim the lights.

Several people got up and quietly left the room.

Those were the easy ones! I reminded myself.

It was not a reassuring thought.

Dr. Sellers started by telling us about Charles Darwin, describing how he had been inspired to formulate his theories. The slides he showed to illustrate this part of his lecture were of the Galapagos Islands and its exotic creatures.

After briefly mentioning the various mechanisms by which Darwin proposed the process of evolution worked—with an aside that we would study them in more detail at a later date—Dr. Sellers went on to say that physical anthropologists believe that there are, among humans, so-called "progressive" traits, such as intellect, that demonstrate that humans are advanced beyond their animal origins. There are also "primitive" traits, which recall our animal ancestry—body hair being one example.

Fascinated, I studied the next slides, which showed a variety of racial types.

Dr. Sellers explained that every group of humans exhibits a mixture of both progressive and primitive traits. "For instance," he said, "many Negroes have wide, flat noses, similar to those of the apes."

Much to my disgust, there were snickers and murmurs of agreement when the face of an Australian aborigine appeared on the screen. Apparently no one was going to object to the idea that Negroes, at least, might be descended from animals.

The next slide showed three faces: one Caucasian and one Negro, with a grinning chimpanzee inserted in between.

"This slide is of particular interest because it illustrates how many similarities there are between Caucasians and monkeys, rather than between Negroes and monkeys, as certain poorly informed individuals might suppose," Dr. Sellers said. "Both the Caucasian and the chimp have thin lips, light facial skin, and plentiful body hair."

The angry buzz that had been a steady accompaniment to his lecture intensified.

"In contrast," Dr. Sellers told us, "we can see that the Negro is quite 'progressive,' with his heavy lips, dark facial skin, and notable lack of body hair."

At this pronouncement, a number of students jumped up from their seats, loudly protesting: "That's blasphemy! God created man"—and there was no doubt in my mind that they meant *Caucasian* man—"in His own image!"

Some of these dissenters had actually brought Bibles to class (it seemed that news of the day's topic had leaked out), and now they waved them above their heads, hissing and booing and acting for all the world like a troop of rowdy baboons.

I held my breath until the room quieted down, at which point the unflappable Dr. Sellers—most likely he had seen it all before—resumed his lecture.

In rapid order, he listed the ways in which man has evolved beyond his animal ancestry. "Man's now-useless appendix and wisdom teeth, for example—and some people in this class were probably born without them, as this is the most 'progressive' trend."

He asked for a show of hands to prove his point, and also reminded us that some people are able to wiggle their ears, a 'primitive' trait. Several students admitted to being able to do this, and one young man actually gave a demonstration, much to my classmates' delight. This provided a welcome respite from the tension that had been steadily building in the room ever since the beginning of the lecture.

Next, Dr. Sellers turned to the embryological evidence. "You know, zoologists have observed that a developing embryo goes through stages that reflect the entire evolutionary history of its species: the biological law that 'phylogeny recapitulates ontology.'"

A rapid succession of slides displayed embryos at various stages of development. Although each slide purportedly showed an animal and a human embryo side by side, it was impossible to determine which was which: in one instance both had gills, in another both had flippers, in yet another a snout-like nose was forming, and so on. Dr. Sellers stated that only in the human embryo is the entire developmental sequence played out.

By now, the audience was muttering again, but with less conviction, uncertain as to what he might be leading up to.

We didn't have to wait long to find out.

"And now, I want to show you the end result of this embry-onic growth process," Dr. Sellers announced, "the final proof that man is an integral part of the animal kingdom and not a result of Special Creation. For although man is superior to animals in many ways, he is indisputably descended from them."

When the last slide appeared on the screen, everyone in the audience gasped. Before us, in monumental size, was a young, white human baby, shown rump-first—complete with a tail!

Furious howls erupted all around me as people surged to their feet, yelling and stamping and shaking their fists, Bibles raised aloft like banners. After a solid minute of cacophonous protest, the entire group turned and stampeded en masse out of the auditorium.

I sat there watching, gnawing steadily on a fingernail, until the last protester had vacated the room.

Throughout all of this excitement and the ensuing exodus, Dr. Sellers had remained standing quietly on the stage with his hands in his pockets, clearly fighting to contain the mischievous grin that was threatening to break out on his face. In the eerie silence that followed, he looked out at those of us who remained, shrugged, and said, "Gee, that works even better than yelling 'Fire!'"

Somewhere around that time, my social life took a definite turn for the worse.

By now it was mid-semester and I had come to expect to hear from my English friend, John Goodfellow, several times a week. Despite the fact that we never went out on what my peers would have classified as an official "date"—we only went on walks together—we nevertheless had a great deal to talk about, and I thoroughly enjoyed our long rambles.

One evening, not long after Pixie had given herself the ink shot and Dr. Sellers had treated us to his Evolutionary Special, John called to invite me to a bluegrass festival that was taking place in Brown County, a two-hour drive from Bloomington.

"It's a famous event," he told me. "Practically everyone in the club is going."

Just the thought of being able to leave campus for a couple of hours would have been enticement enough—not to mention that this might even qualify as a genuine date.

"I'd love to go!" I said right away.

"Jolly good! I'll ring up Derek Stone and some of the other chaps to find out if someone is willing to offer us a ride. And I'll give you a buzz to let you know when we're leaving."

The possibility of spending the day with Derek added a whole new dimension to my interest, and I waited expectantly for John's return call.

But I waited in vain, and my eagerly anticipated weekend arrived without so much as a whisper from John. Still, naïve to

141

a fault, I never gave up hope until late Sunday afternoon, when even I was forced to admit that it was far too late to go anywhere with anyone.

When it came time for the November meeting of the Folk-singing Club, there had still not been so much as the proverbial peep out of John. I was so embarrassed by the thought of having to see him there, or anywhere else, that I hoped he wouldn't show up. But nothing was going to prevent me from attending—not even the humiliation of having been stood up by a date. So I gritted my teeth and went.

To my amazement, no sooner had I arrived than John came bustling over, a happy smile lighting up his bearded face. "And how are you, me darlin'?" he bantered, sweeping me up in a rib-cracking hug.

I was speechless.

To my astonishment, he didn't seem to notice my distress; instead he kept chatting away as if we'd last seen each other only the day before—until finally I could no longer hold back my questions.

"John," I cried, "where have you been? And what happened to the bluegrass festival?"

"Bluegrass festival? Ah, yes, it was quite entertaining. I drove over with Derek Stone—nice chap, very generous. We had a splendid time."

Now I was more confused than ever. John actually didn't seem to remember having invited me, and he was so open about having gone there himself that I didn't have the courage to question him further. Still, something was definitely amiss, because although he kept me company for the rest of the evening, he never phoned again.

In the weeks that followed, I searched in vain for an explanation, thinking that there must be something I'd overlooked. Otherwise, John's behavior was totally illogical.

Had I inadvertently offended him? Or scared him off by being too serious—or not serious enough?

Perhaps he was just too busy to see me.

All of these possibilities occurred to me at one time or another, and each seemed to explain the situation, depending on my mood at the moment I thought of it. But since John wasn't available to discuss my theories, all I could do was keep on guessing and waiting, hoping that he'd have a change of heart.

John's mysterious disappearance gave me all sorts of unwished-for free time, and in a determined effort to keep myself busy, I attended concerts, art exhibits, and other special events, hoping in vain that I would run into him there. I even agreed to go to the International House with Shennandoah, who assured me that the answer to "man trouble" was to meet more men.

It didn't work.

Although she dutifully introduced me to any number of very nice foreigners—graduate students and undergraduates, teaching assistants and assistant professors—none of them caught my fancy quite the way John had.

Meanwhile, back at the dorm, I played cards for hours at a time, sometimes with Pixie and the gang, sometimes by myself. Soon I was an expert on practically every variation of Solitaire in my Hoyle handbook. At other times, I engaged in intense one-on-one card duels with Myrna, who seemed to be as socially adrift as I was.

Every Saturday night, the smaller of our dormitory's two cafeterias was converted into a movie theater in a humane effort to entertain those of us who didn't have anything better to do with our lives. I had studiously avoided all dorm-sponsored events ever since my first and last mixer, but one memorable evening, I decided to attend.

Romantic comedy was the usual fare for movie night—that particular evening, however, as Fate would have it, they were showing *The Diary of Anne Frank*. I had seen it before—in fact, it had been the original inspiration for my diary-keeping endeavors—but I decided to go anyway, on the premise that it was a more constructive way to spend my time than sitting around hoping the phone would ring. And as it turned out, it was: the movie was every bit as enjoyable, and powerful, as I'd remembered, somehow managing to be both uplifting and depressing all the same time.

Afterwards, while I was waiting for the elevator to take me back upstairs, I found myself standing beside two girls, one short, blond, and buxom, the other a slim brunette. Both were red-eyed and sniffling, obviously distraught. And their discussion of the movie, which started out in whispers, grew progressively louder and more shrill until it was impossible to ignore.

Their accents betrayed them as Southerners, and I thought I recognized them as neighbors, girls who lived on the other side of the glass doors that were just beyond our room. If Rachel's information was correct—and I had to admit that it usually was—they were probably Jewish. Indeed, a surreptitious peek confirmed that both girls were wearing necklaces adorned with the Star of David.

"Did you hear about that awful business up in Indianapolis?" the blonde abruptly asked her companion just as the elevator arrived. "They were talking about it all morning on the radio."

"I must have already left for class," the brunette replied. "What happened?"

By now I was eavesdropping like mad. We boarded the elevator together.

"According to the reporter, there's a neo-Nazi movement brewing in northern Indiana. A big one. Believe me, it sounded like something right out of *Anne Frank*."

"Oh, god, not again!"

"He said there were a couple of anti-Semitic rallies over the weekend, and afterwards someone went around burning crosses and painting swastikas on temples—on people's houses, too."

"Rebecca, I'm scared! What if someone like Hitler comes along to lead them? Horrible things might happen."

"I heard that report, too," I interjected, unable to remain silent. "It really makes you wonder if it's safe to be here in Indiana."

"Hey, who asked you to butt in on our conversation?" the blonde—Rebecca—demanded, turning on me.

Her friend gave me a contemptuous once-over. "Don't you worry about a thing, Honey." Her voice dripped sarcasm. "Even if you are foreign, you Christians are always safe wherever you go. No one's gonna bother you."

I was so taken aback that, rather than tell them off as I should have done, I fell back on exquisite politeness.

"Excuse me for interrupting," I told them stiffly. "I just wanted to let you know that I sympathize with your concerns."

"Why?" Once again, it was Rebecca who challenged me. "What's it to you?"

"Because—"

"Say, haven't I seen you around somewhere?" the dark-haired girl interrupted. "You live on our floor, don't you?"

"Who cares where she lives?" Rebecca spat out. "That doesn't give her the right to stick her nose in our business."

"I'm interested because I'm Jewish," I said with as much dignity as I could muster.

"You!" It was satisfying to see her so thoroughly disconcerted. "Oh, my god!" she said in quite a different tone of voice. "I'm really sorry! I had no idea."

"Neither did I. Please forgive us." The other girl held out her hand. "I'm Judy Stein."

I could feel my blood pressure starting to drop back toward normal. "Meri Henriques."

"And I'm Rebecca Goldman, Judy's roommate," the blonde said, also offering her hand.

The elevator stopped at our floor.

"Hey, Meri, about what happened just now," Rebecca said. "Please don't take it personally. It's just that you caught us off guard. What with the movie and all, both of us were pretty shook up."

"So was I," I admitted.

"Well, then I hope you'll let bygones be bygones . . . Say, how about you-all coming on down to our room for a visit? Let us show you some real Southern hospitality."

"Please do!" Judy seconded.

Not wanting them to think that I would hold a grudge, I rather hesitantly accepted. Moments later, the three of us had walked right past my room and through the double glass doors beyond.

"So where are you-all from?" Judy was asking, I supposed as a conciliatory gesture, as we entered their room.

"New York—which is why I'm finding this whole neo-Nazi thing so hard to believe. Nothing like that ever happens where I grew up."

"Really? No trouble?" Rebecca sighed. "Boy, oh boy, let me tell you, there's plenty of trouble in my home town."

"Where's that?"

"Louisville, Kentucky." She pronounced it "Luville."

"And I'm from Nashville, Tennessee," Judy said. "Folks down there are prejudiced, too, believe you me. It's hard to imagine New York—or anyplace else—could be much different."

"Well, I can't vouch for the rest of the state, but I grew up in a Jewish town."

"Lucky you!" Rebecca's envy was palpable.

"What kind of problems do you have back home? Has anything ever happened to you?" I asked, really curious—after all, they might be Jewish, but they were also undeniably white.

"Are you kidding?" Rebecca said.

"I wouldn't even know where to begin," Judy said.

"Tell me," I urged, anxious to show them solidarity and my sympathy.

"Well, for one thing," Rebecca said, "there are stores we can't go into, 'cause no one will serve us. They pretend we don't exist, or else just flat-out tell us to get out. And there are schools that won't let Jews in—restaurants and other public places, too."

I gasped. "Really?"

"Yeah. And mean kids used to wait after school to beat us up. Sometimes my mother had to come rescue us, and when she did, they called her bad names."

"That's terrible!"

"It truly is." Judy sighed. "And you know what's the saddest part? We Jews have never hurt anyone, but some people hate us anyway. That's a fact. So we learn to keep out of their way. We keep to our own kind."

No one said a word for several moments—the girls sitting at desk chairs while I, as their guest of honor, occupied their armchair. Their stories eerily echoed things I'd heard about the way Negroes were treated in the South, and I was just about to say so when Rebecca broke the silence.

"Speaking of the facts of life," she said, "it's a fact that you're out there, all by yourself, and we're in here with the rest of the Jewish kids."

"Yeah, in our own private little ghetto," Judy mocked.

I let out an uneasy laugh. "Oh, I'm just fine—"

"You should have come to us sooner and told us you're Jewish," Rebecca scolded. "We would've looked after you."

"We surely would have," Judy agreed.

"Gee, thanks," I said, hoping to put a rapid end to their concern, "but I'm not sure that's—"

"Anyhow, now that we know, I promise we'll do right by you, Meri," Rebecca said. "Don't you worry: we'll go have a talk with Miss Bell—right away. Today."

"Talk to Miss Bell?" I said, unable to suppress a nervous giggle. "About me? Why would you want to do that?"

"'Cause you're one of us and you belong in here," Judy said. "We Jews have to stick together because, let's face it, those *goyim* are trash."

"Judy!" Rebecca cut in, her voice very stern, before I could voice a protest. "You haven't even mentioned the worst part: not only did they put her in with the Christians, they gave her a nigger roommate."

My mouth dropped open.

"Oh, my god, I can't believe I forgot that!" Judy blurted out. "That's disgusting!"

Suddenly, I was having trouble breathing. The room seemed to be going in and out of focus; one second their voices were coming at me from somewhere very far away, the next from way too close.

"It must be horrible living with one of *them*," Rebecca was saying. "I bet that nigger girl smells bad. Why, she probably stinks!" She wrinkled up her nose in delicate disgust. "How can you stand it?"

Abruptly, without quite knowing how it had happened, I was on my feet, hands fisted at my sides and clenched so tightly that my fingers immediately started to go numb.

Both girls stared at me.

"Are you okay?" Judy asked.

"SHUT UP!!!" I shouted, finally finding my voice. "For your information, Pixie smells the same as you and me. As a matter of fact, now that I think about it, she smells a whole lot better than you do!"

"I beg your pardon?" Rebecca said with true Southern civility.

"Don't bother!" I snapped, "although you *should* ask Pixie's forgiveness . . . How can you have the nerve to sit there complaining about prejudice against the Jews one minute, and then spew out that obnoxious crap about Negroes the next? How dare you!"

"Now hold on just a cotton-picking minute." Rebecca was also on her feet. "Let me get this straight. Are you comparing the Jews to the niggers?"

"For your information: it's Negroes. And you bet I am!"

"Get out of my room!"

"With pleasure!"

I turned and stalked out, heading for the sanctuary of my own side of the glass doors.

———

Pixie was getting ready for bed when I came in. "What's wrong, Meri?" she immediately asked.

Instead of answering, I slammed around our room for several minutes, cursing under my breath and tossing things on the floor, clenching and unclenching my hands to counteract the numbness and trying to force myself to take deep, calming breaths. At last, with a groan, I threw myself onto my bed, and somehow managed to give Pixie a carefully expurgated version of my confrontation with Rebecca and Judy.

She listened without comment, her dark eyes studying my face, until I'd finished venting.

"I'm sorry you're so upset, Meri," she said at last. "I know how you feel . . . But you have so much to learn."

"Like what?" I demanded, unable to keep the belligerence from my voice and hoping she'd realize that my anger wasn't directed at her.

"Like I told you before, this isn't the music festival. It's the Midwest. Do you remember when I said that?"

"Yes," I ground out between clenched teeth. "The first day. Right after I met you."

"Well, everything I said then is still true. Nothing's changed."

"How can you stand it?" I choked on a sob. "How can you live with it?"

"I live with it because I have to . . . You know, it's funny: in some ways it's a whole lot easier to take than what goes on up North."

"How can you say that, knowing how these people feel?"

"But that's just it: I know how they feel. No one tries to hide it. And maybe this sounds crazy, but here I know my place, and as long as I stay in it, I know what to expect. Up North, people act like they're friendly, but inside they're usually at least as prejudiced as any Southerner, only they've learned to hide it better . . . And suddenly, just when you're beginning to trust them, they turn on you. At least no one here pretends to be your friend when they aren't."

"I never thought of that." It dawned on me belatedly that Pixie and her friends had excellent reasons for having both public and private personas. "But doesn't it hurt when people treat you like dirt?"

"Sure it hurts."

"Then why do you let them? Why don't you fight back?

I don't think I could sit around and let people treat me that way, if I were you."

"Yes you would, or you'd find yourself in an awful lot of trouble. Just look at what happened in that Baptist church in Birmingham, back in September, right before school started: four innocent little girls blown to Kingdom Come by the Klan. It was a warning not to step out of line. And don't you forget, you can get in just as much trouble for not keeping your mouth shut around here. Doesn't matter what color you are."

"Then I guess I'm going to be in trouble!"

"You're a damn-fool idealist, just like Rachel!" It definitely wasn't a compliment. "She says Negroes have an obligation to stand up and protest, or things will never change."

"Maybe she's right."

"Maybe so. But there's no future around here for a Negro with opinions like that! Anyway, it's not her neck she's advising me to stick out . . ." She winced. "No, I take that back. She told me she's signed up to do a voter education project in South Carolina this coming summer—on one of those Freedom Buses. She doesn't have any idea what she's getting into. I hope she'll be okay."

"I'm sure she will."

"Ha!" Pixie's mood seemed to shift once again. She ran her fingers through her crinkly red-brown hair and looked me in the eye. "Listen, Meri, it's just that things have slowly been changing for the better for us, over these past few years. And now President Kennedy seems to represent some real hope. Oh, boy, do they hate him around here—almost as much as they do in the deep South. Still, I have to trust that what the Reverend King says is true: if we're patient, the changes will come."

"Well, sometimes you have to give the changes a kick in the pants to help them along!"

"Not me! It's gonna be the dumb white liberal idealists from up North, like you and Rachel, who do the kicking—not the Negroes. You can count on that. We have better sense. And in the meantime, I'll keep in my place, thank you very much. At least I know it's safe!"

chapter 13: dies irae

I was awakened by someone shining a flashlight in my face. "Are you Meri Henriques?" a familiar voice asked.

"Yes."

"And is that Katherine Gates in the other bed? I can't seem to wake her up to ask her."

"Yes, Miss Bell," was my weary reply.

"Thank you. Just making sure. That's all—you can go back to sleep now."

I glanced over at the illuminated dial on Pixie's clock.

It was 2:00 a.m. on the morning of November 22.

Another bed check! I thought, thoroughly disgusted. *Just to make sure that we're really here. As if there's anyplace else to be!*

The next time I awoke, it was seven thirty, and Pixie had already gone downstairs for breakfast.

It was a gloomy day. Rain fell in a soft gray drizzle, puddling on the limestone pavers that formed the paths and courtyards of Wells Quad. But not even the bad weather could spoil my elation.

It was the week before Thanksgiving, and pre-holiday excitement was in the air. Everyone was having trouble concentrating on school routines, yet professors were piling on homework, expecting us—optimistically or sadistically, depending on one's point of view—to hand it in at the end of the vacation.

Pixie was spending the evenings happily drawing, coloring, and cutting out pumpkins, turkeys, and pilgrims for a class project. Rachel put off doing her own homework in order to kibitz.

"Pixie, your lack of artistic talent is truly impressive. What's that thing you're making supposed to be: a turkey or the Michelin man?"

Irked beyond politeness, I hotly confronted Rachel. "So Pixie's pictures don't look professional. So what! They're lively and charming, and I'm sure the children will love them."

Rachel gaped at me, obviously astonished by my sudden bold rebellion.

"And Pixie," I went on, turning away from Rachel, "you know what impresses me even more? The way you patiently put up with Rachel's teasing!"

For once Rachel didn't seem to have a sarcastic wisecrack at her disposal, and for the rest of that evening, at least, she was unusually well-behaved.

For me, though, the most thrilling part of the upcoming holiday was that, thanks to Gineeva, I was going home.

Several days earlier, she had come up to our room for the express purpose of letting me know that her roommate was looking for people who were interested in sharing the cost of driving to New York City over Thanksgiving vacation. She remembered hearing me telling Pixie that I could only afford to travel on Christmas, and had reasoned that I might be able to do so if I could get a cheap ride with her roommate.

I was extremely grateful for her thoughtful suggestion. I had been steeling myself to stay alone in the dorm while everyone else was at home with their friends and relatives, a depressing scenario no matter how positive a spin I tried to put on it. Not even the prospect of being spared my mother's inevitable tongue-lashings seemed adequate compensation for the loss of this most special holiday. However, because of my limited budget, I'd felt I hadn't had a choice.

As it turned out, Gineeva's roommate was delighted to find another passenger. Better yet, the ride was going to be practically free: all I had to do was help pay for gas. The plan was to leave late Wednesday afternoon, immediately after class, and drive straight through the night to arrive in New York City early Thanksgiving morning. From there, I would take the Long Island Railroad out to Great Neck. Three other people had already signed up as passengers, and I was the fourth and last.

Just the thought of going home gave my spirits a lift, and I felt a playful urge not to tell my family the good news. How surprised they'd be when I arrived on their doorstep early Thanksgiving morning!

When I returned to the dorm after my morning classes, it was still raining. I bought a carton of milk from the vending machine and brought it up to my room. After making myself comfortable on my bed, I opened my chorus folder and spread the music out on my lap. In addition to the "B-minor Mass," we were working on Benjamin Britten's "War Requiem," and the soprano line was extremely difficult.

With a tuning fork and my violin on hand to help work out the pitches, I began going over my part, stopping every so often to look out of the window. Rain dripped off branches, shaking loose the last of the dead brown leaves. It was an appropriate accompaniment to the mood of the music.

> *Dies irae, dies illa,*
> *Solvet saeclum in favilla.*
> (Day of wrath, that day
> In ashes the earth shall pass away.)

The men sang that part, while the women wailed:

> Libera me, Domine!
> (Save me, Lord!)

Half an hour later, satisfied that I could do an acceptable version of my part, I started gathering my things in preparation for leaving. I had just finished putting on my raincoat and was rooting through my closet, searching for my umbrella, when the phone rang.

"Get Pixie," a hoarse voice growled, when I picked up the receiver.

"Is that you, Gineeva?"

She didn't answer, but I could hear the congested hiss of her breathing on the other end of the line.

"Gineeva?" I persisted. "Are you there? Why are you calling? You know Pixie has classes all afternoon."

"Shit!"

I was taken aback. She was often gruff, but even by her standards this was unusually rude.

"What's the matter? Why won't you talk to me?"

She didn't answer that either, but I could hear a radio playing in the background. It sounded like some sort of news broadcast.

I tried again. "Is something wrong? Are you sick? Do you need help?"

"No."

Annoyance flared. "Listen, Gineeva, this is a stupid game you're playing with me. Don't you realize you're making me late for—"

"OH NO!!!" she wailed—and suddenly, to my amazement, she burst into wrenching sobs.

This was really too much!

"What the hell's the matter with you?" I demanded. "Tell me right now, or I'm going to hang up on you."

"Oh, Meri, President Kennedy's just been shot! They say he may be dead."

In that single, terrible instant, the whole world shifted subtly, and nothing looked quite the same as it had only seconds earlier. I felt as if I had accidentally blundered into the middle of someone else's nightmare.

Gineeva was still crying, but more quietly now.

I was so shocked that I said the first thing that popped into my head—the stupidest thing imaginable—because I had to deny any possibility that this heartbreaking news might be true: "I don't believe you! You're lying!" I regretted the words the moment they were out of my mouth.

"God damn you to hell, Meri! If you think I'd make up a story like that, you can go listen to the radio yourself!" She slammed down the receiver.

"I'm sorry!" I moaned. "I didn't mean it!"

But it was too late.

In a daze, I hung up and turned on Pixie's radio.

It was true. Every radio station had the same story: twenty minutes earlier, in Dallas, Texas, John Kennedy had been shot. No one was sure of his condition.

I sat on Pixie's bed, listening to the reports coming in and watching the rain washing steadily down the windowpanes. In my mind a single thought formed, repeating itself over and over, with hypnotic regularity: *This can't be real. This can't be real. This can't be real.* After a while, I felt so numb that the thought itself assumed a certain unreality.

The radio reports continued. The announcers sounded as confused and upset as I was. They spoke of the sense of shock people throughout the world must be experiencing. Which made me think about the concern people often expressed for John Kennedy's safety whenever he left the country on a good-will tour: a fear that some fanatic foreigner, lurking in the shadows "Over There," might try to assassinate him. And now, ironically, it had happened, not in some foreign country at all, but right here in the United States!

Eventually, it occurred to me that I was late for chorus. I wondered if anyone else would be there, then decided that I might as well go over to the music building to find out.

I no longer wanted to be alone.

The chorus room was very quiet: only about half of the students had showed up. Somebody had brought along a transistor radio, and the volume was turned down low. The only other sound in the room was an occasional muffled sob.

Not long after I arrived, the chorus director hurried in. His face was pale and haggard, and with a tremor in his voice, he apologized for being late and thanked us for waiting for him. He said he realized that singing was probably the last thing we felt like doing just now, but suggested that we try to make it through the final section of "War Requiem" before he dismissed us.

We sang terribly.

In paradisum: deducant te Angeli.
In tuo adventu suscipiant te Martyres.
Et perducant te civitatem sanctum Jerusalem.
Chorus Angelorum te suscipiat . . .
Requiescant in pace.
Amen.

(Into paradise: may the Angels lead thee.
At thy coming, may the Martyrs receive thee
And bring thee into the holy city of Jerusalem.
May the choir of Angels receive thee . . .
Rest in peace.
Amen.)

After class, I drifted slowly through the music building. People stood around in the halls and classrooms, staring at nothing or talking to one another in hushed voices.

It was like being in church.

When at last I stepped outside, ice-cold rain slapped me in the face, stinging me awake, and I quickly retreated into the doorway. A logical voice inside my head told me to go back to my dorm, if only to pick up my forgotten umbrella—but I couldn't bear the thought of going indoors again, not even for a minute.

My room seemed like a prison.

So instead, I tucked my chorus folder inside my raincoat, hunched my shoulders against the inclement weather, and ventured forth. In an instant I was soaked to the skin, but I was beyond caring about physical discomfort. Besides, walking gave me something to do.

The dreary gray world seemed a fitting counterpoint to the gloom I had left behind in the music building. Although I had nowhere to go and no reason to continue onward, my feet marched mechanically along, step by step. With each step, grim thoughts kept repeating inside my head like the chorus in some Greek tragedy: *He's dead! He's dead! He must be dead . . .*

How on earth could such a thing have happened? How could a single bullet, in one shocking instant, have changed the world so completely?

I kept trudging blindly forward, eyes riveted on the ground, torturing myself with unanswerable questions, until some slightly less foggy part of my brain registered that I was passing the Social Sciences building. It also dawned on me that I wasn't the only person who had taken refuge out-of-doors. In fact, by some strange coincidence, it seemed that a large portion of the school population was standing outside in the drizzle in their raincoats and boots, carrying umbrellas, talking, and listening to transistor radios.

I slowed down, hoping to catch a news update, but all the smiling faces put me off.

What could anyone find to be happy about?

What would make *me* smile? I couldn't think of a single thing that would allow me to forget what had just happened in Dallas.

Immediately ahead, taking up the entire path and also most of the adjacent lawn, a large group of people was discussing something with such animated intensity that they were apparently unaware of the fact that they were preventing anyone else from getting past.

As I came closer, I began to overhear conversations.

"Hey, what's happening?" a newly arrived coed called out. "I would have gotten here sooner if my dumb history prof hadn't kept us in to discuss the shooting. Is there anything new?"

"No," another girl responded. "It's really boring: the reporters are all hanging around the hospital, waiting for the doctors' report. There's lots of speculation, but no one knows for sure."

By now I was on the outer fringes of the gathering.

"Does that mean Kennedy's still alive?"

"Yes—but we're hoping."

It felt like a kick in the stomach.

I must have gasped, because people turned around to look at me.

There must be some mistake! I thought. But deep down inside, I knew with sickening certainty that these people meant exactly what they were saying. This was Hoosier Hysteria in its most terrible incarnation.

Although there was still a great deal of excited chatter going on all around me, the crowd's movement had created a narrow passage, revealing a possible escape route. I almost fell into it: scurrying forward, staring straight ahead, hoping against hope that if I moved fast enough, I would outrun the rest of those loathsome conversations.

But there was no escape.

Everywhere I went, people were standing around talking, and everywhere I looked, I saw smiling faces. And now that I was aware of how my fellow students truly felt, the snatches of questions and answers that I had been successfully ignoring until that very moment began pressing in on me from all sides.

"Wow, I can't believe this is really happening!"

"Neither can I. Isn't it fabulous?"

"I hope we hear something soon."

"Hey everyone: great news!" a male voice cried out over the hubbub. "The doctors have just pronounced Kennedy dead!"

My heart went still.

The next instant a solid wall of noise, like the roar of an approaching avalanche, erupted from the crowd. All around me, people caught each other up in ecstatic hugs and jubilant impromptu dances.

"Hold on a minute—that's not all!" the same obnoxious

voice shouted over the uproar. "The reporter just said that Lyndon Johnson may have suffered a heart attack when they told him the news."

The mob went crazy.

"Oh, my god, this is unbelievable! What an incredible day!"

"It's not just incredible—it's the best day of our lives!"

"What's going to happen if it's true about Johnson?"

"Who knows? Maybe Nixon will take over!"

Manic laughter rippled on rain-swept gusts of wind.

Soul-sickening horror and despair were unfurling inside of me like a poisonous black flower. For the first and only time in my life, I fervently wished that I would suddenly be struck deaf and dumb so I wouldn't have to know, wouldn't have to hear or feel, what was going on around me.

I could scarcely breathe.

Trapped . . . surrounded by a ravening horde of nightmare monsters, ghouls vomiting up peals of merciless laughter.

I ran.

Daniel Weaver came striding toward me through the rain, wrapped in a bulky raincoat, huddled under his umbrella.

I careened straight into him. For a moment, I didn't know who he was or what I was doing there. I struggled, flailing wildly, until his hands reached out and grabbed my arms, enfolding me and pulling me close.

"Take it easy, Meri—it's me, Daniel."

"Daniel, did you hear them?" I sobbed against his chest. "Did you hear what they're saying?"

"I heard." His voice came out knife-edged, perfectly flat and bitter. "Bastards!"

"But why?"

And then both of us were crying.

Daniel dropped his umbrella and we held onto each other, clinging together like drowning children, our faces washed by the rain.

After a while he spoke again. "Look at you, Meri: you're soaking wet. And now I am, too . . . You shouldn't be out here like this." Without another word, he picked up his umbrella and put an arm around my shoulders. Slowly, we started back the way I had come.

While I was within the shelter of Daniel's umbrella, protected by his steady presence, I felt safe. But the moment he said good-bye and left me standing alone in the downstairs lobby of my dorm amidst the crush of revelers, I was back in my waking nightmare. I pushed my way through the giddy throng and, avoiding the claustrophobic confinement of the elevator, fled up the stairs to the haven of my room.

Shennandoah was waiting for me there, huddled in our armchair. I was so relieved to see a friendly face that I fell, sobbing, into her arms.

Eventually, when we were calmer, she told me she'd been alone for the past few hours, until she'd finally decided that she needed company. Myrna, who was at this point nowhere to be found, had let her in.

"Do you mind if I stay with you for a while?" she asked.

I accepted gratefully. Then I went and shut my door, hoping to blot out the harsh reality of the rest of the school. By now I was shivering violently, as much from emotion as from the cold.

I stripped off my wet clothing and rummaged through my closet, searching for something appropriate to wear. I settled at last on my concert dress. It was the blackest thing I owned, but still not black enough to suit my mood. I changed in silence, then sat down on my bed to wait—for what, I didn't know.

Shennandoah had reclaimed her place in our armchair.

We were quiet for a long time, watching as the room slowly darkened and that bitter day drew to its inevitable close.

Someone knocked on my door.

"Come in," I called out.

The door swung open, letting in a dazzling flood of light. Two people were standing on the threshold, backlit by the glare. When my eyes finally adjusted, I saw that it was Myrna and Susan Olsen.

"Hello?" Myrna began in a hesitant voice, peering into the gloom. "Is anyone here?"

"What do you want?" I demanded, too shell-shocked to be polite.

"Why are you sitting in the dark? I can hardly see you."

"Just tell us what you want."

"Oh. Well," Susan began, "Roberta says Myrna and I are supposed to let everyone on our floor know that you're all invited to the party tonight. Have you heard about it?"

Neither Shennandoah nor I deigned to answer.

"I said: There's going to be a Victory Party tonight in the downstairs lounge and everyone's invited. Will you join us?"

My answer stuck in my throat.

"Get out!!!"

I was grateful to Shennandoah for having said it for me. I pulled my knees to my chest and hugged my arms around them.

"Well, okay . . . if that's how you feel . . ." They left, shutting the door behind them.

Once again, we were alone with the dark.

"Shen?" My voice came out in the barest of whispers.

"What?"

"How can they do this?"

"I don't know."

"But you must know!" For a moment I was angry with everyone, including her. "You grew up here."

"You mean, what made them stop being . . . human?" Her voice broke on the last word.

"Forgive me. I didn't mean to snap at you." I, too, was on the point of tears.

"Things like this make me ashamed that I was born here."

"I'm sorry! I know you're not like them. I just thought—oh, I don't know—that since you grew up here, you might be able to explain how things could get so twisted up inside a person . . ." I took a ragged breath and tried again, despairing. "How bigotry and personal interests can warp someone to the point where they're actually celebrating President Kennedy's death."

"Politics. For them it's just politics. Which means any-thing's fair, even an assassination."

"That's sick!"

"You're damn right it is! It's something I've been fighting against all my life. And it's why I am the way I am." She sighed. "I know some people laugh at me because I won't date white men—and some of them would probably like to do a whole lot worse than laugh. You know, sometimes I get so discouraged I think maybe I should give up. Not rock the boat. Conform. Be like everyone else. But then, whenever something like this happens, I know for sure I have to keep on fighting."

"My god, this is a horrible place!"

"It is. But it can also be a good place—if we insist on it, and if we're willing to work hard to change things. Don't let anyone or anything ever make you forget that."

My laugh was as bitter as gall. "Don't worry, Shen, I'll never forget this—all the prejudice and hatred. It's disgusting! In fact, I'm not sure I want to be here for the rest of the semester. When I go home for Thanksgiving, maybe I should just stay there."

"You have to do what you think is right. But if I were you, I wouldn't run away from this—or let anyone *chase* me away, either."

Her words set off a flood of guilt, yet I protested, "Would it really be running away? I can't help thinking that I've made a terrible mistake coming to Indiana. I don't belong here, and what happened today only confirms it."

"But we need people like you. Someone has to act as the school's conscience."

"Not me!" It was a cry straight from my heart. "Anyway, what kind of conscience am I? Everyone tries to pretend I don't exist because not only do I have a Negro roommate, but I also have the nerve to think of her as my friend! That's not socially acceptable."

"At least as unacceptable as going out with Negro men."

"Well, nobody in the dorm ever says anything out loud to me, like they do about your dates—except for those damn Southerners. And their opinion of both of us is obvious."

"They can't help it, Meri. It's what they've been taught."

"That's no excuse! They're in college! My god, you'd think by now they might have tried looking beyond the crap they hear at home. You'd think they'd have noticed there's a fellow human being inside the other person's dark skin." I could no longer hold back my tears.

"Not a chance!"

"Why not?" I scrubbed at my eyes with my sleeve. "You did."

"And look where it's gotten me! I'm not exactly a member of the school's social elite, you know."

"So what do we do now?" I asked, although I knew it was hopeless.

"Forget them. And try to set a conspicuous example with our own behavior."

"I only wish I could."

We lapsed into silence. There was really nothing more to say.

It was getting quite late. According to the luminous dial on Pixie's clock, it was nearly dinnertime.

Suddenly the door opened and Pixie and Caralene walked in, turning on the lights and flooding the room with a harsh, alien glare. I could see right away that both girls were very tense. They barely greeted us, and neither made a single comment about the day's events. When Caralene went next door to change, Shennandoah stood up to leave.

"Are you ready to go to dinner, Meri?" Pixie asked. Her voice was perfectly calm, as flat and expressionless as if she was reading from a phone book.

I was incredulous. First the others and now Pixie!

"Do you mean to tell me you're actually going to eat dinner tonight?" I exploded, nearly choking on my rage. "With those pigs? In spite of what's happened? I don't believe it! Don't you realize they're celebrating out there? I thought Kennedy meant something to you!"

She whirled to look at me, her eyes ablaze with fury. "You

listen to me, Meri Henriques, and you listen good! Remember what I told you? Remember what I said about having to keep in your place around here?"

I nodded, not trusting myself to speak.

"Well, this isn't any dress rehearsal—this is for real! And my place is to go on acting like nothing's happened. I won't let them see how much I'm hurting. I'll cry inside."

"I'm sorry, Pixie!" I blurted out. "I should have known. May I go to dinner with you?"

Her expression softened, and then she nodded and turned quickly away—but not before I'd seen the tears in her eyes.

I walked Shennandoah to the elevator. "What are you going to do now?" I asked her.

"I guess Pixie is right. I should go back to my dorm to eat dinner and try to keep up a brave front. But Meri, before I go, promise me one thing?"

"What?"

"Promise you'll think about what I said earlier. Don't leave unless you're positive it's the right thing to do. And while you're home over Thanksgiving, don't forget: I'll still be here—and so will Pixie, and Caralene, and Gineeva, and all of their friends from the Trees—if you do decide to come back."

"Okay, I'll think about it."

We hugged each other and she left.

With an aching heart, I walked slowly down the hall, dodging revelers, intending to ask Rachel if she'd join Pixie, Caralene, and me in the cafeteria. But she had locked herself in her room, and all I could hear were muffled sobs through the door.

"Rachel? It's Meri. Come out and be with us."

"Go away!"

So I left her alone, but the sounds of her grief followed me down the hall and haunted me throughout dinner. Pixie and Caralene managed to eat a little, but I just stared at my plate, thinking how frightened and lonely a young widow and her two small children must be that night.

Later, it was impossible to sleep, despite my mental and physical exhaustion.

Ironically, it seemed that everyone else in the dorm was wide awake, too. The Victory Party went on until dawn—in fact, although a memorial service was held in the main auditorium, the Victory Parties lasted, in one form or another, right up to the moment Indiana University closed for Thanksgiving vacation the following Wednesday afternoon.

In my opinion, we didn't have much to be thankful for that year.

chapter 14: winter

While I was away in New York, winter had come to the Midwest—and that meant the coldest temperatures and the most snow I had ever experienced.

I was glad it was winter. The relentless cold seemed an appropriate reflection of the way I felt about my life at Indiana University.

More than once over the course of Thanksgiving vacation, I'd found myself attempting to describe my Indiana experiences to my friends and relatives. But it had proved hopeless. Words had been inadequate, and every conversation had ended the same way: with me stuttering out a nearly incomprehensible litany of grievances, shaking with emotion, and choking on tears. In the end, the only coherent statement I'd been able to make was that the school's reaction to President Kennedy's death had depressed me far more than the event itself. On one hand, school officials had authorized memorial services; on the other hand, Indiana University's highest authority, President Elvis Stahr, had issued a harsh proclamation prohibiting anyone from canceling or not attending classes, and threatening any teacher, graduate, or undergraduate student who failed to comply, with expulsion from the school.

As far as I knew, no other university in the entire country had remained open, and I silently vowed that I would never voluntarily return to a place where such callous disregard for common decency was sanctioned.

When I arrived in New York, my family was shocked by my appearance. I was still dressed in my black concert dress, to which I had added a black armband as mute testimony to my despair. I had gotten little sleep since the night of the assassination and was rumpled and depressed, with dark circles under my eyes. Furthermore, as a result of my self-prescribed milk diet, I had lost more than twenty pounds since they'd last seen me in September, and my clothing hung from my body in baggy folds. That first night, right in the middle of Thanksgiving dinner, my mother announced to our guests that her eldest daughter looked like a bedraggled scarecrow.

Her sarcastic jibes were nothing new—I was used to them. Still, being at home caused me an acute sense of disorientation. It was strangely unsettling to find myself among people whose reactions to our national tragedy were reasonable. In Indiana, my mourning dress had been a statement, an expression of my opposition to popular opinion; in New York, where everyone was just as horrified by the assassination as I was, my outfit seemed almost melodramatic.

Which represents reality? I asked myself. *Indiana University or New York?*

The day after Thanksgiving, I was about to pick up the phone to call Gineeva's roommate and let her know that I wouldn't be making the return trip to Indiana, when my parents summoned me for a talk.

My father was the first to speak. "I know how angry you are about Indiana—after all you've told us, I'm furious myself—and we realize that you don't want to go back there. In fact, I'm not at all sure what I'd do myself, if I were in your shoes—"

"Oh, for heaven's sake, Tommy!" my mother said. "Stop beating around the bush and get to the point."

My father gave her a patient but weary look. "Your mother and I think that you should consider carefully before you burn any bridges."

"But I have!" I found that I was close to tears.

"Stop whimpering and pay attention," my mother snapped. "What your father is trying to say, in his roundabout way, is that we're concerned that if you drop out now, halfway through your first semester, it will be your school record, and not Indiana University, that will suffer. You may have a hard time finding another school that will accept you."

My father placed a gentle hand on my shoulder. "Maybe the best thing to do is grit your teeth and finish what you've begun."

It was practical advice, and eventually, after a great deal of soul-searching, I decided to take it. Besides, I felt terrible every time I thought about abandoning my friends to their fate. Surely I could endure the situation at Indiana University if they could.

By the time I returned to campus, my heartache had frozen into a grim determination to work even harder and do well, which would allow me to graduate from IU in three and a half years—should I last that long—instead of the usual four.

—————

The first snowfalls of the winter season were light, followed by crisp, sparkling days when being outside was a pleasure. One mild afternoon, Pixie, Rachel, and I went out to play in the pristine white courtyard in front of Morrison Hall, chasing each other and throwing snowballs, making snow angels in the deep drifts, and laughing like giddy children.

But as the weeks passed and winter closed in, snow began falling in earnest. Sometimes it was so gloomy that the streetlights along the campus roads and byways stayed on continuously, day and night. Temperatures seldom rose above zero, and snow piled up in deep drifts. Footpaths narrowed to treacherous, icy troughs.

Going outside became an elaborate and time-consuming ritual. Each morning, before I left the dorm, I bundled up in all of the warm winter clothing I possessed.

"Seems like you're trying to put on every single thing you

own, Meri," Pixie teased, "all at the same time! You sure you don't want to borrow some of my stuff?"

I was too busy to answer—pulling on thermals over conventional underwear, a full slip, two pairs of socks, a blouse, and two sweaters, one on top of the other, and finishing the entire ensemble off with a pleated wool skirt.

"You look absolutely ridiculous," Rachel opined, observing from our armchair, as I began to struggle into my heavy woolen coat, scarf, cap, boots, and mittens. By the time I pulled on that last mitten, I was so well padded I could scarcely move.

"You'd better be careful," Pixie warned. "If you happen to slip and fall on the snow and ice, you'll never be able to get up without help."

"She's probably hoping some chivalrous knight will come along to rescue her," Rachel suggested. "And if he doesn't, she'll just have to lie there, stuck in a snowdrift like a prehistoric woolly mammoth, until spring returns to thaw her out."

"Well, even if I do look like a fool, at least I'll be a warm one!" I surprised myself by retorting.

Attending classes was an adventure. I skittered along the frozen paths feeling like an Arctic explorer, watching my breath puff out in frosty white clouds in the frigid air. By the time I arrived at my destination, I was usually so overheated that I was anxious to discard my bulky winter outfit. And there it would remain, lying in a steaming heap on the floor beside my desk, until the end of the class period, when I would have to put everything back on again, hurrying so as not to be late for my next class. I soon learned to appreciate zoology lab and Introduction to Drawing, both of which lasted for hours—limiting the need for costume changes.

―――――――

Despite the bad weather, university life went on much as usual, but as the semester drew to its inevitable close, an almost tangible tension entered the air. Workloads increased and we no longer had the luxury of free evenings for card games, entertainment, or relaxation. Even my art class was affected by the accelerated pace.

It all began one evening when Mrs. Burns came to class carrying a human skeleton. My first reaction was that at last we were going to have an interesting project to work on. But after an entire week of making detailed drawings of joints, scrutinizing how each one worked and meshed with the adjacent bones, my interest in human anatomy was as dead as the corpse that had offered up its skeleton for our edification. I concluded that this was just another of Mrs. Burns's tedious lessons in perseverance.

At our next class meeting, however, the skeleton was no longer hanging from its gallows-like stand—instead it was perched awkwardly in a straight-backed chair and beside it, slumped in an identical chair, was a frumpy woman in a faded blue bathrobe.

Before anyone had much time to speculate about our unusual and extremely informal visitor, Mrs. Burns arrived, putting an abrupt end to all conversation.

"Class, as you can see, we have a special guest tonight. This is Miss Green. Miss Green is a model. She is here to assist us in our study of life drawing . . . Thank you, Miss Green, you may begin."

Miss Green's bland, slightly bored expression didn't alter one iota as she stood up and shrugged out of her robe.

There was an audible intake of breath; underneath her bathrobe, Miss Green wore nothing but a g-string!

I'm sure everyone experienced the same flutter of mixed emotions as I did: surprise, embarrassment, and interest, all jumbled together. Doubtless, each of us hoped to appear blasé and unflappable, as if having a nude model in art class was an everyday occurrence. However, if the expressions on my neighbors' faces were any indication, no one was succeeding.

Mrs. Burn's voice cut through the uneasy babble.

"Class: I assume that you have come here to be educated, not titillated. Must I remind you that our lesson has begun?"

We scrambled for our drawing boards, papers, and pencils.

At Mrs. Burns's command, the model began a series of sixty-second poses. It was immediately painfully obvious that it was going to be impossible to draw anything at all in one minute, and it took all my powers of concentration just to scrawl a few hasty slashes on my paper before it was time to move on to the next inadequate drawing. I had to hand it to Mrs. Burns, she certainly knew how to manage us: her busy regime left us no time in which to gape.

Just as I was finally starting to adjust to the frantic pace, the silence of the classroom was shattered by an ear-piercing shriek. I stopped my mad scribbling mid-stroke and looked up in time to see my classmate, a local girl named Barbara Summers, standing transfixed in the doorway.

"NO!" Her art supplies slipped, unheeded, from her hands and clattered to the floor.

Meanwhile, as if in an alternate reality, the nude woman kept revolving, dreamlike in her sixty-second poses. By then everyone else had stopped drawing in order to watch Barbara watch the model.

At that point, Mrs. Burns intervened. With one hand extended in front of her and speaking gently, as if to a skittish animal or a frightened child, she started slowly across the room. "Now, Barbara dear," she soothed, "everything's going to be all right. You're just a little bit surprised because it's our first day of life drawing"—she edged closer—"and I'm sure you must have noticed our special visitor. Aren't we lucky to have a live model to draw?"

At last, Miss Green became aware of the unfolding drama and stopped posing. She stood regarding Barbara with mild, utterly tranquil, curiosity.

Barbara stared back, mesmerized.

"That's right, Barbara. You're doing fine." By now Mrs. Burns had almost completed her cautious approach. She reached for Barbara's hand. "Why don't you come in and join us, and we'll—"

Barbara startled back to life. "NO!!!" she shrieked, turning brimming eyes on an astonished Mrs. Burns. "OH, NO!" And with a loud, ululating wail that sounded barely human, she turned and fled from the room.

After a shocked moment, Mrs. Burns went racing after her—at which point the entire class threw down their pencils and joined the chase.

"Barbara!" Mrs. Burns cried. "Barbara, come back!"

By the time I reached her side, Mrs. Burns had stopped in the hall outside our classroom and Barbara was nowhere to be seen. But I could still hear her muffled cries echoing through the building as they faded into the distance.

Mrs. Burns stood gazing after her vanished charge, surrounded by a gaggle of agitated students. Everyone chattered excitedly, galvanized by this unexpected and most entertaining turn of events.

"My goodness, I've never had anyone react *that* way before," Mrs. Burns confessed. "The poor thing! I guess I should have warned you ahead of time." As if on a sudden impulse, she turned to me. "Miss Henriques, I've noticed that you're her friend. Try to find her and bring her back—if she'll come. The rest of you, let's get back to work."

I looked everywhere: in the lounges and restrooms, the art gallery, and the main lobby. I even went outside, on the slim chance that she might be standing in the snow or sitting on one of the cold stone benches. But Barbara was gone, and after that she never returned to Mrs. Burns's class.

———

In December, with the Christmas season nearly upon us, a number of special events took place at Indiana University: holiday lectures, art exhibits, concerts, parties, and receptions.

In mid-December, the university held its annual Honors Banquet for students who had earned a 3.5 or better grade point average the previous semester.

The night of the banquet, I looked on with envy as Pixie and Rachel presented their engraved invitations at the door to the smaller of our two cafeterias. Peeking past them, I caught a glimpse of white tablecloths and cloth dinner napkins, sparkling silverware and glasses, centerpieces of green fir boughs and red berries, and the warm glow of candles. That ordinarily anti-septic-looking little room seemed magically transformed. And although my friends had assured me that the honorees would be eating the same tasteless food as we were in the main cafeteria next door, I promised myself that, come next year, if I was still at Indiana University, I would be in there with them.

The banquet, which included the inevitable speeches and special presentations, continued long past our regular dinner hour. Afterwards, Rachel came back upstairs with Pixie and stayed to visit. With a groan, she plopped down in our armchair. Her gorgeous green velvet dress was rumpled from hours of sitting.

"Well, how was it?" I demanded. "Tell me everything! Who was there and what it was like?"

"Boring." She stifled a yawn. "It's always boring. I don't know why I bother to go. The food's lousy and we have to put up with those endless speeches."

Pixie, who was watching my reaction, grinned. "Come on, Rae, don't tell that to poor Meri. She's been sitting here all night, envying us, thinking she missed something special."

Rachel giggled. "Gee, Meri, if you want to go next year, you can have my invitation . . . Wait," she hastily amended, "I take that back! I didn't really mean it. You *can't* go for me."

"But you just said it was boring," I reminded her.

"It is. Only . . . well . . . I guess I feel that I owe it to the school to participate anyhow."

"I thought you hated university-sponsored events."

"I do . . . except somehow this is different. It's the school's way of thanking the top students for working hard and doing well, and they go to a lot of trouble to put it on. Besides, whatever else I may think of IU, I *am* grateful for the first-class education they're giving me."

"Why, Rachel, I never thought I'd live to see the day you had a good word to say about this school," Pixie teased.

"Neither did I," Rachel mumbled. "And believe me, it's damn embarrassing!" She smiled, and for a moment her abrasive persona softened. "Anyway, Meri, if you're set on going to next year's Honors Banquet, you'll have to earn your own invitation. I'll even sit with you—because I'll be using mine."

———

Almost before I knew what was happening, Christmas vacation had come and gone. One moment I was at home, enjoying the holiday with friends and family, and the next I was back at school.

No sooner had I walked into my room than the phone rang, as if on cue. Chuckling, I picked up the receiver, sure it was one of Pixie's numerous admirers, already in hot pursuit.

Instead, it was John.

I was completely taken aback.

I had neither seen nor heard from him since the December meeting of the Folksinging Club, and I was still agonizing over the bluegrass fiasco. Perhaps, I reasoned, during one of my marathon soul-searching sessions, his disappearing act had been his unsubtle way of telling me that he wasn't interested in spending time with me any more. But in that case, why was he so overwhelmingly—almost embarrassingly—friendly whenever I saw him at the club?

In truth, John was an enigma. Weeks earlier, I had come to the unhappy conclusion that I really didn't know him at all. I had never heard him say anything direct, never heard him express an opinion about anything important—and he was twice as cagey when we were with friends from the Folksinging Club, as opposed to when we were alone together.

Was he afraid that if he opened up, no one would like him, I wondered? Or was he driven by an almost paranoid fear that something he said or did would eventually get back to his boss and the school administration?

Whatever the cause, he seemed anxious to make sure that all of his actions were as non-controversial and innocuous as possible. The end result was that he often seemed extremely bland, maddeningly vague and ambivalent. Yet now, as if the bluegrass incident had never occurred, as if he hadn't subsequently vanished from my life, here he was, asking me to go out walking!

I hesitated. What if he reappeared only to abandon me again?

In the end his charm won out over my better judgment, and I found myself agreeing to meet him the next day.

We walked across campus in the cold winter sunshine with my hand (at his insistence) tucked companionably through his arm.

"How was your Christmas vacation?" was my eventual cautious question.

"I had a jolly good time with my friends in Indianapolis."

We walked on in silence for several minutes while I tried in vain to think of something appropriate to say that would expand our conversation.

"And yours?" he finally asked.

"It was good to be back home with my family. I saw lots of friends, too." I hesitated, wondering if he missed his family in England. But I didn't dare ask. In fact, I wasn't even sure if he *had* a family to miss!

Afterwards, back in my room, I sat for a long time, thinking about how much I enjoyed his company, and simultaneously doubting that he would ever trust me enough to let me see behind the wall that he had so carefully constructed around his feelings.

Several days later, when we met again at the Folksinging Club, John once again insisted on sitting beside me in my favorite front row seat—and as usual I couldn't help but be pleased and flattered by his attentions.

First, Derek Stone summarized the business that the club's Executive Committee had dealt with since our last general meeting. He told us that he was still trying to negotiate a Joan

Baez concert with the school administration, but nothing had come of his efforts thus far.

Next, John and his fellow officers reported on the recent activities—or, in our case, non-activities—of their various committees. The Poster Committee was standing by, John assured Derek, eagerly awaiting the call to action should there ever be anything to advertise.

The formalities over, we turned to music. To my utter amazement, after several regulars had done their bit, John clambered to his feet and announced he'd like to sing some British sea chanteys. There was a sparkle in his eyes and a roguish smile on his bearded face that made him look positively piratical.

What's come over him? I wondered.

As it turned out, John knew dozens of songs, most of them extremely funny and more than a little bit raunchy—and like any good showman, he saved the best, about a sailor and a prostitute, for last.

The verses were set in nautical terminology, as if the two characters were schooners. In the song the ships meet at sea, make a few passes at each other, and eventually collide. It was outrageously funny, and several times uproarious laughter nearly drowned out the lyrics.

Wild applause greeted the conclusion of John's bravura performance. It would have been an impossible act to follow, so Derek declared an intermission.

But John wasn't about to relinquish his audience. Happily ensconced in front of the room, in a loud voice he began describing his adventures over Thanksgiving vacation. Despite the time lapse, his perspective on a holiday that all of us took for granted was so irreverent and amusing that practically everyone stayed around to listen.

I was dumbfounded. I had never seen this side of John. And it had never occurred to me that he could be so outgoing and open, so sociable and funny.

After a while, I realized with a start that Derek Stone was standing beside me.

"What a character!" he said, nodding in John's direction.

I was almost too flustered to reply—he was actually speaking to ME! All too aware that I was blushing, I was nevertheless determined to preserve my dignity by upholding my end of the conversation.

"I didn't know he had it in him," I admitted, forcing myself to meet Derek's gaze.

"He's usually so serious and proper," Derek agreed with a wry grin. "And now this!"

At his smile, the butterflies in my stomach transformed themselves into a buffalo stampede. I couldn't think of another thing to say, no matter how desperately I wanted to come up with something—anything—that would prolong our encounter.

"Listen, Meri," Derek said. "Could you do me a favor?"

He knew my name!

"Wh-who me?" I sputtered. "Sure!"

"I'd like to discuss a project I have in mind for the Poster Committee," he said, seemingly (thankfully) unaware of my internal tumult, "but John's obviously going to be carrying on for quite a while yet. When he comes back down to earth, tell him I'd like to see him. I'll be free after the meeting."

I agreed to pass the message along.

For a moment, I thought he was going to say something more but instead, to my profound disappointment, he thanked me and left the room.

All I could do was stand there, watching him go and feeling as if I'd just downed a quart of espresso.

As a result of John's antics, the second half of the meeting was late getting started, and since no one was able to top his performance, we adjourned early.

John immediately offered to walk me back to my dorm. When I reminded him about Derek's summons, he once again surprised me, this time by announcing in a booming voice, "Derek Stone can bloody well wait!"

As we left the room and descended the stairs, he was still chattering away, high on adrenaline.

We stepped out of the Student Union and into a snowstorm. Snowflakes came swirling out of the darkness, illuminated by the sudden halos of streetlights, and then disappeared like a mystery into the night. In a heartbeat, the rest of the world was blotted out and all that existed were the two of us in this beautiful, intensely private place.

My face was cold where the wet flakes landed, and I laughed aloud, delighted by their feathery touch.

Neither of us spoke. Apparently John had finally talked himself out, and I was rapt, awed by Nature's beauty. Also, in the back of my mind, I was still mulling over my encounter with Derek. He actually knew my name! I couldn't help fantasizing about what else he might have said if only our conversation could have lasted even a few minutes longer. Why was I always tongue-tied at the most inopportune moments?

I sighed. To distract myself from the gloomy turn my thoughts had taken, I looked over at John and, like a fool, said the first thing that popped into my head: "By the way, did you know that one of your students lives right down the hall from me?"

"No." With that single word, his jovial smile vanished and his voice turned chillier than the drifting snow. "I had no idea. How did you find out?"

"Actually, it was by accident." I was already regretting my impulsive words. "I discovered the coincidence the other night, after our walk."

"I see. What exactly happened?"

"Not much, really. It's just that at suppertime, one of my neighbors—I really don't know her very well . . . in fact, I can't even remember her name . . ." I tried for a chuckle but failed to carry it off. "Well, she came over and started talking to me while we were waiting in line for dinner. She mentioned she'd seen us together earlier in the day while we were out walking, and she teased me about having a date with her teaching assistant."

"Are you certain she meant me?"

"She knew your name."

"Oh." He lapsed into silence.

How on earth was I going to fix this dreadful blunder? I seemed to be getting into worse trouble with every word I uttered.

"Well, don't you want to hear what else she said?" I finally demanded.

"All right then." His mouth was pinched in a harsh line. "What else did she say?"

"Don't look so worried, John: it was good! She said you're one of the best teachers she's ever had."

But he didn't react the way I'd hoped. Instead of being pleased by the compliment, he withdrew even further into his shell and refused to say another word—and the moment we reached the outskirts of Wells Quad, he muttered a hasty good-bye and fled.

You dope! I raged at myself as I watched his retreating back fading into the snow-shrouded night. *Why did you have to open your big mouth and mention that stupid girl?*

Back in my room, I couldn't fall asleep. Instead, I spent what felt like forever agonizing over our disastrous conversation and John's reaction to it.

Did he actually believe that he could go out with me, go walking all over campus, without eventually being seen by *some-one* who knew him? Was he really as upset as he'd seemed to be, just because one of his students had discovered that he had a personal life?

These speculations seemed so absurd as to be hardly worth considering, yet they were the only explanation I could conjure up for his decidedly unfriendly behavior. Still, because he hadn't told me why he was upset—or even admitted that he *was* upset— there was little I could do besides agonize over the episode and curse myself for my own stupidity.

And so I wasn't in the least bit surprised, although I was definitely disappointed, when, once again, John vanished from my life.

chapter 15: semester break

My first semester at Indiana University was almost over. It didn't seem possible. I felt as if I'd just arrived—but also as if I had been there forever.

At our last meeting of Introduction to Drawing, when Mrs. Burns announced that each of us was to come up to her studio for a private critique of the semester's projects, my stomach began doing somersaults. Before she left the classroom with her first victim in tow, she informed the rest of us that she expected us to spend the next two hours working on our final assignment.

I sat at my desk, biting my fingernails, so unnerved by the thought of what she was probably going to say that I was unable to accomplish anything constructive. Sooner than I wanted, one of my classmates returned from his own personal Moment of Truth and informed me that it was my turn to face the Inquisition.

"How'd it go?" I wanted to know.

"She's tough."

I thought seriously about running away. Instead, I gritted my teeth and headed for the elevator.

Art professors and graduate students were assigned studios on the fourth floor, which was ordinarily off-limits to lowly undergraduates. I felt a mild curiosity about what I might find there—but not enough to distract me from worries about my upcoming interview.

How tough was she going to be?

The elevator ride seemed to take forever, but when the doors opened onto the fourth floor, I gasped. There in front of me, taking up most of the opposite wall, was an enormous, life-size, impressionistic painting of a guitar player who was unmistakably Derek Stone: the light brown, curly hair and mustache; the gold-rimmed glasses; the blue work shirt; those pointy cowboy boots—all of it was a dead giveaway.

Mesmerized and barely aware that I was doing so, I crept out of the elevator, drawn irresistibly forward, all thoughts of Mrs. Burns vanished from my mind like so much smoke in the wind. My hand reached out to reverently stroke the rough-textured surface but halted a fraction of an inch away.

Who had done this painting, and when, I wondered? Was the artist a man or a woman, and how well did he—or she—know Derek? The possibility that the unknown painter might be female, sent a stab of jealousy right through my heart.

My heart! Mrs. Burns would probably serve it up on a silver platter if I kept her waiting! That thought was enough to send me scampering down the hall toward her studio. I arrived on her doorstep panting as much from fear as from my headlong dash.

The door was slightly ajar. Peeking in, I saw that she was seated behind a large drawing table at the far end of the room, frowning as she leafed through someone's portfolio—oh god, it was probably mine! But the next instant, I was once again distracted from my purpose because my attention was claimed—in fact, it was positively riveted—by the walls of her room, which were covered with paintings.

And what paintings!

If I had thought about her as an artist at all, should anyone have asked me, I would have predicted that her creations would be as tightly controlled and puritanically stark as she was. Instead, the entire studio was filled with enormous, bold-colored abstracts that were elegant in their proportions, rich balance of colors, and sensitively defined shapes. These paintings glowed with an inner fire, in sharp contrast with the sterile, white-washed walls they hung on.

"Wonderful!" I breathed, slipping into the room, entranced.

She looked up, startled. "Ah, it's you, Miss Henriques. I didn't realize you'd arrived."

"I . . . I'm sorry," I stammered. "I know I should've knocked but . . . Well, I . . . It's just that I wasn't expecting . . ."

"Yes?" she prompted.

"I wasn't expecting your paintings to be so beautiful!" I blurted out, certain my face had assumed the bold scarlet that dominated several of her masterpieces.

"Oh? What *were* you expecting?" The corners of her mouth quirked up slightly.

I tried to take a calming breath. "Gee, I'm not sure. Still lifes, I guess. Class exercises? City streets on a rainy day?" I blundered on. "Something geometric? I don't know."

The smile was threatening to break through, and she quickly glanced away. When she met my eyes again, her face had regained its usual bland expression. She cleared her throat. "Yes . . . Well, I'm flattered to hear that you approve of my paintings, but I believe it's *your* artwork we're here to discuss, not mine."

She gestured to a nearby chair.

Unfortunately, as I ventured across the room, I was once again sidetracked—this time by several far less conspicuous paintings that were lined up in a tidy row on a narrow ledge beneath a large chalkboard. They were minuscule—none larger than six inches on a side—and each depicted a landscape that appeared to have been painted in thick, delicately tinted cream cheese, carefully applied with a diminutive palette knife.

Completely forgetting both my manners and also the rather intimidating presence of my teacher, I moved in for a closer look, convinced that these, rather than the others, must represent the true Mrs. Burns. I peered at them practically cross-eyed, not wanting to miss a single detail.

"MISS HENRIQUES!"

I jumped.

"I'm sure Mr. Burns will be flattered when I tell him how captivated you are by his artwork. Now stop gawking and sit down!"

"*Mister* Burns!" The words just popped out of my mouth, unbidden. Somehow I had overlooked the obvious fact that if there was a Mrs. Burns, there would most likely also be a Mr. Burns.

"Yes; my husband is an artist, too. He's doing graduate work here, although I must admit that we don't always see eye-to-eye on our approach to painting."

"I can certainly understand why!" was my unfortunate response, but she didn't seem to notice.

"And now, if you're ready to settle down, I think it would be more constructive if we spent some time discussing *your* artwork instead of everyone else's."

Meekly, I took the seat she offered. My class assignments were spread out on her table, with "Rembrandt Henriques" and the finger-painted monkey men on top.

My heart sank.

"Miss Henriques . . . I must confess that I don't quite know what to tell you. It's been, um, an experience having you in my class this semester. Your solutions to the problems I've assigned have been unorthodox but innovative—and also rather interesting."

She hesitated, watching me steadily across the desk. Her near-sighted scrutiny was unnerving.

"You haven't exactly been an easy student to grade, you know," she abruptly said. "At times, you've been downright rebellious—in your own self-effacing way."

I experienced an agony of blushing.

"Well, don't you have anything to say for yourself?" she demanded.

"No, Mrs. Burns—I mean, yes! I'm really sorry for all the trouble I've caused you."

To my surprise, she grinned. "I don't know why I'm having such a hard time telling you that I'm giving you an A," she said, shocking the breath right out of me. "I think it's because you remind me a little bit of myself when I first started art school."

I tried—and utterly failed—to imagine where the similarities could possibly lie.

"So let me give you some advice, Meri," she said. "Work hard—even harder than you have for me—and don't do any more rebelling. If you apply yourself, I think you might turn out to be a rather good artist."

"Thank you, Mrs. Burns! I will! I'll do just what you say!"

"Yes. Well . . ." She readjusted her spectacles on her long nose, cleared her throat, and said briskly, "Very well, then; that is all, Miss Henriques. You may return to class."

Three days later, finals week began.

The emotional intensity was amazing. People were up twenty-four hours a day, trying to absorb every last detail of an entire semester's worth of information. Friends no longer had ordinary conversations—we all "quizzed" each other. Even girls who weren't normally on speaking terms could be seen sharing class notes and studying together. Lights were on, day and night.

And then, just as suddenly, it was over. The pressure simply vanished and everyone around me seemed stunned, like sleepwalkers awakening from a highly realistic and bewildering dream. Where had that dreadful week gone to, I wondered? How had we all managed to survive?

Physically and emotionally exhausted, I packed to go home with Shennandoah for semester break. Pixie, who was going north to visit Maggie and Norman, had offered us a ride.

Just before we left, Rachel dropped in to say good-bye. She had arranged to stay on in the dormitory between semesters, and for the next ten days she would be engaged in nonstop writing, attempting to finish all the papers she had put off doing until now.

"You'd better be careful, Rae," Pixie warned, sounding very much like her sister Maggie. "If you're not careful you'll wear yourself out and get sick. I can tell you're over-tired already."

"How do I get myself into this mess every semester?" Rachel sighed. "You'd think I'd know better by now . . ." Abruptly, her mood shifted. "Oh, well, whenever I start feeling sorry for myself, I'll just think of you two. Imagine spending the entire semester break in scenic Indianapolis! If you ask me, anything's got to be better than that. Even writing papers." She giggled. "Come to think of it: I bet Shennandoah's family's going to give Meri a royal welcome. I'd almost be willing to go along, just to see the fireworks!"

The Waters family lived in the finest residential part of town. Shennandoah and I stood in the street in front of their large Victorian mansion, saying good-bye to Pixie.

"You're sure you won't come in for a minute?" Shennandoah asked, leaning in through the passenger window.

I didn't understand why she was making the offer, since, by her own account, her parents were extremely prejudiced. Was she hoping to shock them, I wondered? Based on her stories, I wouldn't have put it past her.

"Thanks anyway," Pixie said, "but I promised Norman and Maggie I'd be there by five, and I'm late already."

As she drove away, I experienced a moment of sheer panic. If these people didn't like Negroes, how were they going to feel about a Jewish houseguest? Was this setup to be yet another test for Shennandoah's parents—and why hadn't I considered this sooner?

But I didn't voice my fears, not wishing to insult my friend.

Shennandoah and I picked up our suitcases and headed up the walk. The house, already enormous to my eyes, seemed to expand the closer we got to it. As we approached the front door, I had the unnerving sensation that the upper stories were leaning outward, looming over our heads.

The Waters's home was no less imposing on the inside. My friend's parents had obviously spent a fortune on the décor. From my vantage point in the entry hall, I observed carefully arranged groupings of Louis XIV furniture with muted silk upholstery, an enormous Asian patterned area rug, expensive china table lamps, and vases of artificial flowers, set off by a number of unremarkable Currier and Ives prints (although, for all I knew, they might have been originals) in heavily carved, gilded frames. Yet standing there, peering into the cavernous living room, I felt uneasy. The place was too grand and over-decorated, too impersonal and traditional for my taste. I had the impression that if an ordinary family moved in, their very presence would tarnish its perfection forever.

By far the most peculiar and jarring aspect of the entire tableau was the picture on the wall immediately to the left of the front door. It hung quite conspicuously: solitary, large, and ornate, proudly displaying a jet-black velvet mat. My hasty glance took in an electrical cord running from the bottom corner to a standard outlet above the baseboard. That was strange enough on its own—but stranger yet, there was nothing at all inside the frame! Coming from an artistic family, I had certainly seen my share of unframed pictures—but a frame without the slightest excuse of a picture? That was a new one for me. What could possibly be the point of it?

Was the frame itself so valuable that it required this prominent position? Or had some precious item fallen out and not been replaced? It seemed an unlikely possibility in this scrupulously tidy home.

These observations were made in a matter of moments, and before I had a chance to question Shennandoah about the missing picture or even make a polite comment about the house's appearance, a woman's voice called out, "Is someone there?"

"Hi, Mom!" Shennandoah shouted back. "It's me, Shen. Where are you?"

"In the kitchen, Dear. Come on back—I'm too busy to stop what I'm doing."

Leaving our suitcases in the entry, we went past the grand living room and a wide staircase leading to the upper floors, then down a long hall and into the kitchen. There we discovered Mrs. Waters, a plump little gray-haired woman who was standing behind a large wooden table, peeling potatoes.

My first impression was that Mrs. Waters looked tired. She was also rather plain, although I could see that she had made an effort to disguise her shortcomings with bright cosmetics and expensive clothing and jewelry. A rumpled apron was tied awkwardly over her flower-print dress, as if it was somehow out of character for her to wear such a menial object. She stopped what she was doing as soon as we came in, methodically wiped her hands on her apron, and hugged Shennandoah. Then she turned to greet me.

"You must be Meri," she said with a cheery smile. "It's so nice that you could come. Shen's told us so much about you."

"It's nice to be here, Mrs. Waters. Thank you for letting me visit over semester break."

"It's nothing. Shen said you had no other place to go, and any friend of hers is always welcome."

As we shook hands, my nervousness subsided. I realized Shennandoah must have been exaggerating when she described her parents as being extremely unfriendly to outsiders.

"Now, girls"—Mrs. Waters' voice was suddenly business-like—"sit down and make yourselves comfortable. Would you like something to drink? You can keep me company while I finish peeling these potatoes."

We offered to help but she wouldn't hear of it.

"Rest. You just got home. And don't worry—there'll be plenty for you to do later. There's always lots of work in this big family."

"Where's Mrs. Jones?" Shennandoah asked.

"She's sick. She said she didn't feel well enough to come in today. It's a real nuisance having her out just now, when we have company. I don't know what's gotten into her lately, she's usually so reliable and not the least bit uppity—not like most coloreds."

Shennandoah avoided making eye contact with me. Instead, she quickly changed the subject. "Where's Dad? I thought he'd be home by now."

"He won't be eating with us tonight."

"Gee, I thought he might at least try to be here since it's my first night back."

"Now, Shennandoah, you know your father's a busy man. And this evening, he's been asked to give a talk on our main radio station."

"Since when is Dad making public speeches?"

"This is his first. Several very influential people urged him to speak out on some important local issues."

"Gee, Meri, not only is my father a shaker and mover in the real estate world, it seems he's also turning into a bigwig in Indianapolis politics." I could hear the resentment in my friend's voice.

"Now don't exaggerate, Dear," was Mrs. Waters's cheery response. "I've told you before, your father says he wants us to think of him as an ordinary businessman."

"Yeah, very ordinary. Only he just happens to be on the Board of Realtors *and* the Chamber of Commerce!" Shennandoah's voice was heavy with sarcasm. "And now it seems he's going in for public speaking."

"What's he going to talk about?" I asked in an attempt to head off what seemed to be an impending quarrel.

"I have no idea," Shennandoah's mother replied airily. "He never tells me anything. It might have something to do with the housing shortage, though. He's been discussing that with lots of people lately."

"Everyone seems to be worried about housing these days," I said, making an effort to keep the conversation going, "even in New York."

"That's right—Shen told us you're from New York. I visited there once."

"I hope you enjoyed it."

"I did. But everything and everyone was moving so fast. And there were so many strange people . . . Which reminds me: didn't Shennandoah mention that you're Jewish?"

"MOM!"

"It's okay. Yes, Mrs. Waters, I am."

"How interesting. You know, I've never met one of you before—a Jew, that is." Abruptly, she stopped speaking and looked me over with undisguised curiosity.

"Mom, please!"

"I don't mean to say there's anything wrong with the Jewish," Shennandoah's mother chattered on, ignoring her daughter's angry glare. "I just want you to be sure to tell me if there's anything, you know, special you need—food or anything like that."

"Thanks, Mrs. Waters, but special food isn't necessary."

"My, but our Shen has such exotic friends! We never know who she's going to bring home next."

Just then, a mob of young children burst into the room, saving us from what was becoming an increasingly awkward conversation. They crowded around the kitchen table, chattering with excitement and greeting their big sister with hugs and kisses even as they begged their mother for a snack. Shennandoah introduced the four, and there were so many active young bodies swarming around me that I had trouble keeping their names straight. Shennandoah's older brother, a young man of twenty-two whom she privately described as something of a juvenile delinquent, and a teenage sister were the only ones, besides Mr. Waters, who weren't present.

The children were boisterously friendly and curious about what their oldest sister and I did at the far-off university. They kept us busy answering questions right up until dinnertime.

After a noisy meal, all seven of the brothers and sisters, Mrs. Waters, and I gathered around the kitchen radio. The littlest ones squirmed restlessly while the announcer made his introductions, and Mrs. Waters had to remind them several times to be quiet. At last, a different voice began to speak.

"It's Daddy!" squealed the youngest, and the others giggled.

"Hush!" Mrs. Waters commanded. "Let's listen."

"Thank you for giving me the opportunity to present my message," Mr. Waters began, addressing his host, "which is surely of vital concern to all the good citizens of Indianapolis."

When he started describing the terrible housing shortages the city was experiencing, I had to suppress the urge to stuff my fingers in my ears.

"Do you realize that a middle-class family that wishes to buy a home in a decent Christian neighborhood can expect to have a great deal of trouble finding one? Sadly, this family will probably end up being forced to buy in one of the less desirable areas."

In graphic and highly charged detail, he went on to paint a verbal picture of an "undesirable" neighborhood. I silently cringed in my seat.

"And this isn't the only way the people of our community are being affected by the housing shortage," he added. "An influx of unsavory elements are encroaching on what were once fine neighborhoods, bringing crime and violence to the streets. There has been an insidious infiltration of Communism and the Jewish element into all levels of the government and educational institutions, as well as the housing market—not just locally but on a national scale."

As he launched into a diatribe about the federal government, which he assured us was "controlled by liberal, Commie Jews," I shot a horrified look at Shennandoah who, noticing my stare, seemed to try to shrink down into invisibility in her chair.

"However, I am speaking to you tonight to give you hope," Mr. Waters continued. "You, the good people of Indianapolis, can use your most powerful tool, your right to vote, to correct this dreadful situation. And this is the American Way. Only by electing the proper folks to run our city government, men who will heed the wise advice of our Chamber of Commerce and Board of Realtors, can we change our course. A strong local government can use the force of its leaders and financial resources to end our current housing shortage, even as we take action to ensure that only the right people move into our neighborhoods. After all, those undesirables really don't want to mix with us any more than we want to mix with them . . ."

By now, the dinner I'd just eaten was threatening to come

back up again, and I heartily wished that Mr. Waters could be there in person so I could spew it out on his undoubtedly highly polished black shoes.

"In conclusion, my fellow Americans," he said, "only when honorable men are once again charge of our government, both at home and in Washington, will the streets of Indianapolis be safe for our beloved children. Only when we no longer have to fear the threat of mixed neighborhoods will the quality of life in our great city improve. I will not shirk my duty. I have taken a vow to work with every available resource to put an end to a situation where decent Christian folks are forced to live side-by-side with niggers and Jews and other white trash. I give you my solemn promise that I will not rest until our neighborhoods are safe. Thank you, and good night."

"I guess he told those darn Democrats!" Mrs. Waters said with evident satisfaction, as she stood up to switch off the radio.

For several long moments, everyone was silent. Inside, I was seething, struggling mightily to keep from shouting, "YOU BASTARD! I hope you stay away from home for the rest of semester break, so I won't ever have to meet you!"

Luckily, I was saved from my angry impulse when every-one in the Waters family began talking at once. The younger children had endless questions, and the older ones and Mrs. Waters busied themselves answering them, all the while singing the praises of their patriarch's vicious harangue. I noticed that, like me, Shennandoah didn't say a word.

A minute later, the telephone rang, and soon a deluge of calls was coming in—enthusiastic congratulations from friends and well-wishers.

I wondered gloomily how I was ever going to survive my stay in Indianapolis.

In the middle of the week, we helped Shennandoah's mother deliver a basket of food to her sick housekeeper, who lived in what Mr. Waters would certainly have labeled one of the more "undesirable" parts of town.

Mrs. Waters refused to take it in, insisting that the only reason she had allowed us to come along in the first place was that we had promised to do the errand for her. She remained in her car, wrapped in her ankle-length mink coat, while Shennandoah and I carried the heavy basket up to the house.

Although the place amounted to little more than a run-down shack—the inside was impoverished, furnished with wooden packing crates and broken-down furniture, castoffs from more fortunate families—it was spotlessly clean. Mrs. Jones, who had a racking cough, seemed embarrassed by Shennandoah's enthusiastic greeting of hugs and kisses; still, I could tell that she and her young children were extremely grateful for our gift of food.

The sick woman insisted on going outside to thank Mrs. Waters personally. Bundled up in worn house slippers and an ancient man's overcoat, she stood shivering on the snowy sidewalk, talking to her employer, who was pleasant in a condescending way.

"Oh, my, didn't that go well!" Shennandoah's mother crowed as we drove off. "Now I can rest easy, knowing I've done my Christian duty by being generous to a poor colored family."

My final day at the Waters home, a Sunday, was the most trying of all. The whole family arose early and everyone, including the oldest brother and the father—both of whom had fortunately been away from home for most of my visit—made elaborate preparations for going to church.

We ate a hearty breakfast of bacon, eggs, pancakes, and toast before setting off walking to the service: Mr. Waters with his pomaded silver hair, tall and gaunt in a smartly tailored suit; his pudgy, talkative little wife dressed in her Sunday best; the seven brothers and sisters; and me. It was the first time I had seen the entire group doing anything together as a family, and they transmitted a mood of holiday excitement.

When we arrived at the church, which was a block away from their home, we were greeted effusively by the other parishioners and the minister, who escorted us to a special place of honor in the first pew, directly in front of the pulpit.

During my summers at the music festival, one of our favorite traditions had been to attend a different church or temple service each week. I always enjoyed the organ music, the hymns and feeling of community. However, contrary to my expectations, once the singing ended, this particular church service ceased to inspire me in any way except negatively.

In his sermon, the minister harped on the moral superiority of Methodist beliefs over all other religious sects, Christian or otherwise, and once he had covered this subject to his evident satisfaction, he launched into a venomous attack on the federal government, which soon degenerated into a bigoted ethnic and racial slur. He elaborated on the themes discussed by Mr. Waters in his radio speech, praising him as he did so for "taking a courageous moral stand on issues of the utmost importance." I was thoroughly disgusted by the time the service ended, and more than happy to escape from the church.

Outside, people stood around talking, smug and self-satisfied, congratulating each other on the splendid ideals of their fine, upstanding congregation. Everyone wanted to shake Mr. Waters's hand. When we finally started homeward, the family seemed content with the morning's experience, but I was seething.

How can people professing to believe in Christ's humane doctrines behave with such a lack of basic human decency? I asked myself bitterly.

Trailing along behind the Waters family, I was the last to enter the house—and when I did, I let out a startled shriek!

Just inside the front door, the mysterious empty picture frame was no longer empty. Someone passing by must have flicked a switch because now, as if by magic, a life-sized, three-dimensional, in-living-color head of Jesus Christ, so realistic that individual wisps of hair stood out all around his face, filled the space, backlit by a halo! In my unhappy state of mind, this apparition reminded me of nothing so much as a big-game hunter's trophy, collected by some insane but enterprising businessman for the benefit of the Waters family.

I stood in the hall, gaping, wondering what Rachel would have to say about this bizarre object.

Shennandoah's mother must have noticed my distress, because she asked if I was ill.

Unable to think of a polite way to explain myself, I told her that I had a headache and needed to rest.

It was a relief to be alone in the room that Shennandoah shared with her younger sisters. I needed time to come to terms with the day's events.

———

I was vastly relieved to bid good-bye to the Waters family and board the bus for Bloomington later that afternoon. Shennandoah, who was sitting beside me, leaned back in her seat and sighed.

"Leaving home always makes me sad," she confessed.

Out of politeness, I said nothing, and instead tried to focus on how glad I would be to return to the haven of my room at school. As the bus reached the outskirts of the city, and began rolling past flat Indiana farmland, I started to drift off—and then Shennandoah spoke again.

"Gosh, Meri, I can't get today's sermon out of my mind."

"Neither can I!" At last, a chance to discuss those ugly words with a sympathetic person! "Parts of it keep coming back to haunt me."

"I know what you mean. Especially what he said about Christianity."

"That was really something, wasn't it?"

"Well, at first I wasn't sure if I agreed with him, but now that I've had a chance to think it over, I realize he's right."

"Right about what?"

"When he said that no one can have a truly rewarding or fulfilling religious experience unless he believes in Jesus Christ."

"Shennandoah, I don't believe it!" I lowered my voice, hoping the other passengers hadn't noticed my outburst, and stared at her. "I didn't think I'd ever hear you say anything that dumb!"

"But it's true!"

"Then what about all the other religions in the world? Are you saying they're worthless—that they have less meaning for their followers than Christianity? Haven't you learned anything at all from dating those foreign students?"

"I sure have. I've learned that they're lost souls."

"What!"

"They are! That's what Reverend Schmidt said today, and he should know. After all, he is a man of God."

"Some man of God!" I muttered, but I didn't have the energy to argue with her.

She chattered happily on, apparently thinking she'd scored a point. "Oh, Meri, I'm so glad I've decided to become a missionary once I've finished my physical therapy courses. Just think: all those heathens out there, and I'll be able to save their bodies *and* their souls."

God help the natives! was my silent addendum.

chapter 16: second semester

Myrna came in. "Look what my mother gave me," she announced, proudly holding up a large, clear plastic package. "See? They're dish towels with pictures of the American flag, the Liberty Bell, and a golden eagle on them for me to embroider."

"Do you mean to tell us you're actually going to wipe your hands on the American flag?" Rachel asked. Her tone was stern, but her eyes twinkled with merriment. She started to giggle.

It was contagious: Pixie and I burst out laughing.

"My god, what's the matter with you?" Myrna cried. We'd hurt her feelings, and anger followed. "Anyone would think you're a bunch of pinko Commie perverts!" She stalked out of our room, slamming the washroom door behind her.

Our laughter slowly subsided as we returned to the sobering task of planning our new class schedules.

Once again, Fortune had smiled on Pixie: she would be student teaching that semester, and therefore didn't have to register for anything. Her only requirement was to show up at her designated elementary school each morning. She assured us that she would be more than happy to keep us company while we worked on our schedules, however. It was loyalty, she claimed—but I suspected she also enjoyed listening to our agonized groans.

As part of my scheme to finish my undergraduate degree early, I was juggling a workload of seventeen and a half units, consisting of eight different courses—and I was rapidly coming to the unhappy conclusion that the only way I was going to be able to do so was by taking another night class. I told Pixie I hoped she was satisfied: I was doing plenty of groaning.

Rachel was attempting to organize her usual overload of esoteric subjects. She complained that all the classes she wanted to take seemed to have been scheduled at the same time: between nine and ten o'clock on Monday, Wednesday, and Friday mornings. By now, she was close to tears.

"Oh, hell!" she cried, crumpling up her worksheet and throwing it on the floor. "You never get what you plan for anyway, so why bother trying? Let's get out of here!"

As far as I was concerned, anything was better than our present occupation. I suggested going out to dinner, a plan Rachel immediately seconded, but Pixie said someone else had already invited her out—and no amount of cajoling or teasing on Rachel's part could make her tell us who it was.

Rejected by Pixie, Rachel and I decided to have dinner together anyway—and Rachel reminded me that there was a meeting of the Folksinging Club later that evening, and offered to go with me after we ate.

I hardly needed a reminder—I wouldn't have missed the meeting for anything—but in light of my last miserable encounter with John, I was happy to have Rachel along for moral support.

As for our dinner destination, it was a foregone conclusion: in our opinion, practically the only decent place to eat in Bloomington on a Sunday—or any other time, for that matter—was the local pizza parlor. However, I was surprised when Rachel asked me to keep her company while she got ready to go out. I'd only been in her room once, briefly, early that past fall, when Pixie and I had come by to pick her up on our way into town, and I'd never had the honor of a personal invitation. Now she preceded me down the hall, chattering excitedly: we seldom had the time—or the money—to eat out.

Rachel lived in an end room, a generous space that was normally occupied by three and occasionally four students—in fact, it was here that the first group of black coeds had been housed, back in the early days of Integration According to Indiana University. For now, though, Rachel had the place all to herself, her eccentricities having driven out every roommate the dorm committee had attempted to assign her. (Her latest victim had complained about Rachel practicing Russian verbs at all times of the day and night, aloud and for hours at a stretch. Rachel had retorted that she needed to hear the unusual sounds in order to learn them, and that in any case they resembled musical phrases, not the ravings of a madwoman, as her ex-roommate so uncharitably claimed.)

Spacious as it was, Rachel's room actually seemed cramped, hopelessly cluttered as it was with piles, and stacks, and mountains of books. As far as I could tell, books had been deposited on every available surface: every inch of the floor, both bunk beds, the desks, and even the chairs. Rachel, I soon realized, collected books compulsively, the way some people collect string or rubber bands, and each was a scholarly treatise on one arcane subject or another.

She read them all. As the semester progressed, more and more books would be added to her hoard. Overdue notices accumulated on her desk like autumn leaves. But she studiously ignored them until every last one of her term papers had been handed in—often several months into the next semester—at which point she was doomed to spend most of an entire day carting everything back to the library.

As a result of her book-collecting mania, entering Rachel's room turned out to be a risky business: one false step could set off a chain-reaction avalanche. Once I'd made it past the threshold, I was forced to rearrange several tottering towers before I was able to sit down. This accomplished, I didn't dare stir for fear of suffering a premature burial, and I looked on with interest as Rachel launched herself into an elaborate cosmetic ritual in preparation for our outing. When her toilette was complete, she announced that she was going to change her clothing. Excusing herself, she vanished into her walk-in closet, modestly shutting the door behind her.

With difficulty, I stifled a giggle: nothing else she had ever said or done since I'd met her seemed to have embarrassed her in the least—and now this! With a conscious effort, I managed to restrain myself from commenting, and it wasn't until years later that I learned she suffered from scoliosis and was sensitive about letting anyone see her spinal curvature.

When at last she emerged from her closet, I had to smile. She looked like a gypsy in her bright makeup, large gold hoop earrings, white peasant blouse, paisley-print skirt, high-heel boots, and Army surplus coat, plus the obligatory colorful bandanna she always wore wrapped around her head like a babushka. She appeared to be ready for anything—even though our destination was just the local pizza parlor and the Folksinging Club.

Throughout dinner, I struggled with a nearly irresistible urge to tease her about her eccentricities. But I restrained myself, for despite her show of friendship, I was afraid of her; I knew she could flay me in an instant with her sarcastic tongue, and once she began, I would never be able to defend myself.

A small room in the Student Union building had been reserved for the monthly meetings of the Folksinging Club, and for the more frequent meetings of its Executive Committee. When Rachel and I arrived, the general meeting was about to begin. Surveying the room, I realized that this was the one place, besides the art building, where I felt truly at home.

Daniel waved at me from across the room; he'd reinstated our friendship since our shared Thanksgiving ordeal. Betsy Walker, the club secretary, said hello and sat down beside us. John came over to talk, positively bursting with excitement, but backed hastily away the moment he realized that I wasn't alone. Even Derek Stone had a smile and a greeting for me as he passed by on his way to the front of the room—and *that* definitely captured Rachel's attention. She gave me a quizzical look, which quickly transformed into an expression that could only mean trouble, and I braced myself for a wisecrack about my apparent familiarity with the club president. But just as she opened her mouth to speak, Derek called the meeting to order, and I was saved—for the moment. I was sure that I would be hearing from her later.

Derek said he had a surprise for us. Instead of our usual format, which was a random assortment of performances by club members, tonight there would be a real concert. At that point, our vice president, Paul Stillman, took charge.

Since our last meeting, he told us, several club members had been bitten by a strange new bug called jug band music. Over spring break, he had attended a New York performance of the Steve Queskin Jug Band, which had so impressed him that he'd bought one of their records. On returning to school, he'd played it for some of his friends, who had been as dazzled by the weird sounds as Paul was. Then and there they decided they had to try making this fascinating new music themselves.

While Paul spoke, the band members began dragging their equipment to the front of the room. A peculiar assortment of bottles and washboards, kazoos and wooden spoons, and various other household items appeared before our eyes—all in all, an impressive pile of junk, although it looked to me as if the group should have been getting ready for a garage sale rather than a concert.

To my utter amazement, John was right up there in the thick of the action. Paul explained how he had "lured my unsuspecting British colleague" into joining them by presenting him with a washtub that had been converted into a string bass by the addition of some clothesline and a broom handle. According to Paul, John was hooked the moment he set eyes on it.

The band was an instant hit. Their enthusiasm, musicianship, and sense of fun were contagious. John looked like a happy little boy with a beard as he plunked merrily along on his washtub. It was one of our most enjoyable meetings of the entire year, and I was sure the band was destined to have a long and successful career.

The next afternoon, John called.

"Late this morning," he told me, "Paul phoned everyone in the band—I guess he was still high on last night's successful debut—and suggested that we do an impromptu outdoor concert. And since it's unseasonably warm for February, he said he wanted to take advantage of the spring-like weather to find out if we would be as popular with the rest of the student body as we had been at the Folksinging Club . . ."

I said nothing, just listened expectantly.

"So around noon, we set up our equipment on the lawn in front of the Student Union, where we played for several hours to quite an enthusiastic crowd. Unfortunately, it turns out that not everyone who heard us was equally impressed, because when I arrived at work, I was summoned directly to office of the head of the Geography Department."

"Oh, no!"

"Apparently my boss's wife also witnessed part of our performance, and she wasted no time informing her husband how shocked and embarrassed she was to discover that a member of his department had been out 'making a fool of himself,' playing 'disgusting music' with people from 'that scandalous Folksinging Club.' My boss says he's disappointed by my lack of judgment, as well as my choice of friends and recreational activities—and that if I'm serious about my responsibilities and our department's reputation, I must quit the jug band at once, nor must I be seen making any more public appearances with the Folksinging Club."

"John, that's horrible! I'm so sorry!"

"That's not the half of it," he said. "My boss admitted that there was little he can do if I refuse to take his 'friendly advice,' but he let me know in no uncertain terms that if I continue to defy his wishes, I will be asked to turn in my resignation at the end of the semester, and that would be a disaster for my chances of future employment." He sighed. "Naturally, the first thing

I did when I left the Geography Office was to call Paul and resign from the band—and now I've called you to ask a favor: would you be willing to put up the posters for the club's upcoming Ramblin' Jack Elliot concert by yourself? To be honest, I'm afraid to be seen doing anything at all that involves the club."

"Of course!" I told him, realizing how embarrassed he must have been to have to admit his disgrace to both Paul and me.

When I got off the phone, I told Pixie and Rachel the whole, troubling story.

"Well, what did you expect?" Rachel demanded. "It's what Pixie and I have been telling you all year. You have to be careful about what you join. Around here, it's a whole lot easier to get into trouble than it is to get out of it."

"But that's ridiculous! What John was doing was harmless!"

"To you," Rachel said. "But obviously not to John's boss and his wife."

"One thing's for sure," I told them, "John won't be sticking his neck out ever again to date an undergraduate—and I was hoping he might change his mind . . ." I sighed. "Oh, well, after today, I'd guess my chances with him are just about zero."

"Too bad, Meri," Pixie said. "I know you liked him."

"I did—in spite of his quirks. Poor John! And to think: he was actually right to be worried about keeping his life private. I thought he was exaggerating."

"If he doesn't drop out of the club completely, you can still see him there," Pixie suggested. "It's better than nothing."

"I guess so . . ."

"Why should Meri waste her time on a nobody like John?" Rachel suddenly piped up. There was a wicked gleam in her eye. "In fact, I think she should thank him for not coming around any more to distract her. Now she can devote her full-time attention to her special friend, Derek Stone."

"Thanks a lot, Rachel!" I muttered, aware of the heat in my face. "We all know where that will get me: exactly nowhere."

Classes began again—but not before each of us had once again passed through another dreaded registration hassle. As I had predicted, I was forced to take a night class: it was an art course, and the one class I didn't have to fight to get into. Determined to graduate in as little time as possible, I was also taking the second half of anthropology, French literature, and English composition with Mr. McGregor, physical education, chorus, and a second, daytime art class.

Anthropology was disappointing. Unlike Dr. Sellers, this new fellow was uninspiring—so much so that I ended up dozing through more than one lecture.

My other classes were more satisfying, even though Mr. McGregor's classroom threatened to erupt into a full-fledged battle zone. This was due in part to his demanding teaching style and the students' negative reaction to it, but the real problem had nothing to do with his teaching methods: it was Hoosier Hysteria all over again.

The trouble started right away, the first day of class, when he announced that our topic of study would be "The Bible as Literature." The room buzzed with angry protests, and the grumbling only intensified as he began passing out the books that we were going to use.

Until now, because of his excellence as a teacher, I had been looking forward to this class, but hearing my classmates' complaints, my enthusiasm quickly turned to apprehension. If there was already dissension before we'd even started, what would the rest of the semester be like, I wondered?

No sooner had the books hit our desktops than one of my fellow students had her hand up, challenging Mr. McGregor.

"Not to be rude, Sir," she said, "but you've given us the wrong Bible."

"Young lady, there is no such thing as the 'wrong' Bible," Mr. McGregor countered. "However, the King James version is regarded by scholars as a standard text"—by this time I knew Mr. McGregor well enough to recognize the signs of suppressed annoyance in his voice, the squint of his eyes, and his tightly pinched lips—"which is why I have chosen it for this class."

"Well, next time I'm bringing my own," the girl retorted.

"Feel free to do so: comparisons are what this class is all about. However, you should be forewarned that you may have difficulty coordinating your text with ours."

I hoped this would put an end to the dispute, but unfortunately the power struggle was only just beginning.

"May I ask a question, Sir?" This time it was one of the young men, a Southerner by his accent.

"Certainly."

"Sir, as everyone knows, the Bible is the word of God, and so . . ." He paused, as if expecting an objection.

"Go on," Mr. McGregor prompted.

"And so, how can it be studied as literature?"

"How indeed?" Mr. McGregor echoed, his dark eyes intent. "That is exactly what we are here to discover. I hope that meets with your approval."

"It isn't a question of approval, Sir, it's a question of what's possible. The Bible isn't literature—so how can we study it that way?"

"You tell him, Larry!" someone hissed.

Larry grinned.

"I'd like a show of hands," Mr. McGregor said. "How many of you agree with this young man's view of the Bible?"

More than a third of the people in the room responded in the affirmative.

"Congratulations to those of you who raised your hands: you should consider yourselves lucky." Mr. McGregor's scowl was ferocious. "You are about to have the enviable experience of becoming enlightened. End of discussion!"

"Don't worry, we'll show him!" I heard someone whisper.

"Yeah, next time we'll all bring our own Bibles to class."

The second session of that class was no less stormy.

"We'll begin our study of the Bible with an analysis of the Creation Story," Mr. McGregor announced. "Did anyone notice anything unusual when you read that section for last night's homework?"

I didn't have the courage to speak out, but one of the other girls, someone I thought I remembered as being a non-dissenter, raised her hand. "It's kind of strange, but it seems to me the Creation is presented twice here, one version right after the other but with slightly different details."

"Excellent! It *is* presented twice! So what we have here are two separate accounts of the Creation, rather awkwardly cobbled together."

"I'd like to dispute that, Sir."

I winced—it was the troublesome Larry.

"What would you like to dispute?" Mr. McGregor asked, with such deceptive calm that I immediately suspected a trap.

"I don't believe there *are* two versions of the Creation here. Why would there be?"

"My point exactly."

Larry looked puzzled.

"If you read the text carefully," Mr. McGregor continued, "you will discover the answer for yourself—because it's really quite obvious. There are two slightly repetitious but different versions of the Creation because the Bible as we know it is, in fact, a compilation of several Bibles."

"But, Sir . . ."

"No more interruptions! As I was saying, what we have here is a written transcription of the oral traditions of the people, copied over and over by a succession of scribes, each adding his own embellishments. The Bible we have today is a marvelously organic thing. Over the years it has grown, accumulating new information, much as a ship's hull accumulates barnacles . . . and therein lies the proof that the Bible is indeed literature. Although it is a collection of knowledge which, according to some, is the wisdom of God—and we will not dispute the merits of that theory here—it did, nevertheless, have human authors. And as such, we can study it as we would study any other piece of literature."

At that point, I think most of the rebels realized that Mr. McGregor could not be influenced to alter the curriculum. At the end of the class period, many requested transfer slips—which was their loss, because those of us who remained were treated to a fascinating study of the Bible. We compared versions of the Creation in several different translations, and we also read creation stories from other cultures: Norse mythology, Hindu and Babylonian texts, American Indian folklore, and Australian aborigine and African tribal tales. We analyzed their similarities and differences, and discovered many parallel themes running throughout.

After that, we examined the rest of the Old Testament, and the entire class seemed as excited as I was by the correlations we discovered.

Still, I was left with a strange ambivalence—both relief and sorrow that the troublemakers were gone. It was certainly easier to carry on without them, but I thought that all of us might have benefited from the exchange of ideas that could have resulted had they stayed.

The class I was most excited about that semester—and this despite the fact that it was by far the most time-consuming and demanding of them all—was my night class, Color and Calligraphy. Nothing could have dissuaded me from going, neither a raging blizzard nor a violent attack of the stomach flu! My enthusiasm wasn't the result of a rekindled passion for art, however; rather, it was inspired by the irresistible charms of my teacher, Mr. Randolph Jefferson.

He was a large man: solidly packed muscle on a six-foot frame. Dark brown hair, streaked with gray, and a neatly trimmed beard and mustache framed his squarish face. His deeply resonant voice barked commands as he strode about our classroom like a captain pacing the deck of his sailing ship. Always immaculately dressed in beautifully tailored three-piece suits, he wore a gold pocket watch on a chain draped across his massive chest. On his right hand was a heavy gold ring set with a large red stone.

More than once I tried—and failed—to imagine him casually dressed. He seemed like the sort of man who would wear silk pajamas to bed.

He appeared to come from another age, an uncanny reincarnation of some hallowed nineteenth-century historical figure such as Ulysses S. Grant. A charismatic and dashing fellow, Mr. Jefferson had everything going for him. A single glance—not to mention an actual smile—was sufficient to melt the hearts of his female students into simpering puddles of lovesick jelly.

But the most intriguing aspect of Mr. Jefferson's legend was the persistent rumor that he occasionally dated students. That this practice was frowned upon by the school authorities was a troublesome detail that had, thus far, failed to discourage Mr. Jefferson's amorous pursuits.

And it was surely this rumor that kept his female students going—for no other teacher would have dared to assign the workload he regularly gave us. We labored like indentured servants, each of us hoping she would be the favored one, the one he noticed above all other rivals. My male classmates did grumble constantly about the length and difficulty of our homework assignments—but as women outnumbered men ten to one, and since none of these males had anything like Mr. Jefferson's sex appeal, their protests were ignored.

Much to my horror, the first homework assignment almost disqualified me from the running. I had the unfortunate distinction of being the only student who misunderstood the instructions. My project was declared unacceptable. Mr. Jefferson had noticed me, all right, but not the way I wanted!

After that, I practically turned myself inside out trying to invent clever and unusual solutions for each new assignment, and I spent hours practicing my calligraphy exercises in an effort to produce absolutely perfect examples of antique penmanship.

With Pixie so often out, Rachel had come to depend on my company, and she was annoyed by my slavish devotion to my pen. Soon she was teasing me about my apparent determination to turn myself into a medieval scribe. She wondered aloud if I was naive enough to believe there was such a thing as a convent that accepted Jewish saints into their ranks, and she reminded me that convents never permitted male visitors, not even those named Jefferson.

But not even her sharpest jibes could dissuade me from my single-minded worship of Mr. Jefferson. Before long, I was staying after class, along with most of the other girls—and Mr. Jefferson seemed to bask in our attention. He obliged us by staying with us in the classroom, long after class was over, discussing music, art, movies, and literature with his rapt audience.

As for myself, despite the fierce competition, for some unfathomable reason I was pig-headedly confident. I knew that sooner or later he would realize I was special.

And when that happened, I was sure that he would ask me out.

chapter 17: easter

Shortly after the second semester began, Pixie became fascinated by my French homework, which, dull though it often was, was taking up nearly as much of my time as calligraphy. Whenever I picked up a French book, she asked to see it, then marveled over the strange combinations of letters, amazed that I understood their meaning. On several occasions, she had me read something aloud just to hear the sound of it, and afterwards she always asked for a translation. I found it hard to believe that, college honor student that she was, she had never studied a language, but she assured me that language courses were not required for elementary education majors.

"It's funny: I used to think I was lucky not to have to take a language, but now I feel cheated," she admitted. "How about it, Meri, do you think I could learn French?"

"Sure."

"You mean it? Would you teach me? French looks a whole lot easier than that weird Russian stuff Rachel's always babbling."

Her eagerness was so compelling that I put down my book. "When would you like to start?"

"Now! What should I do?"

No teacher had ever had a more willing student. She was extremely persistent and had a good ear. By the time I returned to my reading, she was dutifully memorizing the French alphabet, and it wasn't long before she'd mastered the strange new sounds.

"Oh, boy!" she exclaimed. "Listen to this: day—oh—jhay. Did you understand that?"

"Yes. That was good, Pixie: you spelled dog."

"Wow, I can't believe it—I'm actually speaking French!"

"Well, no, not exactly . . ."

"What do you mean? Was that French or wasn't it?"

"Um, yes. Sort of. You spelled the English word 'dog' using French letters—but that's not the French word for dog. In French it's 'chien.' That's spelled say—ash—eee—"

"Now hold on a red hot minute!" she said. "Are you telling me that in French they use all different words?"

"Of course."

"For everything?"

"Almost everything."

"That's ridiculous! What a waste of time."

I didn't know how to respond to that, so after a moment I picked up my book and went back to my reading.

"Meri?"

"Yes?"

"Sorry I snapped at you."

"It's okay. Languages can be awfully frustrating."

"What are you reading now?"

I showed her the book. "It's a modern French re-telling of a Greek myth. You see, according to legend, there was this girl named Persephone, and one day she—"

"For heaven's sake!" Pixie said. "You don't have to tell me the story of Persephone and Hades. What do you think I am, uneducated?"

"HELP!!!"

Pixie's cries jolted me awake and I found myself sitting up in bed shouting, "Pixie! What's wrong? Are you okay?"

I heard her fumbling in the dark, and then we were both squinting at each other in the sudden glare of her desk lamp.

"Wow, what a nightmare!" she groaned.

She looked awful: her eyes were puffy, and her face was ashen and beaded with sweat.

"A nightmare! Is that all? I thought you were dying."

"Oh, you did, did you? You think it's funny! Well, let me tell you something: that nightmare was all your fault."

"*My* fault? What did *I* do?" I pulled the covers up around me for warmth. "Come on . . . out with, Pixie, it or we'll be up all night."

"You and your damn French!" she muttered.

"Huh? What's French got to do with it?"

"Everything. It was that stupid book of yours. See, I dreamed I was walking through this gorgeous field of flowers— you know, kind of like I was Persephone . . ."

As she spoke, I could see that she was starting to relax. She snuggled down under her blankets and propped herself up on one elbow to face me.

"And everything was just fine until I bent down to pick a flower. Then this big hole in the ground opened up and I fell in."

I rolled my eyes. "Gosh, it sounds real scary."

Ignoring me, she continued, "And at the bottom of the hole was a salt mine."

"A salt mine."

"Stop interrupting. You're distracting me . . . See, at first, I wasn't scared at all. In fact, that salt mine was kind of beautiful. There were all these sparkly rainbow colors everywhere, reflecting off the salt crystals . . ." Her voice was growing dreamy and her eyes, glittering in the lamplight, began to have an in-turned, drifting-off look.

"Hey, don't fall asleep on me now, Pixie."

"Huh? Oh—well, after a while I realized there wasn't anything to be afraid of, so I decided to go for a walk. I thought I'd see what else was down there in that old salt mine. And that's when it happened."

"That's when *what* happened?"

"That's when these giant cheese balls came rolling out from behind the piles of salt."

"Cheese balls!" I chuckled. "Pixie, what did you have for dinner?"

She gave me a disgusted look. "If you think it's so funny, you don't have to hear the rest of it."

"Sorry." But I couldn't help grinning.

"Anyway, the next thing I knew, those damn cheese balls were chasing me. I ran like hell! But no matter how fast I ran, they stayed right behind me, yelling that if I didn't stop, they were gonna smother me. And you know what was the worst part of all?"

"I can't imagine."

"Those stupid cheese balls were yelling at me in French."

I burst out laughing.

Pixie glared at me for several moments, but then she began sputtering, and soon her bubbly chuckles filled the room.

"Are you okay now?" I finally managed to ask.

"Yeah, I guess so," was her grudging reply, as she turned off her desk lamp.

I was en route to yet another meeting of the Folksinging Club when the elevator doors slid open to reveal a scene of utter chaos. The downstairs lobby of Morrison Hall was packed with people. I'd never seen so many bodies in there on any other occasion— not on my first day when I registered to live at the dorm, not for any mixer, and not even in celebration of President Kennedy's assassination.

I hesitated, stalled on the threshold, reluctant to commit myself to taking that initial forward step. Glancing around in search of either an obvious explanation or else a safe avenue of escape, I spotted a familiar face.

"Susan!" I called out. "Susan Olsen!"

She skidded to a halt and turned back, impatience twisting her normally pretty features into an ugly frown.

"What's happening?" I demanded. "Why is everyone here? This looks like the biggest mixer of the year."

"Don't be ridiculous! It's not a mixer." She began edging away.

"Hold on a minute! What's going on?"

"I can't talk now. I have to get to the lounge."

"What's in the lounge?"

"Television."

"Huh?"

"You mean you haven't heard?" She sounded incredulous. I shook my head.

"The Beatles are on the Ed Sullivan Show tonight." Her voice was full of urgency, and she shifted from foot to foot in her anxiety to escape, like a small child who was trying not to wet her pants. "I have to go now—I don't want to miss them."

"Ugh, beetles!" I shuddered. You never knew what that Sullivan guy was going to come up with next! "What kind of beetles?"

"You know: THE Beatles!"

It was an extremely unhelpful reply but, that said, she turned and bolted, shoving her way through the crowd like an arctic icebreaker.

Curious, I followed in her wake.

By some miracle, she actually managed to elbow her way into the lounge—which was, if anything, even more crowded than the lobby—and I was right behind her. Once inside, I noticed that the people closest to the television were sitting on the floor so everyone in the back of the room could see.

I peered at the tiny set. There on the screen, were four of the strangest-looking young men I'd ever seen, all of them wearing boxy, lapel-less suits, and every one of them in desperate need of a haircut!

Meanwhile, the girls in our lounge, and in the television audience, were either screaming, crying, or swooning—which made it difficult to hear what else was going on. However, I thought I recognized the same weird music I'd been hearing all over the dorm for the past few weeks, whenever anyone's radio was turned on. And as much as I loved rock 'n' roll, this new stuff was definitely going to take some getting used to.

As I watched, the camera zoomed in on the blissfully smiling drummer in the back of the group, who was tapping along and nodding in time to the music. In bold black letters, his drum heads proclaimed the group's name.

"Oh, it's *those* Beatles!" I said to no one in particular. "Who cares?"

Several people hissed at me to be quiet, but I was already turning away, forcing my way back out, and heading for the familiar sounds of the Folksinging Club.

When I walked in, Derek Stone was standing in his usual place by the door, greeting arrivals, and Daniel was right beside him, expounding on the virtues of protest songs. I expected the night to be a rerun of all the previous club meetings.

I was very surprised to see John, though, and even more so to have him greet me with his "Oh-here-you-are-my-long-lost-buddy!" routine. Apparently he had recovered sufficiently from the Jug Band Debacle to feel comfortable about sitting with me, regardless of who might see us.

But as the meeting progressed, something strange happened between Derek and me. Every time he addressed the group or sang a song, I felt as if he was looking directly at me and smiling in some sort of unspoken understanding. It was extremely unnerving; it felt as if there was an electric current running between us.

Watch out! I chided myself. *You're letting your imagination run away with you. Before you know it, you're going to do something really stupid and make a complete fool of yourself.*

Nevertheless, I was puzzled.

Something was definitely going on—wasn't it?

At intermission, with typical brusqueness, John stood up and walked off without saying a word. Soon he was across the room in animated conversation with several of our mutual friends. Hurt by his lack of consideration, I was about to leave the room when someone spoke my name. The blood rushed to my cheeks as I turned to face Derek.

"Do you have a minute to talk?" he asked.

I was so flustered, I could only nod.

"Let's go outside." His smile was friendly, and I sensed that he was trying to put me at ease.

It didn't help much.

"I've noticed that you always come to our meetings," he said as we entered the hall.

"That's because I really enjoy them," I replied, and I even managed a wavery sideways smile.

He was taller than I'd realized, and I had to hurry to keep up with his long-legged strides. At the far end of the hall he stopped, which forced me to face him directly.

"John says you've been a tremendous help with the Poster Committee."

"Thanks," I mumbled, my attention fastened on his chin. I was afraid to meet his eyes, afraid he'd read my interest and longing—surely he could see how flustered I was. And I was afraid he would brush me off like some annoying freshman fly.

"The reason I mentioned your work with John," he said, "is that I'm looking for people who are especially dedicated to the club. You've probably heard that most of our officers, myself included, are going to be leaving after this semester . . ."

I tried, and failed, to imagine the Folksinging Club without Derek Stone. It would be a far less interesting place.

"Right now, we're scouting for responsible people to nominate for next year's Executive Committee," he went on, unaware of the bleak feeling that was threatening to overwhelm me. "I'd like to be able to sponsor the chairman of next year's Publications Committee. I was hoping it would be you."

"M . . . me?" Greatly daring, I looked upward.

Behind his wire-rimmed lenses, his pale blue-gray eyes held a hint of amusement. For my embarrassment? For our situation?

My face flushed even hotter. "I . . . I'm not sure I'm qualified."

"I wouldn't have asked you if I didn't think so."

"Well, I'd be willing to give it a try . . ." I said at last, and I even managed another shaky smile.

"Good. Let me have your phone number, and I'll make sure you get the details."

By the time I'd given him my number, intermission was over and we had to rejoin the others—but once back inside, I was unable to concentrate on even the simplest details of the meeting. Instead, I kept mulling over our conversation.

It seemed to me that there had been an undercurrent of important things left unsaid.

Calm down, you fool! I chided myself. *There's nothing to get excited about. It's not as if he asked you out. He just wanted your phone number so someone else can contact you. For him, it was nothing but a business deal.*

And, given my lack of self-confidence, I was afraid that it would surely remain that way.

———

The following day, as I had suspected, it was the club secretary, Betsy Walker, not Derek, who called to invite me to the next Executive Committee meeting. I immediately agreed to attend, but I was disappointed. I had hoped for better. My only consolation was that I had had the sense not to reveal my fantasies to Pixie and Rachel.

The Executive Committee, which met later in the week, turned out to be quite interesting, once I got over my initial shyness. I knew all of the club officers by sight, if not by personal introduction, and they seemed to know me as well. It was a close-knit community of good friends as well as fellow-officers—and they included me without hesitation. Derek went out of his way to make me feel welcome, and my election, sponsored by him, was unanimous.

Before long, I was privy to many of the behind-the-scenes struggles of the Folksinging Club—namely, the issues that had to be dealt with in order to keep it going. Despite modest membership fees and fund-raising concerts, the group was barely able to hold its own financially. This was because the University consistently refused to let the club use any of the school's larger auditoriums, apparently for fear they might attract new members or actually—oh, horror!—turn a profit. According to Derek, the University was hoping to put the club out of business. He even had new evidence of their duplicity: He had just received a letter from Joan Baez informing him that the school administration had offered her a considerable sum of money to do a concert for their benefit. This was the same concert that Derek himself had been trying to organize all year—but he had been turned down repeatedly on the grounds that Baez was too controversial a figure to be allowed on campus. Now the University had gone behind his back and made their own offer.

Indignant, Baez had refused.

This was yet another blatant example of campus politics, and I realized that in joining the club's Executive Committee, I was taking a conspicuous stand with the underdogs. Someone higher up, someone who might have control over my future—particularly my financial future—at the University was bound to notice. Only in my most private and sober moments did I allow myself to think about the possible consequences of my actions.

Easter vacation came as a welcome respite from our busy class schedules—although I was sorry that it interrupted my initiation into the inner workings of the Folksinging Club. I had budgeted my precious school funds so I would be able to go home for the holiday; and in return for having allowed me to stay with her over semester break, I invited Shennandoah to accompany me, thinking she might enjoy a change of scenery.

When our plane landed at Idlewild airport—only now it was suddenly JFK—my family was waiting for us: my younger sister, my father, and my mother in her wheelchair.

I felt a pang. Achingly familiar, they meant home to me,

and yet, with the passage of a few short months and many new experiences, they were beginning to seem like strangers. Still, ironically, before many hours had passed, all of this was reversed: New York was undoubtedly home and Indiana was, once again, an unreal and alien landscape.

But how strange it must have been for Shennandoah!

My family was not the sort to have a traditional Easter or even Passover gathering. However, despite their outspoken liberal views and their self-proclaimed status as non-practicing Jews, something had to be done on this occasion: both the holiday spirit and my homecoming demanded a celebration.

That year, it was my parents' turn to entertain. My uncle and his youngest son were our first guests to arrive. Shen's curiosity had been piqued by the information that my uncle was a doctor who had been married to three different women, all now deceased. To her, this seemed to suggest the possibility that he might be a notorious poisoner, and she was eager to meet him.

As for my uncle, he was obviously flattered by the rapt attention of my pert young girlfriend—much to the annoyance of his youngest son, who was the same age as Shennandoah and thought he deserved her notice far more than his father did. Every time she smiled and batted her eyelashes at my uncle, my cousin fumed and made outrageous comments, hoping in vain to divert her attention.

Before long, my uncle's other two children and their families arrived. The gathering complete, we immediately settled into our long-standing traditional roles. Our guests seated themselves around the dinner table, my sister and I served the food under my mother's nagging guidance, my father uncorked the wine—and the conflict began.

Our family debates followed a strict protocol: although they ordinarily revolved around either politics or religion, any subject was acceptable just as long as there were two clearly defined and contrary positions to defend. Debaters did not necessarily choose sides because of personal beliefs; more often than not, it was to maintain the balance of power.

That March of 1964, the topic of contention was abortion, and the opposing factions quickly drew their lines. My uncle squared off against his older son, who was a dentist and seemed to enjoy playing the role of devil's advocate. His younger son, a novice by family standards, joined his older brother, probably because he was still annoyed with his father for monopolizing Shennandoah's attention. My uncle's son-in-law joined their camp, but my father, who was already slightly tipsy from the wine, and my uncle's daughter, who was famous for her brilliant but sarcastic wit, sided with my uncle. My mother acted as referee, in case of ties or undue violence. And my sister and I, who had lived with my mother long enough to know when to keep our mouths shut, and were in any case considered to be too young to have anything worthwhile to add, assumed the role of interested spectators, watching from the sidelines.

Meanwhile, food and wine were steadily consumed—and despite occasional threats by various combatants to get up and leave, nothing was broken or spilled, and there were only a few brief interludes when diplomacy broke down and yelling and out-and-out name-calling held sway.

This was all normal behavior, and it had never occurred to me that other family gatherings might be different. But Shennandoah left me in no doubt about her opinion: she sat through dinner with her round blue eyes open almost as wide as her mouth, not daring to utter a word and eating scarcely a bite of food.

Afterwards, when all the guests had gone home—each having assured us that they had, as usual, had a wonderful meal and a terrific time—Shennandoah vented her anger on me.

"Imagine discussing abortions—and at the dinner table!" she scolded. "It's disgusting! Your family is a pack of barbarians." She burst into tears.

Puzzled and hurt, I loyally defended them. "But Shen, they've always been that way, for as long as I can remember. And my uncle's dinner conversation . . . it might be a little unusual, but isn't really all that bad."

Shennandoah sniffled and reached for another tissue.

"Anyway, family debates are harmless fun," I protested. "Doesn't everyone know that?"

We argued over the relative merits of my family vs. "a normal American family" until it began to sound remarkably like one of our traditional family debates! Shennandoah was so upset, I was afraid she might leave for Indiana that very evening.

Fortunately, we were interrupted by a phone call.

I had already introduced Shennandoah to several of my closest friends—and she had been singularly unimpressed—but the young man on the phone was not ordinary in any sense.

Barry was an extremely handsome, very talented flamenco guitar player. He was several years older than me, and he also happened to be black, though he was of such mixed racial heritage that his skin wasn't much darker than mine. The first time he visited us, after he'd left, my father commented, "What a nice kid—and what a musician! But why didn't you tell us he's Negro?"

"He is?" was my rather befuddled response. My education at the hands of our housekeeper, Mildred Holmes, had apparently left me literally oblivious to a person's color.

My father was highly amused.

Barry and I had long since established a rather romantic friendship—within certain well-defined limits. While I was in high school, he usually arrived at my house at least one night a week to practice guitar. Over the years, I'd probably spent more time listening to his music than anyone in his immediate family, all of whom I knew well and loved dearly. However, I admired Barry, as it were, from afar. Although we spent hours at a time together, he and I seldom spoke: he just sat there strumming, and I watched him and adored.

And how he loved to be adored! He was one of the most charming men I have ever known, and also one of the most elusive. He never arrived at my house when he said he would; he often turned up hours or even days later than I expected. Sometimes he would disappear for several weeks altogether, and then show up again, as charming as ever. He never explained his absences, and I soon learned not to take anything he said too seriously: he was a heartbreaker.

And there were other, not insignificant problems. Barry liked to pretend he was Spanish rather than black—a deception I did not admire. Trying to be Spanish was one of the reasons he'd taken up flamenco, and he often called me "Maria," as if by including me in his fantasy he might legitimize it. Still, he was a marvelous musician, and so charismatic that he could have, as Pixie would have said, "sold ice to the Eskimos."

That Easter Sunday, the moment I heard his voice on the telephone, inspiration struck: if I wanted to restore myself to Shennandoah's good graces, I would have to arrange for them to meet.

He came by the next day—at more or less the promised time—and he seemed genuinely glad to see me. What with all of the hugs and kisses he showered on me, it was several minutes before I was able to introduce him to Shen. And then the sparks really flew! High voltage bolts of blue-white fire seemed to arc directly from Shennandoah's eyes into Barry's, and then back again. Apparently, he had a passion for blondes that matched Shennandoah's for blacks. All that remained for me to do was to step back and watch them admire each other.

I was satisfied with my accomplishment—though I also felt just a bit left out. After all, Barry had never reacted that way to me!

Later that evening, after our handsome guest had departed, Shennandoah was still floating on air.

"Oh, Meri," she sighed, "he's the most beautiful man I've ever met! Why did he have to leave so early?"

"Early? Shen, it's past midnight!" I pulled my nightgown over my head.

"But we're on vacation! And speaking of vacation: oh, how I wish I could pack him up and take him home with me when this one's over."

"I'm not sure he'd like Indiana—or your parents. And that might be mutual . . ."

221

"No, I guess he might not." She shrugged. "Oh, well, who knows what will happen . . . Anyway, he says he'll be back tomorrow, and he promised to write."

"He did! What will Toshio think of that? After all, you've said he's rather old-fashioned."

"What Toshio doesn't know won't hurt him," she announced primly, settling down on her cot, apparently without a second thought for the Japanese professor she was currently dating.

I turned off the light and climbed into bed.

"Meri?"

"Yes?"

"I know this may sound corny, but think I'm in love."

"With Toshio or Barry?"

"Barry, of course!"

"Isn't it a bit early to tell?"

"Don't you believe in love at first sight?"

"I'm not sure."

"Well, I do—and so does Barry. He told me so when I walked him out to his car." Her sigh was dreamy. "It must be fate that we met this way. I'll be grateful to you forever."

However entertaining our time in New York may have been, all holidays must come to an end. Toshio met us at the airport—and when she stepped off the plane, Barry or no Barry, Shennandoah actually got down on her hands and knees, and kissed the dusty pavement of the Indiana runway.

I assumed it was her unsubtle way of letting me know that she was glad to be home, and I supposed, had I been a bit less scrupulous about hygiene, I might have done the same when I'd returned to my room after my visit to her family in Indianapolis.

chapter 18: spring fever

After months of snow and ice and cold gray skies, it was wonderful to see the sun again, and to feel the season turning. The campus was shrouded in the most tender of greens, the air echoed with intoxicated bird trills, and flower petals drifted on warm, sweet-scented breezes. The sunlight was dazzling.

Everyone had spring fever, although each of us manifested it in a different way.

Spring always makes me restless. I took long, solitary walks and daydreamed a lot. I was in love with everyone—Derek Stone, my art teacher Mr. Jefferson, Dr. Kildare—and I even had a tender spot for Barry, who was back in New York writing endless love notes to Shennandoah.

Once or twice a week she would bring me one of his letters, several pages thick, wave it in my face—hoping to make me jealous, I supposed—and then clutch it dramatically to her bosom. But she never allowed me to so much as touch one, let alone read it. Depending on her mood, she was either madly in love with Barry or speaking earnestly about bringing Christianity to the Orient via her Japanese professor.

Spring smoothed the rough edges from Rachel's cynical personality. She reminisced with longing about the past summer, which she'd spent with her boyfriend, Steve—a cub reporter for *The New York Times*—traveling around the country on the back of his motorcycle.

Pixie was dating heavily. Although she tried to keep it secret, we all knew what she was up to, what with the flood of telephone calls she received practically every day and night. When Norman called, he was still "Lover," in that throaty purr, but now there was also "Sweetie-pie" and "Big Boy," as well as a very persistent "Tiger."

"I hope you know what you're doing," Rachel warned Pixie.

We were in Pixie's old brown '56 Chevy, driving into town on our way to the pizza parlor. She had the radio on, turned down low, but none of us was paying much attention.

"Of course, I know what I'm doing," Pixie retorted, taking a right turn just a bit faster than I thought she should—the tires screeched around the corner. "I can take care of myself."

"Oh, sure," Rachel said. "For your information, if you don't keep track of your men and Norman ever finds out, you're going to be in big trouble."

"So what?" Pixie said. "If you really want to know, it doesn't matter one iota who I'm dating right now, because I'm considering giving them all up, including Norman."

"What!" Rachel cried. "I don't believe it."

"Well, I am. For your information, I'm madly in love with someone else."

"So who's the lucky guy?" A smile of pure devilry curled Rachel's lips. If I'd been Pixie, I wouldn't have dared to answer. Rachel looked like she was ready to telephone Norman the moment she heard Pixie's confession.

"You really want to know?" Pixie asked. "All right; by a lucky coincidence, here he is. Just listen to this." She cranked up the volume on her car radio.

A man was reciting poetry; long, rambling verses in convoluted rhyme with an aggressive, staccato rhythm. His voice was loud and brash, and he was obviously more than a little bit pleased with himself, since he kept referring to himself as "The Greatest."

"Who *is* that?" I demanded.

"Cassius Clay," Pixie said. "He's a boxer. Isn't he wonderful?"

Rachel snickered.

"Don't laugh, you nasty thing—he's special. Whenever he fights, before he goes into the ring, he makes up these poems about how he's the world's greatest boxer and all, and how he can't be beaten. And you know what? He never has been, although plenty have tried."

"So this is the guy you're gonna dump Norman for?" Rachel kept right on giggling. "Too bad his poetry isn't as good as his boxing."

Pixie silenced her with a stern glare.

We were quiet for the next few minutes, listening as his monologue wound down.

"Okay, Pixie," I said, at the end of the performance, "enlighten me. What makes him so wonderful? Besides being unbeatable, that is."

"Well, he's incredibly handsome," she said dreamily. Her expression sobered. "But you know what's the most special thing of all?"

I shook my head.

"He actually says he's proud to be a Negro. I've never heard anyone say that before. Ever!"

Our dorm was full of women in love—or perhaps it would more properly be termed "lust."

Myrna was constantly singing, warbling away at all hours of the day and night like a canary in heat. She was busy reading *Fanny Hill* every chance she got, and unwittingly entertaining us with her titillated *oooohs*, which were audible even in our room.

Dressed only in a half-slip which she wore pulled up to her armpits, Roberta Kruger sat for hours at a time in the third-floor lounge, poring over a marriage manual. She was always willing to take time out to inform anyone within hearing how, ever since she was five years old, she'd been saving ten cents a week toward her wedding day. Now her dreams were about to come true: in June she was going to be married to her fraternity-guy sweetheart, swathed

225

in yards of white satin and lace, at a ceremony that sounded like it would almost certainly rival a royal coronation.

Nearly every evening, from across the hall, we could hear Susan Olsen's loud complaints about the "test dinners" Roberta was subjecting her to. Roberta had smuggled a hotplate into their room, and was using Susan as a guinea pig so she could practice cooking for her future spouse.

Susan's moans drifted down the hall. "But everyone knows you have to cook spaghetti before you serve it!"

"I *did* cook it!" was Roberta's equally aggrieved reply.

"You can't just put raw spaghetti in a pot with a can of tomato sauce and expect to be able to eat it!"

"Be reasonable, Sue." Even as she spoke, Roberta was walking past our room, headed for the bathroom with a scalded pot that was emitting a cloud of noxious smoke. "Look at it this way: by the time I actually get married, my cooking will have improved tremendously."

"Great. And I might be dead of food poisoning!" Susan grumbled from their doorway.

Later that same evening, Rachel and I passed Roberta, who was sitting in her usual state of semi-undress in the lounge, consulting her marriage manual. "Darn it—what's *that* supposed to mean?" she muttered.

Rachel couldn't resist the temptation to meddle. "What's *what* supposed to mean?" she asked sweetly.

Roberta looked up. "Oh. Hi, Rachel. Meri. This stupid book! I can't figure out what they're talking about."

"I have some experience in these matters," Rachel said. "Maybe I can help."

"Gee, thanks. Okay, listen to this: It says here that when you're . . . er, you know, fooling around, you should always have a glass of ice water handy next to the bed. It says here"—she paused to locate the passage she was referring to—"quote, 'your husband will be delighted when you use the ice water at the appropriate moment,' unquote. But it doesn't say what you're supposed to *do* with it!"

"Maybe you're supposed to give it to him to drink," I said, as clueless as Roberta.

"You dummies." Rachel's lips quirked upward in one of her most mischievous expressions. "It's obvious: you're supposed to pour it over him to cool him off!" Unable to maintain her serious expression, she started to giggle.

I couldn't help it; I burst out laughing, too.

"Thanks a lot, Ladies!" Roberta grumbled. Turning pointedly away from us, she dove back into her book.

———

Even Daniel was intoxicated by the spring weather. He came by one evening right before dinner, insisting that he had to speak to all three of us immediately. We joined him in the courtyard, just outside the front door of Morrison Hall.

"What on earth's the matter with you, Daniel?" Pixie demanded. "Stop wiggling. You look like you've got ants in your pants!"

Rachel snickered.

Daniel stopped pacing and went over to perch precariously on the limestone railing that edged the wide front steps.

"Come on, Pixie, be serious," he said, a hurt look on his face. "I've got something really important to tell you, and it's not a joke. In fact, it's an idea that could revolutionize this whole campus."

"Well, I'm all for that!" Rachel announced, immediately sobering up.

Daniel watched us, his eyes begging us to ask him to divulge his secret, but we waited, knowing very well that he wouldn't be able to hold out on us for long.

"Okay, it's this," he began in a rush. "Last month I was reading a magazine article about nudist colonies in Florida and I was thinking—"

"Nudist colonies!" Pixie echoed in disbelief.

"In Florida. The article described how they got started, and how popular they are down there. And it suddenly dawned on me that there's no reason why we couldn't start one ourselves—right here."

"Here," Pixie repeated. "At IU?"

"It really wouldn't be all that difficult. All we have to do is—"

"You're crazy!" I blurted out.

Daniel glanced over at Rachel and Pixie. Their faces gave nothing away, and his eager expression faded just a bit. "That's what they said at the Yipsell meeting last night," he admitted. "I tried to get them interested, but they wouldn't even listen. And they're supposed to be a radical organization! I was hoping you'd be more open-minded."

"Sorry, Daniel, I don't want to be a wet blanket but . . . well . . . Doesn't a nudist colony at Indiana University sound a bit far-fetched?" I felt compelled to ask.

Daniel's sad gray eyes sought Pixie's, but she was busy inspecting her fingernails. Rachel, meanwhile, was examining something that only she could see in one of the dormitory windows.

"It is *not* far-fetched!" Daniel insisted, forcing their attention back to him. "Look at this. I wrote to the author of the article and he—"

"You actually wrote to him?" Pixie's eyes were wide.

"Yes. See, he's the director of a nudist colony in Florida, so he's an expert on the subject"—Daniel hurtled on as if he expected us to try to prevent him from finishing his story—"and he sent me a whole bunch of information about how he got started. He even included a brochure."

"Let's see!" Rachel was grinning with delight.

The three of us crowded around Daniel, anxious to have a look.

The glossy pamphlet was liberally illustrated with photographs of chubby, middle-aged couples sitting in lounge chairs, smiling happily and sipping fruit juice in the golden Florida sunshine. Much to my disappointment, however, all anatomical details had been carefully airbrushed out.

"Well, I don't know about the rest of you," Rachel said huffily, "but *I'm* certainly not getting involved with any organization that requires everyone who joins to have his or her genitals removed!"

As she made her exit up the steps, I wasn't sure if she was coughing or choking on laughter.

Daniel turned his puppy-dog eyes on Pixie.

"It was really sweet of you to think of me, Daniel." She patted him on the cheek. "But I'm afraid I can't help you. My mother says it's very tacky to go out without your underwear—besides, I just don't look all that good in basic black."

"Meri?"

"Sorry, Daniel, I catch cold too easily."

We left him standing on the steps, hugging his brochure and looking extremely forlorn.

Spring fever brought out the silliness that most people had been suppressing all winter. One of the fraternity houses decided to include our dorm in their antics, and by the time anyone realized what was happening, it was too late to stop them.

Late one Saturday afternoon, a noisy crowd of rowdy young men rushed up the front steps of Morrison Hall and into the lobby. They immediately headed for the upper floors, where some of the girls were studying, while others were relaxing or taking showers in preparation for their Saturday night dates. It was several minutes before anyone noticed the trespassers and someone sounded the alarm.

"MEN!!!"

Shrieks chorused up and down the halls. "EEEK! A PANTY RAID!!!"

The place was in an uproar. Girls ran around in various states of dress and undress, squealing in terror as they raced for the safety of their rooms, herded along by happily yelping boys.

Miss Bell quickly recruited several helpers—girls who had

been caught more or less decently clad—and they began trying to round up the invaders.

At the first sign of trouble, Pixie jumped up and slammed our door. The lock engaged with a satisfying click, and I heard Caralene do the same thing over in her room.

By that time, Miss Bell and her posse were gaining control of the situation. They systematically cleared out the dormitory, starting from the top down. Once our uninvited guests had been escorted from the building, Miss Bell locked the front doors and secured the side exits, as much to give the resident girls a chance to calm down as to keep the men out.

From our window, Pixie and I looked down at the fraternity boys, who were now standing outside in a group, jabbering excitedly and waiting to see what would happen next.

It didn't take long to find out.

Once my dorm mates realized they were safe, doors and windows burst open and girls came pounding out of their rooms and out to the lounge balconies, where they leaned as far out over the railings as they dared and tossed their panties down, shouting, "Take mine! Take mine!"

The men below went crazy.

———

The next evening brought a second visit from the same crew, only this time it was for a more serious purpose. One of my dorm mates had been pinned by a fraternity member—perhaps this was what had inspired the previous day's panty raid—and now the same jokers were back to perform an engagement ceremony for the happy couple.

The young man and his fraternity brothers assembled on the grass outside our front entrance, carrying candles and dressed in their best, looking as honorable and decent as they possibly could—indeed, they looked as if butter wouldn't melt in their mouths, and yesterday's shenanigans might have been a figment of our imaginations. When the engaged girl appeared in the entry at the top of the steps, the whole group burst into song.

The rest of us stood at our windows and out on the balconies, listening to the strong male voices singing about true love, faithfulness, and never-ending happiness as the young lady waited in her place of honor, framed in the open doorway, her white dress shimmering in the twilight. As we watched, her boyfriend went to join her. After placing his fraternity pin on her dress, he escorted her back down the stairs. And at that point, the serious business over, the whole group, now shoving, laughing, and joking, hurried off into the night to celebrate.

Not all of my dorm mates had such happy involvements with "The Greeks," as they were popularly called. Spring was the time when fraternities and sororities traditionally pledged new members. Each house had its own set of rules about who was or wasn't qualified to join, and this discrimination inevitably led to disappointments.

Rebecca and Judy, the Southern girls I had argued with the previous semester, were happily packing their things. They were joining the all-Jewish sorority, and as far as I was concerned, they were welcome to it.

There was a definite division of opinion among us "dormies" when it came to the subject of sororities. We were, however, unanimous in our dismay over the fate of one of our dorm mates, a girl named Karen Chandler.

Karen was an average freshman. Originally from a small town in upstate Indiana, she wasn't remarkably smarter or duller than the norm. She studied neither more nor less than most of her peers, and schoolwork never seemed to interfere with her social life. Tall and willowy, with long, light brown hair and a model's physique, she had plenty of friends and no lack of boyfriends. Perhaps she was a little bit louder and more daring than some of the other coeds—and she wasn't the least bit apologetic about the

231

fact that she had twice been called before the dorm committee for smoking in her room. But no one held that against her.

Right from the first week of school, she'd let everyone know about her obsession: she had to get into a sorority. But not just any sorority would do—it had to be the one her mother had been in when she was a student at Indiana. As spring advanced and the day approached for the sororities and fraternities to announce their choices, Karen became more and more vocal about her desires. Then, one day, she was ecstatic. She ran up and down the halls, laughing and shouting that she'd been invited to tea at "her" sorority! This was what sororities did for prospective pledges, she announced joyfully: they called you back for tea to look you over one final time before asking you to join.

Karen was so radiantly happy the day of her tea party that even those of us who weren't otherwise interested in sororities wished her luck.

But it wasn't to be. We never learned why—whether it was her mediocre grades, her troubles with the dorm committee, her personality, or some other unknown quality—but when the new pledges were announced, Karen's name was not among them.

For two days, she locked herself in her room and cried. She wouldn't speak to her roommate or anyone else, and she refused to eat.

On the third day, when Karen finally emerged from her room, she was very angry and anxious to tell everyone within earshot what she thought of sororities: they were just plain dumb, and she'd been a fool for wanting to join one! After ranting on like this for a while, she stalked out of the dorm, and no one knew where she had gone.

By late the next morning, it was all over the quad.

After somehow managing to procure a large quantity of liquor, Karen had hunted down one of her boyfriends, a fraternity man, and, together with a group of his friends, they had gone to one of the deserted local limestone quarries, where everyone had gotten rip-roaring drunk. At the height of the party, Karen had attempted a balancing act along the quarry rim, but she was so drunk that she lost her footing and fell into the water far below, probably losing consciousness before she even hit the water. Fortunately, her boyfriend and his buddies had been sober enough to save her from drowning, but by the time they'd gotten her to the campus infirmary, her condition had been serious.

They kept her there for several days, and when she returned to us, a very subdued girl, she was a painful sight: every visible inch of her body, from head to toe, was black and blue. That day, she made her third appearance before the dorm committee and was restricted to the dormitory for an entire month, with time out for classes. She was warned that her next offense would be her last.

She behaved for nearly a week—until the following Sunday afternoon, when she sneaked out with the same boyfriend. The campus police found her drunk and dancing nude in the middle of the fountain in the plaza by the main auditorium. After that Karen departed for good, and we whispered about it among ourselves for weeks afterwards. The general feeling seemed to be that it was unwise to let oneself be carried away to excesses, whether or not it was spring.

Not long after that, some fellow on campus went a little bit berserk and took to lurking about at night in the woods between my dorm and the art building, surprising young women by jumping out of the bushes wearing nothing but an unbuttoned raincoat.

"I wonder if he saw Daniel's brochures and is advertising for a nudist colony," I said to Pixie. "If so, his approach probably isn't gaining any converts."

"It isn't funny!" she scolded. "I'm worried about you going through the woods at night, every time you have that calligraphy class."

"Don't worry," I told her, "I've got everything under control. From now on, I'll be carrying my umbrella."

Pixie's forehead wrinkled. "What good is that?"

"Hah! I'd like to see that guy try to attack me!" Brandishing my umbrella, I executed a perfect lunge, one we'd been working on all week in my fencing class. "My teacher says I'm really good at this, you know."

"Terrific!" Rachel commented from in her usual seat in our armchair. "Now all you have to do is hope that the Flasher has taken fencing lessons, too—and that he sticks to fencing etiquette instead of trying to grab you!"

But not even the possibility of encountering the Flasher would have kept me from going to art class. Spring fever had only intensified my crush on Mr. Jefferson, and I was more determined than ever to attract his attention, still mulishly convinced that it was only a matter of time before I met with success.

Each week I planned interesting topics to discuss with him—just in case, should the chance for a tête-à-tête arise when I stayed late after class with the rest of my rivals.

Then, one evening, by some miracle—or so it seemed at the time—Fate smiled upon me.

My big break came at the end of the regular class period. Just as we hangers-on were settling in for yet another siege, Mr. Jefferson stood up and announced that it was fine with him if we all wanted to stay late, but tonight he was going to leave on time.

Naturally, his departure took away all incentive for the rest of us to remain. Mr. Jefferson might have been amused if he could have seen the dejected looks we gave each other and heard our unhappy grumbling as, not five minutes later, we groupies packed up our art supplies and vacated the room.

Encumbered by my artwork and my trusty umbrella, I stepped outside into the warm spring night. My route took me across the plaza in front of the main auditorium, where Karen Chandler had made her last watery appearance, and then along the path that sloped downhill toward the woods and the dreaded Flasher's Lair. Up ahead, at the very edge of the plaza, a man passed beneath the streetlight, and I caught my breath: it was Mr. Jefferson.

Was it really possible? Was this my chance to have a private word with him, away from the competition? I quickened my pace, hoping to get close enough to at least say hello.

By then, he was turning toward the auditorium, and I would certainly have lost him if he hadn't stopped at the bottom of the steps to rummage through the pockets of his jacket and pants, apparently looking for something. He must have heard my scurrying footsteps, for at that point he stopped and glanced over his shoulder.

"Hi, Mr. Jefferson!" I called out, sounding rather out of breath, even to myself.

"Meri? I thought you were staying late."

"I changed my mind."

"Damn! Where are those tickets?" he growled, still rummaging through his pockets. For a moment, he seemed to forget my presence. "Wait a minute . . . Ah! Here they are." His teeth flashed white in his beard when he grinned. "Well, now that I've found my tickets, are you sure you want to go right home? I'm on my way to a concert, and it just so happens that I have two tickets. Would you care to join me?"

"I'd love to!"

"Come on, then. We don't want to miss the whole thing."

Taking my elbow, he hustled me up the steps so quickly that I was even more breathless by the time we entered the lobby.

Was this really happening?

The second half of the concert had already begun. People in the audience looked up as we made our way down the darkened aisle.

What a coup! Surely they must be noticing, even in the dark, that I, Meri Henriques, was the guest of the dashing Mr. Jefferson!

Our seats were far down toward the front of the theater, and they were located dead center, in the middle of a row. We had to climb over several individuals in order to reach them. I could never have afforded to sit that close to the stage.

As I searched for someplace to stash my portfolio, I exulted silently. *My wish came true*, I thought. *I have a date with Mr. Jefferson!* No matter that I had practically engineered the situation by forcing myself upon his attention; in the end, he was the one who'd invited me to join him.

Once I began to calm down, I realized that Mr. Jefferson was speaking to me, giving me a running commentary on the orchestra's performance.

"Listen to that!" He had a loud, booming voice and whispering was obviously a foreign concept to him. "They played that passage all wrong."

Someone in the brass section hit a sour note.

Mr. Jefferson guffawed. "Oh, my god, this is great. They're really awful!" He hooted with laughter.

Several of our neighbors hissed at him to be quiet.

Mr. Jefferson put his hand over his mouth and looked at me with feigned embarrassment. Above his hand, the eyes of a naughty little boy twinkled with mischief.

The orchestra played several more wrong notes, and Mr. Jefferson reacted with peals of delighted laughter. "Bravo!" he shouted over the mooing of the French horns.

I slid downward in my seat. How could the suave Mr. Jefferson be so unbelievably uncouth? I was beginning to hope that no one had seen us come in after all—or that, if they had noticed, they'd noticed only him.

Mr. Jefferson leaned closer. "Pretty bad, huh? Is that why you're hiding under your seat? It won't help, you know."

He had such a loud voice!

I struggled to return his smile.

Moments later, the piece came to a crashing conclusion, entirely out of sync and terribly off key.

Mr. Jefferson leapt to his feet, applauding wildly. "Encore! Encore!" he yelled. "You don't get to hear a performance like that every day! Hey, Meri, what do you think? It sounded to me like they played Beethoven, and Beethoven lost!"

I cringed.

He was in a wonderful mood as we joined the crowd filing up the aisles and out of the auditorium. I was buffeted around quite a bit because of my portfolio, and although I was sorely tempted, I didn't dare use my umbrella to defend myself.

Mr. Jefferson noticed my distress. "Here, let me carry that for you," he offered, reaching for my portfolio. "Let's get out of here and go someplace quiet where we can have some coffee. I want to talk to you."

I clung to my portfolio like a life raft. "Gosh, Mr. Jefferson, I'm really not sure I can . . . I have to be back at the dorm before lockout."

He looked as if he was going to argue—after all, it was Friday night, and he knew as well as I did that I had plenty of time to spare—but just then, to my infinite relief, a voice called out: "Randolph! Randolph Jefferson!"

He turned toward the speaker.

"I thought that was you down there, bellowing in the fifth row!" Laughing, his friend gave him a hearty slap on the back.

Almost immediately, several other people joined us—grad students and a couple of teachers—and plans were quickly made for going out on the town.

"You sure you won't come with us, Meri?" Mr. Jefferson asked.

When I once again declined his offer, he didn't waste much time trying to persuade me. Perhaps it was the presence of his friends, who were anxious to leave, that made him abandon his efforts.

Not long afterwards, I found myself hurrying through the woods towards my dorm, thinking, *Well, isn't it nice to have gotten that out of your system. Just think: you actually had your dream date with Mr. Jefferson . . . and thank goodness it's over!*

chapter 19: pizzlum sieve

Derek Stone's bluegrass band finished playing "May the Circle be Unbroken," and with that, the April meeting of the Folksinging Club was over. Derek put down his guitar, thanked us all for coming, and reminded us not to miss the next club-sponsored concert in two weeks, as the room filled with the sound of creaking chairs, shuffling feet, and people's voices.

I had been there since early that evening; we'd had a short Executive Committee meeting before the regular meeting started. I was tired and a little stiff from sitting for so long, and I was looking forward to a much-needed breath of fresh air. I got up and stretched, then turned to my companion.

"Well, good-bye, John," I said. Unable to resist the temptation to tease him, I added, "See you next month."

"Ah, you're a cold, cruel lady, me darlin'!" Smiling, he stood. "Wait while I fetch my coat, and I'll walk you home."

He was a nice person, I decided as I watched him strolling across the room and greeting acquaintances—even if he was only friendly during club meetings.

When I turned to retrieve my own jacket, Derek was standing beside me. "Can I give you a ride home?" His heavy guitar case was in one hand and his car keys were in the other.

Without a moment's hesitation and only the tiniest twinge of guilt, I replied, "Sure! Thank you very much!"

"Where do you live?" he asked. "GRC?"

I panicked. *Oh, my god, he thinks I live in the Graduate Residence Center! He'll be horrified when he realizes that I'm just a freshman!*

"No . . . actually, I live nearby, in Wells Quad. It's not really far enough to drive."

And that's the end of that! I thought. *Oh, well, at least I gave him a graceful way out.*

But to my astonishment, he said, "Wells Quad? That's even better. It's a beautiful night; I'll walk you home."

"Oh, I'd like that! But, well . . . There *is* one small problem . . ." I looked meaningfully in John's direction.

"Ready to go then, Meri?" John boomed in a hearty voice, as he rejoined us.

"She is—but *I'm* taking her home," Derek announced, before I could say a word.

The two men faced each other expressionlessly. I was too surprised by the suddenness of their confrontation to interfere, but I desperately hoped that Derek wouldn't be the one to back down.

John shrugged. "Well, Derek, you're the boss here. So, as you said yourself, Meri: 'See you next month.'"

And he was gone, leaving Derek and me standing there, facing one another, Derek grinning at me like we were co-conspirators.

I felt a flood of relief—and then, unexpectedly, I was stricken with a bad case of the jitters. This was what I had been hoping for all year: a chance to talk to Derek. But now that it was actually about to happen, how was I going to manage?

I doubted my ability to meet his expectations—whatever they might be. And although I very much wanted to find out all I could about him, the truth of the matter was that I was a mere freshman, while he and his friends belonged to a world of graduate students, professors, and intellectuals. By comparison, I wasn't very interesting at all.

I jammed my hands deep into my coat pockets, as much to stop their trembling as to keep myself from chewing on my fingernails.

Suddenly, Derek laughed. "I've wanted to do that for months!" he confessed to my amazement, nodding in the direction of the retreating John. "Come on, let's get out of here."

And we walked out of the meeting room.

"You seemed kind of tied up with John all year," he said as we left the building, "and I didn't want to interfere."

"I'm glad you did," I said, astonishing myself. At this point, though, the unexpected seemed to be the norm, and the truth just popped out of my mouth, uncensored.

"Let's go this way," he said. "I want to put my guitar in my car."

We approached an old green Dodge.

"John and I are just friends," I felt compelled to say, "but it took me a while to figure that out."

"Unfortunately, that doesn't leave *us* much time to get to know each other." Derek unlocked the trunk and deposited his instrument, then slammed the lid closed and turned to face me. "The semester's nearly over and my thesis is almost finished—and the minute it is, I'm leaving for California."

His directness was disconcerting. It wasn't exactly what I'd imagined a conversation with him would be like. No one I knew was quite *that* blunt.

Without another word, we began walking.

"There's something else you should know," he said. "I wasn't totally honest with you back there at the meeting when I offered to drive you home. I already knew exactly where you live—room 312 in Morrison Hall—and I also know that you're a freshman, not a graduate student."

I was speechless.

"But I wanted to take you home," he went on earnestly, "and it was the only thing I could think of on the spur of the moment. It was really stupid, and I'm sorry."

By now I was entirely off-balance. He kept making such unexpected statements—I had never known anyone who did so little beating around the bush! I was fascinated and wanted to keep him talking, hoping he'd surprise me again.

"You don't have to apologize," I told him. "I'm glad everything worked out the way it did." I could feel a smile tugging at the corners of my mouth. "Are you always this bad at keeping secrets?"

"Secrets?" He glanced over at me. "I can't afford to have secrets in my personal relationships. I believe in honesty. Don't you?"

"Well, yes . . . But sometimes being too honest can hurt someone you care about."

"They'll get over it eventually. Anyway, they'd get hurt just the same, sooner or later, when they found out that you'd lied to them."

"I guess you're right." I realized that he was telling me something important, but I needed time to think it over—and time was something we definitely didn't have. I found myself wishing that my dorm was five miles away, instead of five blocks. We were almost there.

"Well, this is where I live." It was difficult, but I was determined to be as honest and direct about my feelings as he was. "I'm really glad you walked me home. I wanted to get to know you better. I hope I'll see you again."

He stopped walking and put one booted foot up on a stone bench that was just below the stairs to the front door. He studied me intently, considering. "I'm not sure that's such a good idea. There are lots of reasons why we shouldn't see each other. As I mentioned, the school year's almost over, and I'm leaving. And there's my work. My thesis isn't finished, and my advisor is giving me a hell of a time." He ran a hand through his curly hair. "I need to think this through."

"I understand," I said, although I didn't. How could he approach me like this and then turn away?

"I'm not sure you do understand." He shrugged. "Oh, well, I'm not sure I know exactly what I want, either . . . Anyway, I'm glad we had a chance to talk, and to get to know each other a little better."

"Me, too."

"Well, then, good night, Meri. I'd like to say you'll be hearing from me—but you shouldn't count on it."

"Okay. But I can hope."

He removed his foot from the bench and stretched.

I stifled an unexpected reaction: I wanted to reach out and put my hands on his chest, feel his arms close around me.

His smile was enigmatic, almost as if he could read my mind. And then he was gone.

I ran upstairs, the words of our strange, candid conversation racing through my head. I couldn't stop thinking about his last smile, and the question in his eyes. I burst into my room and, not unexpectedly, found Rachel visiting Pixie. They both looked up, startled.

"What happened, Meri? Did you run all the way home?" Pixie demanded with a smile—and then abruptly, bolting to her feet: "Oh, my god, tell me it wasn't the Flasher!"

"Derek Stone walked me home!" I said between gasps for air.

"I don't believe you!" Rachel was also on her feet now, glaring at me. "He never dates anyone."

Pixie just smiled like a sphinx.

"It wasn't exactly a date, Rachel. He only walked me home."

"Yeah, well, he never walked *me* home," she grumbled. Then her expression softened. "I'm jealous as hell, but I wish you luck."

"Thanks," I said. "Only I think it's going to take a lot more than luck, if I'm going to spend any more time with him."

"So do I," she admitted.

———

All the following week, I waited for his phone call. I told myself I was a fool for expecting to hear from him after he'd expressed such doubts. After all, why would someone like him be interested in someone like me?

But nothing could prevent me from hoping. And all those things he'd said . . .

Finally, on Friday afternoon, Pixie said, "Rachel, we've got to get this girl out of here. She's been moping around the dorm for almost a week."

"Let's take her out to dinner," Rachel suggested.

I felt a warm rush of gratitude for these friends who clearly really cared about me.

The three of us piled into Pixie's Chevy, and we headed into Bloomington.

The local A&W Root Beer stand was a classy establishment: not only did they have the usual drive-in arrangement, they also had inside table service. We chose a bright orange vinyl and Formica booth by the front windows, overlooking the parking lot, and ordered hamburgers from a not-very-friendly waitress.

We must have been a strange-looking trio: a Mediterranean Jew, a mischievous black imp, and a New York gypsy in a bright red and green babushka. By comparison, our fellow diners were ordinary to the point of dullness: plump, middle-aged, Indiana farm couples having a night on the town. But we weren't much interested in our surroundings or how we fit into them—rather, we were out to have a good time.

Pixie began describing her week's teaching experiences. She was a wonderful actress and raconteur, and the stories she told about her kindergarten class were highly entertaining.

"Today, we learned about puff adders," she announced. "They're real scary. See, they rear back—like this—and they puff out their cheeks—like that—and they sway back and forth from side to side—like this," she mumbled around a mouthful of air.

It was a remarkable demonstration. Her bulging cheeks were rapidly turning a brilliant shade of scarlet, her eyes bugged out, and she swayed back and forth in her seat like a top that was about to run down.

Just then, I happened to glance out of the window. An elderly couple was watching us, open-mouthed, from their car, staring at Pixie and pointing. They probably thought she was having some kind of fit.

Pixie and Rachel both noticed our audience at the same moment, and all three of us burst out laughing.

"Is something wrong, girls?" It was our waitress, looking very stern.

Sobering up quickly, we assured her that we were fine.

"If you think that was funny," Pixie said, as soon as the woman was out of earshot, "listen to this: today, I heard the craziest story."

"From who?" Rachel asked around her hamburger.

"Mrs. Butler, my supervisor. She's a real serious old lady—she never jokes around. As a matter of fact, she hardly ever smiles, and if I didn't know her so well, I'd have sworn she was telling me a whopper."

"Well, come on, let's hear it!" I urged.

"Okay. According to Mrs. Butler, this happened a long time ago, when she first began teaching, back in the hills of Tennessee. The problem was that people there were so poor and ignorant that many of their kids didn't come to school at all, and there was never a class list the first day because some parents waited until the last minute to decide whether or not to send their kids to school. So every year, Mrs. Butler had to spend part of the first day of school having the students come up to her desk, one by one, to tell her their name, birthday, parents' names, address, stuff like that, for the school records. And it wasn't easy, because kindergarten kids don't always know all the answers . . ."

When Pixie saw that Rachel and I were avidly listening, she continued. "Anyway, that year everything was going pretty much as expected until this one little girl came along. She was real cute, Mrs. Butler said, all scrubbed and shiny looking, dressed in what was obviously her best dress—it wasn't fancy or new, but it was real clean. So Mrs. Butler asked the little girl what her name was, and the little girl answered right out, polite as can be, 'My name is Pizzlum Sieve Johnson, ma'am.'"

Of course, true to form, as she told her story, Pixie was having a grand time acting out each part, changing her voice to suit the character. "Well, Mrs. Butler was sure she'd heard wrong, so she asked the girl to repeat it. 'Yes'm,' says the girl. 'It's Pizzlum Sieve Johnson.'" Pixie shook her head. "Now that was a new one for Mrs. Butler—she told me she'd never heard a name like that before, and she wasn't quite sure what to do about it."

"It was a nickname, right?" Rachel suggested.

"That's what Mrs. Butler thought. But the girl said no, it wasn't. So Mrs. Butler asked her to spell it, although she didn't really expect a little kindergarten girl to be able to spell that peculiar name any more than she could. 'I don't know how to spell anything yet, ma'am,' the little girl answered. 'That's why Ma sent me to school.'"

Pixie paused while Rachel and I chuckled over that, then resumed her story. "Well, as you can imagine, Mrs. Butler told me she was good and truly stumped, and she was beginning to think she wasn't going to get past square one registering that kid. But then she had a bright idea: she asked the little girl if she had any older brothers or sisters at the school. 'Yes'm,' says the girl. 'My big brother Zeke's in the first grade.'" Pixie grinned. "Mrs. Butler says she breathed a sigh of relief and sent the girl to get Ezekiel Johnson, hoping he'd be able to solve the mystery, because she had to do something about registering that child."

"Well, what happened?" I pressed. "Did it work?"

"Sort of. You see, when Mrs. Butler asked Ezekiel Johnson what his sister's name was—her real, Christian name—what do you think he said?"

"Pizzlum Sieve Johnson!" Rachel and I chorused.

"Yup."

"Did he know how to spell it?" Rachel asked.

"Of course not—which left Mrs. Butler right back where she'd started."

"What happened then?" I asked.

"She said that at that point, the only thing she could think of was to ask Ezekiel to bring a note from his mother or father with all of the necessary information. Meanwhile, she went ahead and registered the rest of the kids. But the next day, instead of a note, who should show up but the little girl's mother.

"'I hope my little 'un ain't been causin' you no trouble, Miz Butler,' the woman said. 'I told her I'd give her a good lickin' if she has.'

"'Oh, my goodness, no!' Mrs. Butler said. 'And I certainly didn't mean for you to go to all the trouble of coming here in person.'

"'I ain't too good at writin', so here I am. Now what's all this fuss about?'

"'Well, you see, Mrs. Johnson, I'm trying to register your daughter for school and I need certain information, but neither she nor her brother seems to know her given name . . . By the way, what *is* her given Christian name?'

"'It's Pizzlum Sieve Johnson, like they both told you.'

"'Forgive me, Mrs. Johnson, but it's such an unusual name that I assumed it was a nickname.'

"'Humph! And I thought you schoolteachers were supposed to be so smart! What kind of teacher are you, that you don't know your Bible?'

"'Of course I know my Bible, Mrs. Johnson, but I . . .'

"But Mrs. Johnson interrupted. 'Maybe I cain't read or write as good as some folks, but I do know my Bible inside out. I've memorized whole parts of it and I named every last one of my children after the Good Book.'

"'Well, all I can tell you is that I've never heard of Pizzlum Sieve—and I certainly don't know how to spell it.'

"So Mrs. Johnson tells her, kind of snooty, that she doesn't know offhand either, but if Mrs. Butler will just find her a Bible, she'll be glad to point out her daughter's name.

"By that time, Mrs. Butler was pretty annoyed by all the trouble one little girl was causing her, but she was also kind of intrigued—and she still had to get that child registered. So she opened up her desk and got out her Bible. It took Mrs. Johnson a while to find what she was looking for, and Mrs. Butler says she was real curious by the time she finally gave the Bible back to her, pointed, and said, 'Here it is: Pizzlum Sieve, just like I told you.'"

Pixie paused dramatically.

"Well, what was it?" Rachel demanded.

Pixie giggled. "Psalm One-Oh-Four, of course. You know: Psalm C-I-V!"

Rachel and I burst out laughing. Soon, all three of us were

laughing so hard that we couldn't stop. If one of us began to slow down, the sight of the other two was enough to get her going again.

Rachel looked up. "Uh-oh, here comes the waitress!"

We decided to leave before we were thrown out.

⸻

It was fairly late by the time we arrived back at the dorm. We were in high spirits, with an occasional giggle still erupting every now and then. Myrna heard us come in and joined us in our room, wanting to know what all the hilarity was about.

"Oh, by the way, Meri," she said when Pixie had finished an abbreviated explanation, "you got a phone call while you were out."

"Who was it?" I almost shouted, scarcely daring to breathe.

"Oh, some guy with a weird name. Durrell. Dorrick. Or was it Darryl?"

"It wasn't Derek Stone, was it?"

"That's it: Derek," she said with evident satisfaction.

"For god's sake, Myrna!" Somehow I resisted the urge to shake her. "Tell me what he said!"

"Um . . . Let me think . . . Oh, yeah, he didn't say what—just that you should call him back if you got in before seven thirty."

I groaned.

"Even though it's too late, I saved his number for you."

"Where?" I gasped out.

"I think it's on my desk."

I followed her into her room in a torment of anxiety, close enough on her heels that I would have run her over if she'd stopped walking. Pixie and Rachel were right behind me.

Myrna rummaged around on her desk, taking forever, and finally produced the promised slip of paper.

I grabbed it out of her hands.

"Gee, Meri, too bad you missed him," Pixie said. "Try calling anyway."

I hurried into the washroom and dialed. There was no answer.

After going to bed that night, I tossed and turned for hours before I finally fell asleep. I was burning with curiosity about Derek's phone call, and bitterly disappointed that I had missed him.

chapter 20: a party

Saturday passed with no further word from Derek. I was frantic, but loath to try phoning him again. After all, there was an almost sacred rule that nice girls didn't pursue men.

And I was confused. What did he mean by saying that he wanted to get to know me better but didn't think he should? By calling me, and then not calling back?

What was I supposed to think? Or feel?

By Saturday night, I was an emotional wreck.

Hoping to avert a total meltdown, Pixie and Rachel suggested an outing. *Tom Jones* was playing at our favorite movie theater next to the coffeehouse, and none of us had seen it. But even though it was supposed to be one of the funniest movies of the year, I declined their kind invitation, determined to spend every moment roosting by the telephone—just in case. I had no intention of making the same mistake I'd made the evening before!

As soon as they were gone, I regretted my decision.

I tried to study but was unable to concentrate. I sought solace in the Zen-like discipline of my calligraphy exercises, but the wavers in my penmanship were a clear indication of my true state of mind. In desperation, I turned to Myrna, pestering her until she agreed to a game of cards.

Ours was a longstanding rivalry. As the school year progressed, our group card games had all but ceased, more often than not because Myrna and I were the only players left in the dorm. Pixie and Caralene, as well as most of their friends, were usually out socializing. Rachel didn't date, but she didn't play cards, either. In the end, it was Myrna and I who proved to be the true cardaholics.

Our battleground was a game called Pounce, which required split-second physical reactions, as each player attempted to stack her cards in numerical order on a central pile before her opponent could outmaneuver her. Myrna was slow; I was fast. I always won, yet she kept coming back for more punishment, angrier each time we played.

Before long, Rachel had joined the mix. Once she discovered what we were up to, she began showing up faithfully for our almost nightly duels, which she seemed to find irresistible. Her chosen role consisted of teasing Myrna mercilessly and cackling like a fiend every time she made a clumsy mistake—which only made Myrna angrier and more clumsy than she already was, much to Rachel's delight.

As for myself, I enjoyed being in Rachel's good graces. Apparently she appreciated my ability to provide her with such reliable entertainment. As an added bonus, from my point of view, she was usually so preoccupied with harassing Myrna that she ignored her second-favorite victim: me.

After these evenings were over, I was always disgusted with myself for having had a good time by making a fool of someone else. However, my scruples didn't prevent me from continuing to play cards with Myrna while Rachel kibitzed, and Myrna continued to come back for more abuse. Eventually, I realized that the three of us filled a void in each other's lives: none of us had much of a social life, and all of us would otherwise have been terribly bored and lonely.

Of course, that particular night Rachel was out at the movies with Pixie, but even without her nagging, our game proceeded pretty much as usual. Myrna and I sat on my floor facing each other across the cards, our faces set in what were presumably identical expressions of grim concentration—the "Life-and-Death-Struggle Look" was what Rachel called it.

And we were still hard at it, a couple of hours later, when Pixie and Rachel returned from their outing. Pixie looked suspiciously nonchalant, but Rachel was fuming.

At the sight of her nemesis, Myrna groaned and stopped shuffling the cards. "Why are you back so soon?" she demanded, noticeably peeved. "I thought you went to the movies."

"We did," Rachel growled, dropping into our armchair, "but Pixie got us kicked out of the theater."

"You're kidding!" I exclaimed. "I thought the management didn't care who comes in."

"Oh, it was nothing serious," Pixie said with great unconcern. She sat down on her bed and started to remove her shoes.

"Right: nothing serious," Rachel said with a sneer. "Katherine Gates, I am never going to the movies with you ever again!"

"Come on!" I urged. "Tell us what happened."

"You should have gone with us, Meri," Pixie said in an obvious attempt to sidestep the issue. "It was a great movie."

"What we saw of it," Rachel amended. "And Pixie was fine, too . . . for a while. Until they got to this eating scene—"

"I wasn't the only one who was laughing," Pixie protested.

"Yeah, but did you have to laugh so hard?"

"How could I help it? Listen Myrna and Meri, you tell me if you wouldn't have been laughing, too . . . See, Tom Jones is this playboy kind of guy; he's real cute, and there's no way he can resist women—and they can't resist him either. So he meets this sexy lady at a country inn, and there's an immediate mutual attraction. They sit down to eat this huge dinner together—whole pigs, and lobster, and chickens, and legs of lamb—kind of like in *Henry VIII*. And the two of them start making eyes at each other right across the dinner table. It was really funny."

"Not *that* funny!" Rachel grumbled from her chair.

"Was, too," Pixie insisted. "And Tom Jones sort of nibbles his way up a chicken leg, real suggestively, like it's her leg—kind of like this—and the whole time he never takes his eyes off the lady. And she gives him this smoldering look and starts sucking on a lobster claw real slow—like this—until they're practically having an orgy, in pantomime, right there at the dinner table. It was the funniest thing I've ever seen."

"Yeah." Rachel's voice was full of disgust. "So funny that Pixie started laughing. And you know her: before I could stop her, she was moaning and groaning loud enough to wake the dead . . . And then she started howling and carrying on about how the movie was absolutely killing her! And *then* she fell out of her seat and started rolling around in the aisle . . ."

"Oh, dear," I said.

"And that's when the manager threw us out," Pixie finished up cheerfully. "So we went and got something to eat. I was starving after that eating scene anyway!" She sighed. "I would have liked to have seen how it ended, though . . ."

Rachel's face was bright red. "Pixie, how could you—"

Our phone rang.

Still chuckling, I went to answer it.

"Hello?"

"Meri? This is Derek Stone."

"Derek!" I squeaked.

My friends were abruptly silent.

"Sorry I missed you last night."

"I'm sorry, too," I answered, making a conscious effort to regain my composure.

"I was going to ask you to the movies, but your roommate said you were out. I suppose you went to see *Tom Jones*, since that's what everyone else is doing . . ."

"Oh, no!" I moaned, barely audible.

"So I went by myself tonight," Derek said. "Did you enjoy it?"

"No! I mean, I didn't go. Some friends took me out to dinner last night, but I stayed home tonight, hoping you'd call."

Did I really say that?

"Gee, I'm sorry," Derek commiserated, apparently willing to overlook my social gaffe. "It would have been fun to see it together. On second thought, though, maybe you're lucky you didn't go tonight. Halfway through there was a big commotion, and I think someone actually got thrown out of the theater."

"Yeah, my friends told me about that . . ."

"Oh."

At this point, our conversation suddenly seemed to hit a brick wall. I heard him take a deep breath before continuing, "Well, I guess you're wondering why I'm calling when I sounded so doubtful the other night."

"I was hoping you'd have second thoughts."

Apparently his blunt honesty virus was contagious.

"I couldn't stop thinking about how disappointed you looked when I told you not to expect to hear from me." He paused. "I decided that maybe we should go ahead and take a chance anyway, even though time is so short. What do you think?"

I couldn't believe he needed to ask! As far as I was concerned, the situation had long since passed beyond my control. I knew what I wanted: to spend time with him. *He's the one with decisions to make,* I thought—although I did find it a bit disconcerting, with all that we'd already said and also left unsaid, to realize how much those decisions might affect my life. At the same time, I was thrilled and a bit overwhelmed by his sudden change of heart, so he'd barely finished asking my opinion before I blurted out my answer: "Yes! We should definitely go ahead. What have we got to lose?"

"Plenty. But never mind—the telephone isn't the place to discuss this. I'd rather do it in person. That's why I'm calling: to invite you to a party at my house tomorrow night. Most of the Executive Committee will be there, as well as some other friends. I'd like you to come. Will you?"

"Of course!" My disappointment over our lost movie date vanished like mist in warm sunshine.

"Good. You'll need a ride, won't you?"

"I guess so . . . Where do you live?"

"A couple of miles outside of town. I could ask someone else to get you, but I'd rather do it myself. I'll meet you in front of your dorm at seven o'clock. Okay?"

"Sure! And thanks!"

"Don't thank me until it's over and you've decided whether or not it was worth it."

"What a pessimist you are!"

"Not a pessimist—just cautious," he answered, but it sounded to me as if he'd said it with a smile.

The moment I hung up, my friends crowded around, deluging me with questions, and I was already wondering how I was going to survive until the next evening.

Derek lived down a long, bumpy, dirt road in a small white house he rented from a local farmer. On the way there, he told me that some of his guests had already arrived.

"But we'll manage to find some time for ourselves," he promised. "We need to talk."

Right then, talking didn't seem very important, I was content just to be off campus with him, with the whole evening ahead of us. And in truth, the prospect of discussing our possible future relationship made me rather jittery.

When we arrived, most of the Executive Committee was already there, and none of them seemed particularly surprised to see us together. It was twilight, and someone had built a huge bonfire in the front yard. People were standing around outside in the gathering darkness, talking and enjoying the spring weather and the fire's warmth. Behind the house, a stone wall edged a dense fir grove. The air was redolent with the scent of pines and wood smoke.

No other houses were in sight.

Derek greeted his guests and then invited me to come inside, saying that he wanted to show me his place. It was strange to enter his private world, and I belatedly realized that it was the first time I'd visited anyone in Bloomington who wasn't living in a dormitory room—which made his invitation seem all the more intimate.

Derek's house was furnished with uncluttered simplicity. Although I was still struggling with the strangeness of being there with him, I immediately felt comfortable. The knotty pine walls, decorated with prints of modern paintings, glowed warm in the candlelight. A bookcase covered one wall and an antique clock stood on the mantle. Facing the fireplace was a rich brown corduroy sofa.

What a wonderful place! I thought, thoroughly envious. *School would be almost bearable if I had a retreat like this.*

But I kept these thoughts to myself as I followed Derek through the rest of his tiny house. There was a small bedroom directly off the living room. Beyond that was a long, narrow hall that served as an art gallery, which led to a bathroom and a galley-like kitchen in the back of the house.

"Well, what do you think?" he wanted to know when our tour was completed.

I felt that he was asking for more than my approval of his house.

We were standing very close together in his tiny kitchen. Our eyes met and held.

"I love it!" I breathed.

After that, neither of us said a word: we just stood there, smiling into each other's eyes.

Unfortunately, Paul Stillman, the club's vice president and jug band impresario, chose that moment to intrude. Clumping noisily down the hall, he burst into the room with, "Hey, Derek, where the hell's the beer!"

"Damn! I knew I forgot something."

"You went all the way into town and back, and didn't get the beer?" He grinned. "Oh, well, at least you got your girl."

I knew I was blushing.

Derek started to apologize, but Paul put up a hand. "Don't worry about it. I'll go myself if you promise to hold the troops at bay."

"Thanks, Paul. Take my car."

As soon as he was gone, Derek turned to me. "I guess it's time I started acting like a host . . . Stay with me, will you, Meri?"

"Of course."

We joined the others outside, and there was plenty of good-natured teasing about Derek's social priorities. Soon more people were arriving, many of them with instruments, and everyone cheered when Paul drove up with a trunkful of six packs.

After that, there was hardly a moment when Derek wasn't busy serving refreshments and talking to his guests, but he always remained aware of my presence, letting me know that he was thinking of me, even if it was just with a smile.

I said little, preferring instead to listen to the conversations that were going on all around me, making occasional comments when they seemed appropriate. I was filled with happiness just to be there, and I wrapped my contentment around me like a cloak, soaking up the serenity of the place and enjoying the lovely spring night.

The sky glittered with stars. Red sparks from the fire rose up against a jet-black backdrop of pine trees, swirling and mingling for a brief moment in the diamond-studded sky before they winked out forever.

Later, Derek and several friends who regularly played bluegrass music together, took out their instruments and gave an impromptu concert. Their music flowed around us, drifting off into the night.

And then, suddenly, it was time to go. The next day was a school day, and my curfew was fast approaching. I turned to Derek, who at that point was sitting beside me on the stone wall, taking a break from music making. "I should really go home now," I said, my voice full of regret.

"Is it really that late?" he asked.

I nodded.

"Damn the dormitories and their damn lockout!" he said, surprising me with his vehemence.

I sighed. "I agree. But it's a fact of life."

"It's just that we never had a chance to talk."

"Oh, well, that gives us something to look forward to next time . . ." It was less a statement than a suggestion. "Do you know if anyone's going back yet? I need a ride."

"I'll drive you home myself."

"I don't want to take you away from your guests," I said, hoping that he wouldn't believe me.

"They'll do just fine without me." He sounded rather grim.

As we drove away, I gazed wistfully back at the party. "It looks like your friends will be here all night."

He gave a short, mirthless bark of laughter. "No doubt about it."

"I wish I could stay."

"So do I."

We were silent during the return trip. My mind was full of images of the evening, and he seemed preoccupied with his own thoughts. Before long, the country road had widened, and we were entering the familiar outskirts of town. When he stopped near my dorm, I turned to say good night.

"Thank you for a wonderful evening, Derek. I'm glad you asked me." I started to open the car door.

"Wait!" His hand closed over mine. "I don't want you to go! There's so much to talk about and so little time. The party just wasn't the place for it. Can I see you again . . . soon?"

"Yes!" That one word left me breathless.

Then neither of us seemed to know what else to say. We just sat there, wordless, our hands clasped. His felt warm and reassuring.

"I'd better go," I finally said. "It's almost eleven."

"I guess I'll let you go—for now." He squeezed my hand and then released it.

I ran all the way back to the dorm, but I wasn't sure if my feet ever touched the ground.

"He's toying with you, Meri," Shennandoah said, "the way a cat plays with a mouse. You know he is." Her eyes, watching me over the rim of her coffee cup, were full of concern. "You're in way over your head."

We were having dinner at a small restaurant in downtown Bloomington. The food wasn't particularly good and I, for one, couldn't really afford it, but at least it got us out of the dorm.

"Maybe so . . . But it just doesn't feel that way." What could I say to make her understand? "Shen, I can't explain why—you'll just have to take it on faith—but I'm certain of one thing: Derek would never purposely hurt me or lie."

"Then why haven't you heard from him?"

I winced.

"It's been nearly a week since his party," she persisted.

"I'm sure there's an explanation."

"Of course there is: Freshmen have no business getting involved with graduate students. Graduates are never serious about undergraduates, they just take advantage of them."

This was fine hypocrisy, coming from her! "Shen, that's so cynical!"

"It may be cynical, but it's also realistic."

And it was true: Derek had disappeared, and nothing I said in his defense would alter that fact. I was worried and hurt, afraid that I might, indeed, have made a fool of myself.

"Forget Derek—there are lots of other men," Shennandoah was saying.

"I'm sick of men!" I cried, sure that she was about to suggest her usual remedy: another visit to the International House. "Thanks for your concern, but I don't need any more men."

"No, I suppose you don't." She paused. "Why are they all such a pain?"

"Are you having problems, too?"

She nodded, suddenly miserable.

"Tell me."

"Forget it. You've got enough troubles of your own."

"Come on, Shen. It'll be a relief to have something else to think about besides my own misery."

We paid for dinner and began walking back towards campus. On the way, she admitted that she and Toshio were becoming seriously involved indeed; in fact, the previous evening, he'd asked her to marry him.

"Did you accept?"

"I said I'd have to think about it."

"Good. Don't rush into anything."

"Why, oh why, do I still have doubts?" she moaned.

"Barry?" I asked, more out of a desire to let her know I cared than because I thought he was in any way responsible.

"Yes," she said, so quietly that I had to strain to hear her.

"He's still writing?"

She nodded. "He's very persuasive."

"About what? A serious relationship?" That certainly didn't sound like the Barry I knew.

"Yes. Well, no. Not exactly. He wants us to spend a weekend together, to see how we get along."

"Oh, Shen, don't count on anything with him. I know he's my friend, but . . . Well, he has a way of wriggling out of things just when you think you've got him pinned down."

"You've said so before, but he doesn't seem like that in his letters. He really wants us to be together. Still, I suppose I should begin by dealing with the problem at hand, which is Toshio."

"I think that's very sensible."

"But whenever I think about Toshio, I start thinking about Barry—not to mention all the other men I haven't met. I'd hate to have to give them all up for marriage."

"Then maybe Toshio isn't the right person."

"But what if he is? Oh, Meri, I'm so confused! And that's where I thought you might be able to help me out."

"Me! How?"

"You could spend some time with us. You know, talk to him, see what you think of us together—how we get along, stuff like that. Then you can tell me if I should marry him."

"You shouldn't decide something as important as that based on *my* opinion!"

"I won't. I promise. But every little bit of advice helps. Will you do it? Please?"

"Okay," I said, although I wasn't at all sure I wanted to accept the responsibility. "Do you have something definite in mind?"

As it happened, she did. "Tomorrow night, Toshio and I have a date to go to the movies. I want you to come along."

"Gosh, Shen, don't you think Toshio might not like that?"

"I'm sure it'll be fine. And afterwards, we're invited for tea at the house of a Japanese couple. I'm sure they wouldn't mind if you joined us."

Her request was becoming more complicated and problematic by the moment. Still, despite my reservations, I agreed to her plan, provided Toshio and his friends didn't object.

After all, it wasn't as if I had any other, more pressing social engagements.

<hr />

Shennandoah and Toshio met me at my dorm at precisely seven thirty. They were certainly a striking, if unusual, couple—Shennandoah tiny, blond, and all-American with her softly rounded curves, and Toshio tall, gaunt, and angular. He wore a conservative, charcoal-gray business suit, immaculately tailored, and a dark red tie; and his graying hair was cropped very short. His manner towards both of us was quite proper, if somewhat distant, and I suspected that he wasn't at all pleased to be saddled with a chaperone. I guessed him to be somewhere in his late thirties or early forties.

On the way to the Oriental Studies building, there was no conversation; instead we received a lecture on *The Seven Samurai*, the movie we were about to see. Briefly, Professor Yamamoto explained the history and customs of the samurai warrior sect, as well as life in feudal Japan. He went on to tell us about the Japanese filmmaking tradition, and how we should view this movie in particular. It was a fascinating discourse, but the way it was delivered left no doubt in my mind that he considered both of us to be his intellectual inferiors—and possibly even culturally disadvantaged barbarians.

Amused but also rather insulted, I finally dared to interrupt with a series of questions about several aspects of what he'd just told us about Japanese movies. I wasn't searching for enlightenment; I was simply hoping to knock him off his professorial pedestal and make him relax so he would talk *to* us instead of down *at* us.

He hesitated, regarding me with solemn curiosity, before answering. When he finally spoke, it was more as to an equal than an underling. Apparently I had earned the right to at least a modicum of respect.

I enjoyed the movie. Its concepts were familiar in some ways, entirely alien in others. It was an experience somewhat akin to sampling a foreign cuisine for the first time and finding it to be tasty, but definitely different.

We were joined after the movie by Toshio's friend and associate, a darkly handsome, aggressively intelligent, and very vocal New York Jew who turned out to be one half of the "Japanese couple" who had invited Toshio and Shennandoah to tea. The four of us walked across campus, discussing the movie, until we reached the apartment complex that housed many of the married professors.

There, we were greeted by a Japanese woman who was wearing a traditional kimono and an elaborate Asian-style coiffure. Standing in the doorway, backlit by the bright lights of her living room, she was a lovely and exotic creature.

She bowed very low to her husband and Toshio, and delivered what sounded like quite a formal speech in Japanese. Then she turned to Shennandoah and myself and, in halting English, punctuated by a great many little bows, bade us welcome. This accomplished, she indicated that we should enter. But before I could step across the threshold, Shennandoah grabbed my elbow. "Hey, your shoes!" she hissed.

Puzzled, I looked down and saw that everyone else had placed their footwear in a neat row beside the front door. Immediately stooping down to remove my shoes, I vowed that from then on that I would watch carefully; I didn't want to make any more embarrassing social gaffes.

Meanwhile, Toshio's friend Sammy was speaking to his wife. In harsh, guttural tones, he barked what sounded like military commands, and she went scampering from the room. Yet when he turned to us, chameleon-like, he was once again our affable American host. With gracious words and a kindly smile, he indicated that we should join him at a long, low table. I carefully copied the others when they knelt on the carpeted floor.

As talk began, I glanced surreptitiously around the room. It was completely Japanese, down to the last detail, without any reminders of Western culture.

Sammy must have noticed my silent inventory. "Well, how about it, Meri? What do you think of my place?" he suddenly demanded, interrupting something he'd been telling Toshio.

"It's wonderful!" I said. "I feel like I've stepped into another world."

He beamed.

I considered how to phrase my next question without offending him. "Have you always been a Japanese American?"

He laughed, as I'd hoped he would. "Not at all. I grew up

in Brooklyn. But right after the war I was stationed in Japan, and that's when I was bitten by what I guess I'd have to call the 'Oriental Bug.'"

Just then his wife came gliding back into the room bearing a handsome red and black lacquer ware tray that contained many small, artistically arranged dishes. With meticulous care, she set her offering down on the table in front of her husband, left the room again, and came back with a teapot and four cups. Kneeling, she placed these items on the table beside the food.

Throughout her preparations, Sammy continued his monologue about his experiences in Japan. I was utterly distracted, torn between watching his wife's humble domestic rituals and paying polite attention to my host's story. Sammy, however, seemed completely oblivious to his own wife's presence as he told us about how, once his tour of duty was over, he'd decided to stay on and study the Japanese language and culture. Soon after, he had met and married Michiko.

Meanwhile, Michiko was pouring our tea with silent concentration. The task completed, she shuffled over to a corner of the room directly behind her husband's back, squatted down, and tucked her hands neatly into her kimono sleeves. Her gaze was riveted on the floor, and I was unable to catch her eye.

Was wifely subservience a Japanese custom, I wondered, or was it a unique but peculiar aspect of this couple's personal relationship?

Still chatting amiably, my host and friends began to eat. As unobtrusively as possible, I watched what they were doing. I had never used chopsticks before, but I wasn't about to admit that. I observed for several moments, thankful that as both an artist and a violinist I had been trained to execute complex manual tasks, and when at last I picked up my own chopsticks, I felt that my performance was awkward but acceptable.

My first reaction to Japanese food was keen interest. There were so many textures and flavors that were new to me—and although the rice was certainly familiar, even that had an unusual, sweet flavor. Everything was parceled out in elegant, bite-sized portions, and the food itself was prepared and displayed like pieces of art—it almost seemed like sacrilege to bite into it.

Meanwhile, talk continued around the table, still as if Michiko didn't exist—about Sammy's interest in the Orient, about Toshio's language students, of which Shennandoah was one, and once again about the movie—but for me, the forgotten woman was a definite presence, silent and disturbing.

Abruptly, Sammy confronted me. "You're so quiet, Meri. You haven't said a word since we started eating." He leaned toward me, the intense interest in his eyes quite disconcerting—and, in my mind, more than a little bit inappropriate.

"I'm studying art," I said, flustered and blushing.

But he persisted. "That's not good enough; I want to find out all about you."

While my friend and her presumptive fiancé continued their own conversation, I made an awkward attempt to describe my various classes to Sammy, convinced that they were of little real interest to him, and unhappily aware that there was a not-so-subtle undercurrent of sexual interest coming from his side. He kept leaning closer, grinning and winking, as if we had some sort of private understanding.

Then, much to my relief, the tea ran out and Sammy turned aside to grunt a brusque word over his shoulder to Michiko, who jumped to her feet and hurried away to refill the teapot.

I was becoming more uneasy by the moment. Michiko's self-effacing behavior and her husband's unsubtle flirtatiousness made it almost impossible for me to pay attention to Toshio and Shennandoah—which was, after all, my purported mission. So I was quite relieved when Shennandoah suddenly announced that it was time for us to go. Michiko showed us to the door, and I was grateful to escape, unescorted, into the cool night. Toshio stayed behind.

"Well, Meri, what do you think?" Shennandoah immediately demanded, when Michiko shut the door after us.

"It was interesting," I said, unable to stop thinking about

Sammy—and his wife. I kept seeing her crouched in that dim corner like a lonely waif.

"You don't sound very enthusiastic."

"Shen, what about Michiko?" I blurted out.

"What *about* Michiko?"

"Is she always like that?"

"Like what? Oh, I see what you mean—sort of quiet and unobtrusive, and in the background and all . . . Toshio says that's the way Japanese wives are supposed to behave."

"Do you think she's happy?"

"It's what she expects." She sighed. "I admit, at first it really bothered me. I tried to make friends and get her to talk. But Sammy told Toshio that I shouldn't—that I was embarrassing her. So I stopped trying."

"How much of that do you think was Sammy, and how much what she wanted?"

"I'm sure it was her. Why do you ask?"

"I was just wondering what it would be like to be treated that way . . . Is that what Toshio will expect if you marry him?"

"I don't know. I never thought about it. And I've certainly never asked."

"Well, you'd better! Michiko's little more than a human doormat."

She laughed. "That's *her* problem. Believe me, nothing like that is going to happen to me! All I want is to be a good wife and take care of Toshio and our children. And eventually, in a few years, when the kids are older, I'll have my career . . . Toshio wants to move back to Japan, and he says that lots of people over there need physical therapy. And many of them are heathens, so I'll be able to teach them the Word of God as well as cure their bodies."

"Sounds like you've already made up your mind."

"I guess I have."

We were entering Wells Quad, and there wasn't time to say much more. Somehow, I had to make her think about the reality of being married to Toshio, yet I wasn't at all sure that she really wanted my opinion, despite what she'd said.

"Well, there *is* one other thing I'll have to check out before I agree to marry him," Shen said.

"What's that?"

"One of these nights—it'll have to be when no one's likely to be doing bed checks—I'll have to sneak out of the dorm and go to Toshio's. Before I make any decisions, I've got to find out what he's like in bed."

"Oh!" Unexpectedly, I felt queasy. Was it the strange food I'd just eaten?

Or was it because the moment I heard her plan, I immediately thought of Derek?

The days since Derek's party turned into a week. Just when I had finally given up all hope, he called again.

"You must be wondering where I disappeared to."

"I thought maybe you'd decided to run off and go home to California a bit early," I said, trying for cautious humor.

"No, I didn't." He cleared his throat. "I want to tell you why I didn't call, when I'm sure I led you to believe I would."

"Well, I *did* wonder . . ."

"It wasn't that I didn't want to see you!" he said in a rush. "I started to pick up the phone a dozen times every day. But something always stopped me."

Bracing myself for disappointment, I waited in silence for him to continue.

"I don't think we should see each other again," he said at last, confirming my sense of impending doom. "This isn't going to work."

"Why not?" I had no idea how I managed to sound so calm when my emotions were tossing about like a boat in heavy seas. A week earlier he had seemed so eager—and then he'd vanished. Now, here he was again, and I had the distinct impression that he'd frightened himself off by feeling more interested than he'd intended.

I wasn't sure whether to be happy to discover that he was as drawn to me as I was to him, or depressed because he seemed about to end our possible relationship before it had even begun.

"Okay," he was saying, "here it is: last Sunday night, when I drove you home, I was very upset that you had to go back to the dorm so early."

"So was I."

"Those dumb rules!"

"They *are* dumb."

"And then, in the car, when I held your hand, there were so many things I wanted to tell you, to explain what a complicated person I am. And I wanted to kiss you. But when you left, you seemed satisfied with just that little bit of closeness . . . Well, I'm not! I want more from you than you can possibly imagine."

"But, Derek, I—"

"No. Let me finish. There's so much you don't know about me. Things that might make you uncomfortable."

"What could you possibly tell me that would make me uncomfortable?"

"For one thing, I'm twenty-five. Did you know that?"

"I made a pretty good guess. So you're six years older than me—so what?"

"That's six years' worth of experiences you haven't had."

"Such as?"

"I've been married before . . . when I was quite young." He paused. "Well, doesn't that bother you?" he demanded, when I didn't respond.

"No . . ." I said slowly as I digested and then accepted this unexpected piece of information. "No, I don't think it matters too much. Anyone can make a mistake, Derek. It doesn't have to be the end of the world."

"Well, it really screwed me up for a couple of years, I can tell you that. And I'm still not sure I want to get that involved with anyone ever again . . . But how can you possibly understand?"

"I do."

"Really?" He sounded surprised, as if he'd expected a different response.

"It explains why you're having so much trouble figuring out what we should do—and how hard it must be for you to tell me all these personal things."

"Then you agree with me?"

I felt as if I was fighting for my life: one false step, one wrong word, and it would be over. And that wasn't what I wanted!

"Yes. And no . . ." I searched for just the right way to say this. "Whenever two people get involved, they make themselves vulnerable. After all, the better someone knows you, the easier it is for them to hurt you, purposely or by accident. But I don't agree that the best way to prevent that from happening is to avoid involvements at all costs. That's impossible. You'll never be happy if you live your life that way."

"But this isn't just about me!" he protested. "I'm thinking of you, too. If we go on seeing each other, I guarantee we'll get involved—very involved. We won't be able to stop it from happening."

How could his words make me frightened and thrilled, all at the same time?

"And everything will be new for you," he went on. "What if you expect more from me than I'm able to give? Both of us could get terribly hurt."

"I certainly don't want you to be hurt by anyone, ever again," I said earnestly. "But I'm not afraid for myself. If that happens, it's part of life." I was beginning to panic, afraid I'd said too much, or not enough—or the wrong thing.

"But we haven't got time!" Derek insisted. "We'll only be able to begin finding out about each other before the semester ends and we have to go our separate ways. All we can possibly accomplish in a couple of weeks is frustrating ourselves because we've begun a relationship that we can't continue."

We argued like that for several more minutes, each of us hoping, I suspected, to convince the other that it was possible to go on seeing each other.

At last, Derek said wearily, "Listen, Meri, there's no way we can work this out over the telephone. Let's do this: we'll see how we feel as we go along. As we musicians say, we'll play it by ear."

I agreed. What else could I do? After all, it was more than I'd hoped for, considering the way this conversation had begun.

"I won't call you again," he told me, "but I'll see you Wednesday night at the CABS concert. We'll see what happens then. In the meantime, think about what I said tonight. Okay?"

And so, in this extremely roundabout way, it seemed to me that we had decided to continue on—for a little while longer, at least.

chapter 22: derek

Derek looked exhausted. He told me he was fighting off a cold and hadn't slept well. For that matter, neither had I. I was too nervous about what might happen that evening, which I realized might very well turn out to be our last one together.

We sat, neither of us saying much, in the front row of the same auditorium where Dr. Sellers had offered up his infamous Evolutionary Special, waiting for the concert to begin. It was an emergency event—a hastily organized fundraiser.

Two weeks earlier, Daniel had called to say that both the president and vice president of our local chapter of the Young People's Socialist League had unexpectedly been arrested, charged by the University administration with conducting "subversive activities" on campus. A local judge had decreed that they could be held without bail.

In colleges all across the country, angry students were protesting and attempting to raise money for the YPSL officers' legal fees. It was a frightening incident, reeking of oppression in its most totalitarian form. Regardless of one's political leanings, there was no doubt that the two young men were being denied their basic constitutional rights. Ironically (though none of my friends were surprised by it), our school was the last in the country to organize, despite the fact that the arrests had been made on our own campus.

When he called, Daniel had wanted to know if I, as a member of the Executive Committee, would ask the Folksinging Club to sponsor a benefit performance for the Indiana University chapter of CABS (the Committee to Aid the Bloomington Students), and I was happy to finally be able to support one of his crusades.

The decision of the club officers was immediate and unanimous. We understood that the administration would not look kindly upon our efforts. Nonetheless, we felt a moral obligation to support YPSL—after all, any one of us, any suspect person or organization, might be next on the school's hit list.

The first half of the concert, although poorly attended, went well, and Derek was among the guest performers. But when he rejoined me at intermission, rather than sitting back down, he abruptly announced, "Let's get out of here."

He didn't sound in the least bit friendly.

We packed up his guitar and left it in his car. "Let's walk," was all he said.

He took the path away from the auditorium in rapid, angry strides, and I trotted after him, trying to keep up, feeling more uneasy by the moment, afraid of what he would say when he finally calmed down enough to speak to me. For I knew beyond a doubt that it was our problem that was responsible for his terrible mood.

Suddenly, up ahead of me, he sneezed. "Damn this miserable cold," he growled.

"If you feel that bad, maybe you should go home."

He looked back over his shoulder and immediately slowed down, allowing me to catch up with him. "Sorry, Meri, I didn't mean for you to have to chase after me."

"Are you all right?"

"No. And it's not just this stupid cold."

Oh god, here it comes! I thought, bracing myself for the worst.

"I'm sorry I'm so grumpy." He sighed. "I had another fight with my thesis advisor this afternoon, and this time he really has me worried."

"What happened?" I said, infinitely relieved to learn that it wasn't necessarily our unresolved relationship that was making him so irritable.

"He's giving me a hell of a time because I'm writing about bluegrass music. He's one of those purists who think that any music written after the Pilgrims landed doesn't qualify as 'folk music.' Well, I suppose that's a bit of an exaggeration . . . Anyhow, you've heard some discussion about this at our club meetings. There's a certain amount of scholarly debate over what folk music actually is, and I've spent a couple of difficult years trying to convince him that bluegrass is a legitimate topic for a master's degree."

"Surely he wouldn't let you get this far along with your work if he didn't intend to accept it."

"Oh, he's made it perfectly clear he's going to accept it—in his own good time. He's already made me do a couple of major rewrites, and now he's looking at my latest revisions and suggesting more changes. Says it's for my own good. Ha!"

"It sounds like a nightmare."

"It is. The only thing that's keeping me sane is the support of one of my former teachers back in Berkeley—that and the fact that I've already gotten extremely positive responses from several scholars who've read the articles I've published in the folklore journals."

"If there's outside interest in your work, I can't imagine your advisor will dare to hold you back much longer."

"Probably not. But in the meantime, he's determined to make my life hell."

I was flattered that he was telling me his professional woes. In return, and to forestall any discussion of our possible—or impossible—future, I began talking about my own problems with the university, starting with my introduction to the school and Pixie. I told him I'd been aware from the start that I wasn't like most of my classmates, and how depressed I was by the prejudice that seemed to be an integral part of life at Indiana University.

"Believe me, after growing up in a liberal New York Jewish family, all this Indiana conservative nonsense is really hard to take," I complained. "But that's exactly what Pixie says I have to do: learn to take it. And I can't! I feel obligated to speak out, to take a stand on every issue—from integrated rooms to the reason for the CABS concert . . . And I know I'm a fool, because every time I stick my neck out, I get one step closer to ruining my chances of getting a scholarship next year, which is the only way I can afford to come back. My grades are fine, but my political affiliations stink!"

Derek seemed surprised by this outburst, but he didn't comment; he just kept walking along beside me, watching me intently.

I paused for a moment to catch my breath, and then went on. "Actually, to tell the truth, I'm not really sure I want to come back next year. Still, it would be nice to have a choice."

"If it's any comfort, you're not a minority of one around here, although I'm sure it must seem like it sometimes," he said with a bitter smile. "Lots of us feel the way you do, but we're so busy hanging on to our precious teaching assistantships that we've learned to suppress our consciences and keep our mouths shut—which isn't something to be proud of." He looked away.

"As for me, I'm looking forward to going back home and seeing my folks. I think of Indiana as a strange interlude, and I suspect it'll be that way for you, too . . . You know, if you're really thinking about changing schools, you might want to consider UC Berkeley. I'm sure you'd like it. Or would you prefer to go back to New York?"

"Definitely not! One thing this year at Indiana has done is give me is a taste of independence. There's no way I'm going home!" Amused by my own vehemence, I smiled. "Tell me about California. I have relatives in San Francisco, but I've never visited them."

He began describing his hometown, Berkeley, and it sounded like it was a lot more congenial place than Bloomington.

And so our walk continued, contrary to all of my pessimistic expectations. Before long, we were talking about our families and all of the other personal things two people tell each other when they're still getting to know one another. Time flew by. I had no idea where we were, and probably wouldn't have noticed if we'd walked right off campus and straight into the Pacific Ocean.

Eventually our discussion turned to music, which was an important part of both of our lives. I told him about the music festival and how happy I'd been there.

"So thanks to my musician friends, I decided to apply to IU," I said, summarizing a long explanation. "I was supposed to take music ed courses, only once I got here, I realized that the whole idea of teaching terrifies me."

"Why?" He seemed genuinely interested.

"The thought of standing up in front of a bunch of people and telling them what to do is repugnant. And the prospect of auditioning or performing for an audience scares the hell out of me."

"But you have a great voice. I noticed that right away, last fall, at our first Folksinging Club meeting. You sang so well, and I could hear you in spite of everyone else."

"I hate to be noticed," I muttered. "Except maybe once in a while . . ." I knew I was blushing.

Derek was smiling at me. I smiled shyly back.

"Well, in my case," he said, "I don't mind having an audience. I suppose I might have at first, but now I'm used to it. Still, when I'm performing, I sometimes get the uncanny sensation that all the audience sees is a façade. That each person sees a different 'me,' colored by his or her own fantasies, but no one ever knows who I really am. Maybe no one wants to. Maybe when I'm on stage I'm just someone for other people to hang their dreams on."

Abruptly, he stopped walking and faced me, his eyes challenging. "And what about you? You don't know much about me, but I'm sure I must seem very glamorous: president of the Folksinging Club and a graduate student. What are your fantasies? You're obviously attracted to me, but are you interested in the real-life, everyday person, or are you dazzled by what you imagine I'm like?"

He stood there in the middle of the footpath, this tall, lanky fellow with gold-rimmed eyeglasses, and I wondered exactly what it was that made him so attractive, so unique.

"What do you expect from me?" he was asking. "When I turn out to be an ordinary person with problems that are no different from anyone else's, will you still be interested?" He was out of breath by the time he'd finished, and even seemed somewhat embarrassed. His smile was a bit sheepish, but he didn't offer to take back anything he'd said.

His sudden intensity, almost anger, was startling, but as usual his directness challenged me to match his. I chose my next words with care, knowing that we were finally confronting his doubts about our possible relationship.

"I understand why you're asking those questions, Derek, but I'm not sure how to answer them . . . It's true: I don't know you very well, and of course I've filled in some of the blanks with my imagination. That's only natural. I'm sure you've filled in some 'blanks' about me, too. But I'm certainly not trying to invent some sort of glamorous movie-star fantasy about you."

Derek seemed about to interrupt, but he stopped himself and allowed me to continue.

"Sure I'm curious. I've never met anyone like you before. You're an intelligent, sensitive person who's afraid of getting hurt but not afraid to admit it. I admire your honesty—and that you've let me see behind what you call your 'glamorous façade.' That takes courage, and I appreciate it."

"It's not a question of courage," he said. "I told you before, it seems to me it's the only way to avoid getting badly hurt."

"Well, you may not call it courage, but most of the people I know hide behind their words. They're afraid to say anything direct. I suppose it's a way of protecting themselves. They purposely construct façades to cover up their fears and weakness."

As we began walking again, I thought about Daniel, the hard-bitten radical with his easily hurt feelings, defending himself with cutting words; Barry, who thrived on evasion; and then, unexpectedly, John, the master of neutrality. I had spent most of the school year trying to understand him, and I wasn't sure I would ever know all the answers. Besides, who was I to criticize? I had to admit that I hadn't been very honest with any of them either, or with myself, regarding my own feelings. Rather than trying to discuss our misunderstandings, I had purposely avoided all confrontations.

"You know, Derek," I mused aloud, "I can't help wondering if it isn't possible to be too honest. People don't always appreciate hearing the truth."

"You're right, of course," he said. "I know lots of people like that, and I don't feel comfortable with any of them."

"They probably don't feel comfortable with you either."

He laughed, and then, to my astonishment, reached for my hand. "They probably don't. But somehow I feel comfortable with you." He smiled. "I'm glad we've had this chance to talk. I feel much better."

In the course of our long conversation we had gone around campus in an enormous circle. We were nearly back at my dorm, and it was almost ten thirty. A walk that had begun at twilight was ending in darkness.

"You don't have to go in quite yet," Derek said when he noticed me checking my watch.

I didn't want our time together to end, not knowing if I'd ever see him again, or if we'd ever have a chance to talk the way we had these past few hours.

Why did we always seem to get into the most intriguing conversations on the nights when I had an eleven o'clock curfew?

On the other hand, after tonight, is there really anything left to say to each other, I wondered, *except good-bye?*

Still, even if I never saw him again, I would always have the memory of this evening. He was a fascinating person, one who demanded such uncompromising directness. His intelligence was a challenge—and I knew that I would never regret anything that came of our short, intense friendship.

Meanwhile, we were walking more slowly as we approached my dorm.

"Let's sit down," he said unexpectedly, interrupting my somber musings. "I think there's a bench over that way."

I peered at him in the darkness, trying to make out his expression.

Was this his way of setting the stage for telling me we'd come to the end of our first and last personal conversation?

Still holding my hand, he led me over to the cool stone bench. Inexplicably, as we sat down, he laughed, and I wondered what he was thinking. All of a sudden, he seemed like a total stranger. Even his voice sounded unfamiliar when he asked, "How would you feel about sharing my cold?"

A feeling of unreality crept over me.

"Sounds like fun!" I tried to say, attempting a joke, but the words wouldn't come out.

Derek's arm went around my shoulders, and he pulled me closer and kissed me before I could reply.

It wasn't a gentle kiss. I was acutely aware of the texture of his shirt, the roughness of his mustache, the damp, earthy smell of the shrubbery behind us, and the warmth of the spring air. It seemed to me then that the night somehow became darker and more private, contracting until it held just the two of us.

And then I began to understand the truth of his warnings. He was much more experienced than I was. His kisses were far more passionate and intimate than any I knew how to give, and my desires suddenly seemed vague and immature compared to his. I was uneasy about the way he was making me feel, and I was no longer quite so sure about what I wanted.

When, sometime later, I stumbled dizzily up the steps to Morrison Hall, my thoughts and senses were full of him. The ordinary appearance of the brightly lit lobby and the familiar faces of my dorm mates, superimposed over my inner turmoil, was disorienting. I discovered belatedly that I was covered with mosquito bites.

As Miss Bell closed the doors behind me, shutting out the night and all that it contained, I realized with a shock how narrowly I had missed being locked out.

Pixie glanced up from the papers she was grading when I entered our room.

"Gee, what are those red marks all over your neck?" she inquired, coming closer to inspect me.

I knew that I was blushing.

"I wonder what you've been doing?" she teased.

I was too embarrassed to reply.

"Oh, well, you don't have to say anything. Judging from your appearance, I can tell you had a good time."

Just then, I couldn't talk about Derek—not even with her. It was all too new and strange. Instead, I mumbled something about being tired and went straight to bed. But I couldn't sleep, even after Pixie had turned out the lights. I kept thinking about Derek and this sudden change in our relationship.

It was astonishing. Until tonight we had been cautiously inching our way along, testing every step before we took it as if we were crossing a rotting bridge. I had been expecting the end to come at any moment—yet now, suddenly, there we were on what I had to admit seemed like the brink of becoming lovers!

I wondered just how honestly we were going to be able to face that possibility.

chapter 23: mothers' weekend

The next night, Thursday, was art class, but it was impossible to concentrate on my work, and Mr. Jefferson might as well have been a waxwork dummy, for all the notice I took of him. I was totally preoccupied with thoughts of Derek: what had happened the night before, and what might happen the following evening, when he had asked me to have dinner with him at the home of his best friends.

By late Friday afternoon, I was so jittery that I could scarcely breathe.

When I walked out of Morrison Hall at 5:00 p.m., Derek was there, waiting for me. He took my hand and led me across the quad to a nearby parking lot, and only then, in the relative privacy of his car, did he kiss me.

Afterwards, he held me away at arm's length, inspecting me. "Well, did you miss me for two whole days?" A smile turned up the corners of his mouth.

Blushing must be my curse! I thought, almost angrily. But I smiled and said, "Yes. I missed you a lot."

"Good!" He started the car. "I missed you, too . . . I'm glad we're going to spend the evening with Cassie and Terry," he added, as we drove away from campus. "I've been working so hard on my thesis that I haven't had much time to see them lately, and they couldn't come to my party."

"Have you known them long?"

"We were undergraduates together at Berkeley. The three of us hit it off right away, as soon as we met. I know you'll like them."

The Stevenses lived in a small house on the outskirts of Bloomington, not far from where I'd attended my first and last YPSL meeting with Daniel back in September. Cassie Stevens greeted us at her front door and enveloped Derek in a hearty bear hug. Then she turned to embrace me.

"Hey, don't look so surprised, Meri," she said, grinning. "If Derek likes you, so do I. Consider yourself part of the family."

No one gave me a chance to fall into the shy silence that usually plagued me whenever I encountered strangers. Soon we were all seated on their front porch in creaky old rocking chairs, sipping frosty glasses of Cassie's homemade lemonade, and both of the Stevenses were plying me with questions about places and people in New York—which, it turned out, was Terry's home town.

Derek commented that he was beginning to feel as if all of his friends were from either New York or California.

"Well, of course they are!" Terry gloated, his eyes twinkling with mischief. "Haven't you noticed that the only people worth knowing around here are from either the East or West Coasts? We're the elite of Indiana University. I just hope the rest of the school realizes that and gives us our due."

"Don't be silly, Honey." Cassie gave her husband's arm a playful squeeze. "What will Meri think of us?"

But she needn't have worried: I already liked them.

Cassie asked about my musical interests—it turned out that she, too, was a musician. And then Derek and Terry started reminiscing about their undergraduate adventures, most of which seemed to revolve around sneaking Cassie into and out of dormitory windows.

"I had the toughest time convincing her to move out of the

dorm and into my apartment," Terry told me, winking broadly at Derek.

"Berkeley's changed a lot since then," Derek said. "No more dormitories—unless you're nutty enough to want to live in one. And they abolished curfews years ago."

Eventually, the four of us adjourned to the kitchen, where Derek, who was far more relaxed than I'd ever seen him, took charge. Cassie and I were assigned the task of preparing a salad; Terry was put to work chopping garlic, onions, and mushrooms for spaghetti sauce; and Derek insisted on doing the cooking. He looked so comical in Cassie's tall white chef's hat that I had to chuckle.

"Don't laugh at him," Cassie said with a pout, pretending to sulk. "That hat was part of my last year's Halloween costume, and if you embarrass him, he'll take it off. Then my feelings will really be hurt."

Derek was an enthusiastic chef, wielding a wooden spoon in one hand and a large glass of red wine, which he alternately drank and poured into the sauce, in the other.

I wondered aloud if that much wine in the spaghetti sauce could make a person drunk.

"Of course not!" was his emphatic reply. "Haven't you heard? Wine's an excellent remedy for the common cold. Here, have some of mine, Meri—it's supposed to be great for preventing them, too."

Our laughter was interrupted by the telephone.

"Hello?" Cassie's voice carried in to us from the hall. "Yes, this is Mrs. Stevens. Who are you? Oh! Yes I am, if it's any of your business . . . All right; just a minute." One hand over the receiver, she leaned into the kitchen. "Meri, it's for you."

With an uneasy, queasy feeling in the pit of my stomach, I took the phone.

"Hello?"

"Is this Meri Henriques?"

"Yes, Miss Bell."

"You recognized my voice! How nice. I'm just checking

up to make sure you're where you said you'd be. We can't be too careful about these things, now can we? . . . Meri? Are you still there?"

"Yes, Miss Bell."

"Good. Well, have a nice time, and make sure you're back before lockout."

When I hung up, Derek and his friends were watching me, their expressions carefully neutral.

"What was that all about?" Cassie finally asked.

"It was my dorm counselor," I admitted, so embarrassed about having to explain the school's demeaning dormitory regulations that I was on the verge of tears. "We're supposed to sign out whenever we go off campus—and leave an address and phone number where we can be reached. Also, there has to be a married woman present who's at least twenty-one."

"So that's why she asked me all those dumb questions," Cassie said. "When she asked if I was over twenty-one, I was tempted to tell her to go to hell."

"My god!" Terry exclaimed, "Berkeley was never that bad. It sounds like the Gestapo!"

Derek didn't say a word, but he looked very grim.

"I was afraid of what would happen if Miss Bell found out I'd gone off campus without letting her know," I went on, speaking mostly for his benefit, hoping he'd understand. "So I wrote that I was coming here. She must have looked up the address and phone number. I'm so sorry! I didn't think she'd actually call, or I wouldn't have—"

"I'm glad you did!" Cassie said, giving me a fierce, impulsive hug. "What an awful woman! Don't let her upset you, Meri. And in the future, any time you need to get off campus, feel free to sign out to our house. I'll cover for you wherever you are."

"Gee, thanks, Cassie, but I'd hate to get you in trouble."

"Nonsense! I'm more than old enough to take care of myself—just ask Miss Bell."

"Enough of this idiotic dormitory crap!" Terry growled. "Let's have dinner. I'm starving!"

It was a while before Derek's mood improved.

Dinner was delicious in spite of—or perhaps because of—the soused spaghetti sauce, and afterwards the four of us went to a drive-in movie, the first I'd ever been to. Terry drove, with Cassie beside him, and Derek and I sat in the back. However, when I returned to the dorm at midnight, I wasn't really sure which movie, if any, we'd seen.

Although it was late, Pixie was still out—visiting Rachel in her room, I guessed. I knew that she would never be so foolish or careless as to miss our curfew and get locked out of the dormitory.

I was glad to be alone. I needed privacy to think. In the silence of my room, I tried to come to terms with my conflicting emotions: happiness and worry, excitement and uncertainty, all jumbled together.

What was I going to do?

I sat on my bed with my head in my hands, trying to think it through.

Pixie came in. "Are you okay, Meri?" she asked the moment she saw me.

I looked up. "Yeah. I guess so."

"Trouble with Derek." It was a statement, not a question.

"Not exactly. Things are fine . . . Pixie?"

"Yes."

"How can I be happy and miserable, all at the same time?"

Chuckling, she sat down on the edge of my bed. "Want to talk about it?"

"I'm so confused!" I admitted, and then I sighed. "You already know a little bit about Derek. That I was interested in him all year, and that he's older than I am. Also, he's divorced." I took a deep breath. "None of that bothers me. But every time we're together, we seem to get more and more involved, just like he said we would."

"You like him a lot, don't you?" Her voice was kindly.

"Of course I do—he's the most interesting person I've ever met. I'm crazy about him!"

"So what's the problem? You like him, he likes you. That's the way these things are supposed to work out . . . Are you worried about going to bed with him?"

All I could do was nod.

"You know, I've never understood the big deal about virginity," she said, quite casually. "Surely you weren't planning on hanging on to yours forever?"

"No, but . . . Well, my parents taught me that it's not right to go around sleeping with just anybody."

"Derek isn't just anybody, is he?"

"Of course not! But they said you're supposed to really care about the person."

"You've already said you really care about Derek."

"But it's all so sudden!"

"Sometimes that's the way it happens."

"Why are you talking like this?" I suddenly flared. "We both know that girls like us don't go around sleeping with their boyfriends."

Her arched eyebrows went up another notch. "Is that so? What makes you so sure of that?"

"Who?" I demanded. "Anyone I know?"

She watched me without saying a word.

"Come on, tell me!" I took a guess. "Rachel?"

"Are you playing dumb or are you just plain naive? What do you think Rachel and Steve were doing all last summer? Holding hands? Of course not. They lived together."

"Oh. Well, Rachel isn't like the rest of us. She can get away with stuff we can't. Who else?"

Pixie didn't answer.

"Caralene?" I immediately answered my own question: "No, she wouldn't. She's a lady."

"She *is* a lady—but she's also a woman."

"Oh."

"What do you think all those people are doing out there in the bushes every night before lockout?"

"In the bushes? Really? Daniel told me that, but I thought he just said it to embarrass me."

"He was telling the truth."

"That's kind of cheap, isn't it?"

"I think so. But Derek isn't trying to drag you off into the bushes, is he? He respects you too much for that."

"I know he does, but—well, it's such a hard decision."

"Then don't make it. Wait and see what happens. When and if the time comes to choose, you'll know what's right."

"I hope so."

I wondered how she could be so sure—if she was speaking from personal experience. But I decided not to ask. It was really none of my business.

"Just remember," Pixie said, "what people say about morality and what they actually *do* about it are usually two different things."

"I'm beginning to realize that."

Smiling, she stood up.

"Thanks, Pixie."

"Don't worry. I'm sure everything will work out. From what you've said, Derek sounds like a really nice guy."

Lying in bed afterwards, it was easier for me to accept the direction that my relationship with Derek seemed to be going in. Somehow, the thought of ending our romance seemed far more drastic than breaking some hypocritical social taboo.

By the time I fell asleep, I realized that I was willing to follow my fate with Derek.

Whatever it might be.

Once a year, toward the end of the spring semester, the University invited all the mothers of its undergraduate coeds to spend a weekend in the dorm with their daughters. The purported object of this exercise was to give the mothers a chance to experience, firsthand, the university atmosphere—and also, not incidentally, to discover for themselves how extremely well cared for their precious daughters were.

The day after the Stevenses dinner party, Rachel's mother arrived.

Rose Perlman was a warm, compassionate woman—quite the opposite of what I'd expected, given the feistiness of her daughter. She was the archetypical Jewish mother, and I liked her right away. As soon as Rachel told her that my mother was unable to visit me, she appointed herself Official Substitute Mother and invited me to join Rachel and herself for a day of shopping.

I was touched by Mrs. Perlman's generosity, and very grateful to have something to do besides brood over my entanglement with Derek.

It was a lovely spring day, warm without the mugginess that sometimes occurred at that time of year. The three of us spent several happy hours wandering through shops in the local business district, where Rachel tried on scarves and jewelry and sampled cosmetics and perfume. Mrs. Perlman looked at coats. I vacillated between buying a record or a paperback book, and instead ended up choosing a willow leaf that had been dipped in liquid nitrogen and then molten silver.

It was a trivial, relaxing way to spend the day. But as the afternoon drew to a close, I once again found myself preoccupied with thoughts of Derek. We had arranged to meet at another Folksinging Club event that evening, and I couldn't help but wonder what would happen afterwards.

"Oh, look!" Mrs. Perlman exclaimed, forcing me back to the present. "A Howard Johnson's. Their food can't be too bad, no matter what you girls say about Indiana cooking. Let's have dinner. My treat."

A real meal! Rachel and I promptly accepted.

Inside, it was just like every other Howard Johnson's I'd ever been in. We sat in a booth with bright orange vinyl cushions and ordered dinner. Lost in a daydream of the previous evening, when the waitress asked me what I wanted, I promptly answered: "Spaghetti!"

Then I laughed. However, rather than admit that I'd been daydreaming about Derek, I told Rachel and her mother about my lifelong passion for pasta and how, as a child, my father had nicknamed me "The Spaghetti Queen." Then, after my discourteous lapse, I forced myself to pay scrupulous attention to and participate in the ongoing conversation with Rachel and her mother. I didn't want to be an ungracious or ungrateful guest.

The waitress returned with our food—and I gasped in horror when I saw what she had set before me: a heaping platter of limp, pasty white spaghetti that looked for all the world like a plateful of pale white slugs, topped by a gooey brown mound of baked beans. (I didn't even want to think about what *that* looked like!)

Rachel's mother commented on the peculiarity of the dish, and Rachel made a joke about Indiana's backward culinary ways. Unfortunately, I was the one who had to eat the stuff!

I nearly gagged on my first mouthful. I was already feeling queasy, no doubt due to nervousness about my upcoming date with Derek, compounded by PMS, and I immediately realized that, impolite or not, there was no way I was going to be able to force that slop down.

I apologized to Mrs. Perlman, who urged me to order something else. But rather than waste any more of her money, I decided to forgo the meal, and instead spent my time consuming large quantities of milk and talking with my hostesses while they ate the grilled cheese sandwiches they had so sensibly ordered.

On the way back to campus, I tried to thank Rachel and her mother for their kindness, but I wasn't sure how sincere I sounded. My thoughts were already racing ahead to Derek.

I left them standing together at the top of the steps of Morrison Hall, waving good-bye as I walked away. I felt a bit lost, as if they were seeing me off on a long, uncertain journey.

Derek didn't look at all well. His cold seemed to have taken a turn for the worse since the night before.

I asked him how he felt.

"Lousy! Woge ub dis bordig feelig terrible."

I had difficulty understanding him; besides having an obviously stuffy nose, his speech was strangely slurred. He also seemed to be having trouble with his balance. It took me a moment to decipher what he was trying to tell me: that he'd awakened that morning feeling awful.

He grinned lopsidedly, and I mentally translated his next words: "Don't feel too bad now, though. Started in right away on my favorite home remedy: shot of whiskey every hour or so. It really helps." He sneezed, and then he giggled. "Must've had about half a quart so far today. Sort of makes you forget how bad you feel . . . Until the next day, that is."

My uneasiness intensified.

Derek dozed through the first half of the concert. I hoped the nap would do him good. He roused himself at the beginning of intermission and turned to me.

"Too hot in here," he mumbled. "Need to go outside."

The fresh air apparently revived him, and before long he was pacing back and forth across the parking lot, slapping his forearms and taking deep breaths. In the darkness, he turned to look at me, considering.

"I don't feel like staying for the rest of the concert," he said. "Do you?"

"Not really."

And then came the words I'd known I'd hear sometime in the course of that evening: "Want to go to my place?"

The critical moment had come a lot sooner than I'd expected. For a heartbeat I hesitated, taking silent inventory, and then I shrugged.

"Sure. I'll be glad to drive if you don't feel well enough."

In silence, we walked to his parked car.

We left town without another word. While Derek carefully negotiated the dark country roads, concentrating on the curves,

I thought to myself that this was turning out to be a strange evening indeed—not at all what I'd expected, with Derek sick and more than a little bit drunk.

As for myself, I was very nervous. Where was that inner certainty I was supposed to feel?

But when we got out of the car at his house, the distinctive, intensely lovely atmosphere of that place enfolded me like a warm comforter, and immediately I felt calmer. The smell of the pine woods, the sound of the frogs and crickets down by the creek, and the faint tang of wood smoke somehow gave me the sensation that I was coming home.

Hand in hand, we entered the cold house—quietly, so as not to disturb the peace of the night. Derek lit some candles, which he kept by the front door.

"I'll have the fire going in just a minute," he said, and he sounded much more like himself again, not the sleepy, drunk stranger of earlier in the evening. "Should warm things up pretty quickly."

He went outside and came back, stamping his feet, with an armload of firewood and kindling. Then he crouched down on his hearth and began to build a fire. Hugging my coat around me, I went to stand beside him, and he glanced up, smiling.

The wood smoldered and caught.

Derek straightened up with a satisfied grunt, rubbing his hands together, and put one arm around me. We stood like that for several minutes, gazing into the flames. Then he turned to me with a private, almost shy smile, and kissed me once, gently.

"So here we are, with no one else around and all the time in the world," he whispered, his lips just brushing mine. "Are you afraid?"

I looked into his eyes and shook my head.

"I'm glad." He gave me a quick, hard hug. "Make yourself comfortable while I put on some records."

The sound of a Vivaldi concerto came drifting down the hallway. When Derek returned, he had a drink in his hand.

"This is for purely medicinal purposes," he assured me,

setting it down on a small table by the sofa. He took off his red and black lumberjack coat and hung it over the back of a chair. "Would you like some?"

Once again I shook my head, not trusting myself to speak.

He came over to where I was still standing by the fire and led me by the hand to the sofa, pulling me down beside him.

"Are you warm enough to take off your coat?"

I said yes, and he helped me out of it. And then we were in each other's arms.

When he kissed me, I felt the tension in his wiry body, tasted the bitterness of alcohol on his breath. His face was rough and unshaven and his mustache bruised my mouth, but I didn't care. I was swept up in the immediate, fierce intensity of his passion.

After a while, he took off his eyeglasses. Without them, he seemed terribly defenseless and vulnerable.

In what seemed like no time at all, we were lying entangled on the sofa, the thick corduroy cool and soft against my hot skin. His body was so strange, so hard and angular, so different from mine.

Now he was more gentle, and less rushed. In a vague way I knew that he had taken off my dress and most of my underwear, and that somehow most of his clothing was also lying scattered on the floor beside the sofa.

Somehow, in the passage of that timeless eternity, the fire had burned down low, leaving the room in slowly gathering darkness. The stack of records had long since finished playing, and now the only sound in the room was the hiss and crackle of glowing coals in the grate.

We were so close, and soon all the mysteries would be solved.

"Derek," I murmured. I was reluctant to speak but felt that I had to. "I don't know what to do."

His laugh was ironic, a sound that was as quiet as the rest of the room. "Don't worry, I'll take care of everything . . . Will you wait for me?"

"Of course."

His mouth sought mine. "I'll be right back."

I lay on the sofa, relaxed and a little bit dazed, watching him go. I listened to his bare feet retreating down the hall and into the bathroom. Then he turned on the light and closed the door.

It felt so strange to be lying there in his living room. Strange and somehow right.

How had Pixie known?

For several moments, I looked at Derek's glasses, discarded on the table by my head, and then my eyes moved around the room, taking in the warm wood walls, the embers glowing in the fireplace, the open door to the bedroom and, beyond that, the bed.

His bedroom windows faced east. Did the rising sun wake him each morning, I wondered? If it did, I would never know—never be there to share it with him. I would be back in my own bed in the dorm, safe from Miss Bell's prying eyes. She might suspect, but she could never be sure . . .

Idly, thinking of her watchdog mentality, I glanced down at my wristwatch. "JESUS CHRIST!!!" I shouted before I could stop myself.

The bathroom door crashed open and Derek came running down the hall in his boxers.

"My god, Meri, what . . . ?"

"Jesus Christ!" I shrieked like an idiot. "It's twenty minutes to twelve!"

"OH, MY GOD!!!"

"The dorm. I'll be locked out! What am I going to do?"

"Get up!" Derek commanded, pulling me to my feet.

The two of us ran around the living room, getting in each other's way, wrestling with our clothing, finding my purse, his glasses, our coats. In some other time and place, it would have been the stuff of high comedy—but not today.

Seconds later, Derek was propelling me out the front door. Shoes in hand, we raced for the car, yelping in pain as the sharp gravel bit into our bare feet. Before the car doors were properly closed, we were lurching down the driveway.

"Derek," I groaned, "how did this happen? We'll never get back in time."

"Oh, yes, we will!" His face was set in a grim scowl, and he gripped the steering wheel like a drowning man clinging to a life raft. "I'll get you there in time if it kills me!"

We raced down deserted country roads, jolting over potholes, tires squealing around corners. Soon we careened onto the county highway heading back toward Bloomington.

I didn't dare look at the speedometer.

My watch said eleven fifty-six.

Incredibly, we arrived in the dorm parking lot just as Miss Bell was starting to pull the big front doors shut. There wasn't even time to say goodnight. I jumped out of the car and raced up the steps, still clutching my shoes. Once safely inside, I turned back to wave good-bye, but it was too late: Miss Bell had already locked the doors behind me.

Out of breath and trembling with fright and a rush of adrenaline, stunned by my narrow escape, I started walking shakily back upstairs to my room.

Pixie was grading papers when I came in.

"Meri! What are you doing here? I thought you were with Derek."

"I was."

"What happened? Did you two have a fight?"

"A fight?" I repeated, feeling angrier and more cheated by the minute now that the danger was safely past. "No, we didn't have a fight!"

"Then what went wrong?"

I was amazed by her denseness. "Nothing went wrong—except that it's midnight, and I had to come back . . ."*And I'm still a virgin*, I told her silently, in the privacy of my mind. It was something I would never have dared to say aloud.

She was looking at me blankly. "Why did you have to come back?"

"I almost got locked out!"

"But I thought you were staying with Derek tonight."

This was truly surreal. Our conversation seemed to be going around in circles, rapidly getting nowhere.

"Pixie, are you crazy? Do you think I want to get expelled?"

"Why would you be expelled?" She sounded genuinely curious.

"What about bed checks? What about Karen Chandler? They expelled her! Why would they treat me any differently?"

"Oh, no! You poor kid." Her voice was very gentle. "Don't you know it's Mothers' Weekend?"

"Of course I know it's Mothers' Weekend! So what? What's that got to do with Derek and me?"

"Didn't anyone tell you that on Mothers' Weekend you can do anything you want?"

A feeling of unreality began to creep over me. "Anything?"

"Sure. They never check up on us on Mothers' Weekend," she explained patiently, as if to a child.

"Never?"

"Of course not! Think how embarrassing it would be for the visiting mothers. Imagine Miss Bell coming around in the middle of the night, shining a flashlight in their faces."

My fingers were starting to go numb and a chill was spreading upwards into my heart.

"So there aren't any bed checks," Pixie said. "In fact, you could have stayed out all *weekend* and no one would have been the wiser."

I groaned. My shoes clattered to the floor, unheeded.

"Oh, I almost forgot," Pixie added, "Shennandoah called this morning, just after you and Rachel left. She asked me to let you know that she was spending the night with her Japanese professor. I told her you were with Derek, and she said if I saw you I should wish you luck."

Her words barely registered.

A tear trickled down my cheek.

My lovely fantasy had just come crashing to an end.

chapter 24: good-byes

The next morning, the phone rang, waking me from a troubled sleep. I staggered out of bed, vaguely aware that I must have overslept, since Pixie was nowhere to be seen.

It was Derek, and he began without preamble. "I feel terrible. I woke up this morning before dawn, and started thinking about last night. I don't remember a whole lot about what happened, but I'm sure my hangover isn't the main reason I feel bad. It's us."

His words, coming at me in a rush, made me feel like a glass of ice water was being thrown in my face.

"But last night was all a big mistake!" I protested. "Only I didn't find out until I got back here, and Pixie told me—"

"You're right," he said, "it *was* a mistake. For both of us."

"You don't understand!"

"I do. The truth is, there just isn't enough time for us to work out a relationship. We should stop now, before we do something we'll both regret. I don't think we should see each other again."

I must still be asleep, I thought, without much conviction. *This can't really be happening.*

"Wait, Derek—what did you say?"

"I said we'd better not see each other again."

He went on, explaining the reasons for his decision, but they barely registered. His words, each of which slipped quickly past me, made no sense. All I could think was that I really must be awake, because not even my worst nightmares were this bad. And it occurred to me that, had I known ahead of time about the rules on Mothers' Weekend, we might at that very moment have been eating breakfast together, chatting contentedly in his cozy kitchen, instead of having this bizarre conversation over the telephone.

I *had* to talk to him in person, see him face to face and explain what had gone wrong. I was sure I could make him understand. But did I dare ask him to meet me now, in light of what he'd just said? And even if he did agree to meet me, what could I say to convince him that he was mistaken?

I wouldn't stoop to begging him to change his mind, to ask for another chance. That would be childish and demeaning. No matter what, I didn't want to lose his respect or further distress him by making a nasty scene. He already sounded so miserable that I was sure he would end up hating me if I did.

All of these possibilities and more flashed across my mind while Derek continued talking, and each train of thought led to the same inevitable conclusion: if I really cared about him, if he meant that much to me, I would have to gather my courage and let him go. So instead of protesting, instead of heeding the frantic voice in my head that was shrieking at me to hang on, and not give up without a fight, I said, "I'm sorry you're so upset, Derek—but I do understand why. It's not as if you haven't warned me all along about your uncertainties."

"Oh god, Meri. I've tried so hard to do the right thing. I didn't want it to happen this way, believe me. But now this seems like the only sensible course of action."

Who wants to be sensible? I wanted to cry out. Instead I simply said, "If that's what seems best to you . . ."

"Me! I'm talking about what's best for both of us."

I struggled to suppress a sob. *If this is really what's best, why does it feel so wrong?* that irrepressible inner voice clamored, but I only said, "I told you right from the start that I wasn't afraid to try."

"And I told you from the start that I was afraid we'd both get hurt."

"Getting hurt is a small price to pay for the good times we've had together," I dared to say.

"Yes, there were some very good times. But from now on, I think we'd better stay out of each other's way."

It felt like a death sentence.

Unfair! UNFAIR! wept the voice inside me. "All right, Derek," I said quite calmly. "If that's the way you feel, I accept your decision."

"Thank you. I was afraid you'd be angry. I want you to know that I'll always think of you as a friend."

A friend. Not a lover.

"I'm glad. I feel the same way about you."

At least I had the self-control not to cry until after I'd hung up.

And so Derek and I parted calmly, but with finality. Afterwards, I spent many hours thinking about what else I might have said or done, wondering whether or not it would have made the least bit of difference. Somehow, I felt cheated that I didn't even have his cold to remember him by.

Meanwhile, school went on as usual, but some special quality, some magical feeling of hope and endless possibilities, seemed to have vanished from my life. My daily routine was stale. Classes were dull.

I missed Derek terribly those last few weeks of school. At times the pain was almost unbearable. But I was also so busy with my work that often I simply felt numb, and that was even worse.

The end of my involvement with Derek also marked the end of my interest in staying on at Indiana. With his disappearance from my life, all the fight seemed to go out of me. I had neither the energy nor the desire to continue doing battle with Indiana University's Hoosier Hysteria.

Weeks earlier, at the end of March, my advisor had summoned me to her office to warn me of the dangers of getting involved in campus politics. It had come to her attention (she didn't say how) that I had joined the Folksinging Club's Executive Committee, and she also knew about my one fling with YPSL. Blacklisted students, she reminded me, never received scholarships—and I would certainly find myself blacklisted if I persisted in making such foolish and politically unwise alliances.

I had ignored her advice; the lure of the Executive Committee had been too tempting to refuse. Yet now, if certain sinister rumors proved to be true, I was about to commit an even worse offense, and doom myself forever in the eyes of the school administration. For there was a disturbing report circulating on campus about the upcoming commencement exercises—specifically, concerning the University's choice of guest speaker for this most important and highly symbolic event. And if those rumors turned out to be true, I knew beyond a doubt that I had a moral obligation to participate in whatever protest might take place, even if I turned out to be the only protester, even if it meant forever losing my chance of winning that elusive scholarship.

And so, in my spare time, I began investigating alternate possibilities for the coming fall semester. I spent hours in the campus library researching college catalogues, and soon I was an expert on grade requirements and registration costs at any number of schools. I wrote to Queens College in New York and the music school at Western Reserve, both of which had accepted me the previous year, to find out if they still wanted me—and, with a certain grim determination, I wrote to the University of California, Berkeley, to see what that institution might have to offer.

As dismal as my personal life was just then, I had the dubious consolation of knowing that I wasn't the only one who was having romantic troubles. The weekend after my fiasco with Derek, Norman called just as Pixie was getting ready to go out.

"Hello, Lover," she cooed. "Oh, nothing—just sitting around, grading papers." She smiled contentedly. "Well, of course I miss you." Then her expression changed. "Who told you that? Why that . . . Well, for your information, that guy doesn't know me from Adam Orfox!"

Or was it Madam Orfax? Even at this late date, I still wasn't sure.

"It's not true!" She listened some more. "What?" she gasped. "You're where? Downstairs in the lobby!" She looked ill. "What a wonderful surprise! Of course I'm not too busy to see you, Lover! I'll be right there."

Pixie hung up and turned to me with a stricken look. "Oh, Meri, what am I going to do? Norman's here and I have a date with someone else. They're both gonna kill me!" Before I could say a word, she rushed back into the washroom and picked up the telephone.

"Hello?" she said in a strange, growly voice. I noticed that her washcloth was partially covering the mouthpiece. "Is Bobby there? Oh, Tiger, I'm so glad I caught you before you left!" Relief left her sounding much more like her normal self. "Listen, Tiger, I'm really sorry to call you at the last minute, but I've got the most awful stomach flu . . . Yeah," she growled, abruptly reverting to her "sick" voice. "Real bad." She listened for a moment. "No, I'm definitely not well enough to go out . . . Yup, I sure will—the minute I feel better."

She hung up. "Well, that takes care of that!" she announced, looking very smug. "What they don't know won't hurt them." And she dashed out of the room.

———

Several hours later, Pixie and Rachel came in together. Pixie was crying, and Rachel was attempting to comfort her.

"What happened?" I demanded. "Pixie, are you okay?"

Pixie sniffled.

"As well as can be expected," Rachel answered for her, "under the circumstances."

"What circumstances?"

Before Pixie could reply, Rachel fairly threw herself into the story: "Well, you know Steve's been visiting me all week . . ."

"Pixie mentioned it."

"And we decided to go out tonight for dinner. But just as we were about to order, who should come walking into the pizza parlor but Pixie and Norman. So I waved at them to come join us—only when they reached our booth, a commotion broke out at the next table . . . And guess who it was."

"I can't imagine."

"Bobby," Pixie moaned as Rachel succumbed to a momentary fit of giggles.

"That's right, Meri," Rachel recovered enough to say, "it was Pixie's jilted date, Bobby—*and* his two roommates. It turns out that Bobby was just a little bit peeved to see his supposedly sick girlfriend out with another man."

"Ouch! That sounds like trouble," I ventured.

"And how! Anyway, things got pretty lively after that. It seems our friend Pixie has been a very naughty girl. Not only has she been dating Bobby, she's also been seeing both of his roommates—that's 'Sweetie-pie' and 'Big Boy' to you and me. It turns out that each of them was under the impression that Pixie was dating only him— and boy, was Norman mad! He marched Pixie right out of the pizza parlor. Naturally, I tagged along to make sure she was okay . . ."

"You tagged along because you're nosy!" Pixie piped up.

But Rachel went right on talking. "And Norman told her flat out that from now on she's going to have to behave herself or they're finished."

"I tried to explain there was no real harm done," Pixie grumbled. "I was just having a little bit of innocent fun. But Norman wasn't buying that . . . And it's really so unfair! I think I deserve credit for carrying off my deception for as long as I did without getting caught."

"Yeah, Norman really appreciated that argument!" Rachel chortled. "I mean, come on, Pixie, what did you expect him to do? Give you a medal?"

Pixie glowered at Rachel.

"Anyway, Meri," Rachel continued, "right there on the sidewalk in the middle of downtown Bloomington, Norman gave Pixie an ultimatum: she's either got to marry him immediately, as soon as this semester's over, or she can forget she ever met him."

"Well, I said I'd marry him, didn't I?" Pixie demanded, scowling at Rachel, who grinned insolently back at her and continued her narrative: after Pixie's showdown, Rachel, ever the interested bystander, had escorted my unhappy roommate back to the dorm so she could recover her composure.

"Cheer up, Pixie," Rachel counseled, "the worst is over. You may as well face it: you got yourself into this mess, and it was inevitable that sooner or later you'd have to pay the piper."

"Besides," I added, "you know as well as I do that you love Norman. You'll never find a better man."

Pixie sighed. "True. Well, girls . . ." Abruptly, her face lit up with its familiar expression of devilish mischief. "I'll tell you one thing: it sure was fun while it lasted!" She elbowed Rachel in the ribs, chuckling. "I really had 'em fooled, didn't I?"

All three of us burst out laughing.

The last week of classes found everyone frantically writing papers and studying for exams. Partly as a break from school work, but also to satisfy a desperate need to see Derek one last time, I decided to attend the final meeting of the Folksinging Club.

The moment I walked in, the first person I saw, despite the crowd, was Derek, and he immediately saw me. Then both of us looked quickly away, unwilling or unable to acknowledge each other's existence. The pain of that brief encounter cut through all of my carefully constructed defenses like a knife. Only my sense of dignity prevented me from turning right around and bolting for the exit.

So we played a game, each of us trying to keep as far away

as possible from the other—all the while pretending that neither of us was doing it on purpose. I soon began to feel as if the meeting would never start. But then, at long last, Derek walked to the front of the room and everyone else settled down to listen. He had changed since I'd last seen him: he seemed tired and edgy, unhappy and less sure of himself.

He began by saying how much he'd enjoyed his presidency and that he would think of all of us fondly in the years to come. Abruptly, he blurted out, "Well, I'm sure no one wants to listen to me ramble on forever, so I'll turn the meeting over to your new president, Peter Radcliffe." Without another word he sat down, looking somehow diminished but also relieved.

Under Peter's direction, the meeting continued much as it always had, and I thought to myself that officers might come and go, but the Folksinging Club would undoubtedly remain the same—provided the university continued to allow it to exist. There were a number of performances, including a farewell by Derek's bluegrass band. Watching him up there with his group, singing and playing his guitar, I thought my heart would break.

At last it was time for intermission. In the confusion that followed, caught up in the milling throng, Derek and I accidentally found ourselves together in the same small gathering of friends. An awkward moment, and then we greeted each other, both as polite as could be. Then we ran out of things to say. It occurred to me that he was having as much trouble as I was, concentrating on our friends' comments, and I was certain that each of us was desperately trying to think of a graceful way of escaping without being too obvious about it.

The entire situation was slightly out of control, as if we were characters in a Fellini movie. It was worse than being strangers. I felt as if someone I had known and loved had died right there in my arms. At the same time, I was furious with both of us, disappointed in the stupid, awkward way we were behaving. Where was the candor and trust that had been the hallmark of our entire relationship?

I bitterly regretted ever having come that night.

Mercifully, I was saved by the club secretary, Betsy Walker, who came over to ask to speak with me privately. I excused myself from the group and followed her out of the room.

"I'm sorry I interrupted your conversation," she said.

"It's okay," I assured her. "We weren't talking about anything important. Besides, I was about to leave anyway. What can I do for you?"

"We're planning a surprise party for the outgoing officers, and I could really use some help setting up. We'd have to leave right away in order to get everything ready in time, so you'd miss the rest of the meeting."

"That's fine." Any excuse for a premature departure sounded like a good one. "I'd be happy to do anything I can for you." If all went according to plan, my reasoning went, I would help her and then, before the party actually began, I would excuse myself and go home.

Such was my foolish fantasy.

"Great!" she responded. "Let's get started—it takes almost half an hour to get to Derek's place."

The ground seemed to drop out from beneath my feet. But it was too late to back out.

As we drove out of town, Betsy chatted happily about the party and the club activities that were planned for the coming year, oblivious to my distress.

I found it hard to match her enthusiasm. Derek's house was the last place on earth I wanted to go to. How had I managed to get myself into this mess?

And what would he think when he came back home and found me there?

My conscience demanded that I rouse myself from my bleak thoughts and participate in the conversation. However, at that moment, given my gloomy state of mind, the best I could come up with was the information that I might not be attending Indiana University in the fall.

"I don't want to mess up the club," I told her, "so I've been thinking that I should resign from the Executive Committee tonight. I'd like to give them time to elect someone else."

"Gosh, I'd hate for you to do that," she said. "What makes you think you're not coming back?"

Briefly, I told her about my problems with the school administration, my financial issues, and how I'd never really felt comfortable in Indiana, right from the start. At the end of my explanation, I asked what she thought I should do as far as the club was concerned.

She advised me to discuss it with Peter Radcliffe, the new president, and give him a written statement so he could appoint a standby, in case one was needed.

By then we were in front of Derek's house, and I knew with sick certainty how very difficult it was going to be to make it through the next few hours. Panic cramped my stomach when I thought about being in that house when he inevitably arrived. I had to get away before that happened! But for now, all I could do was grit my teeth and keep my promise to Betsy.

So we got out of the car and I located the hidden front door key—because I knew where he kept it—and entered his home, turning on the lights. I lit some of his candles, opened his windows, and started a fire in his fireplace.

The whole time I was there, I felt like an intruder.

Betsy trailed along behind me, blissfully unaware of my distress, and made herself useful in a busy, cheerful sort of way until at last, much to my relief, she went off to inspect his record collection.

In his kitchen, we fixed drinks and prepared snacks. And then there was the sound of cars coming down the gravel driveway . . .

People were arriving.

Doors slammed.

I heard voices.

Derek walked in.

And there we were, together again in that house. Suffocating, drowning in a sea of extraneous people . . .

Without a word, I shoved past him and ran out of the kitchen.

Brushing aside strangers, I blindly fled into the safety of the night. Heart pounding, I stumbled down the front steps and across the yard, away from the brilliantly lit house. But I only ran a short distance before I stopped.

After all, where could I go? Campus was miles away, and I had no hope of getting there on my own.

As my eyes adjusted to the darkness and my racing pulse slowed, I rediscovered the infinite beauty of that well-remembered place—the sky strewn with stars, the cool air with its distinctive piney tang, and the deep, underlying silence of the night—and my breath caught in my throat. In such a setting my troubles seemed minor indeed, a mere spasm in the vastness of the cosmos. Gradually, a sense of peace settled over me.

After a while, I realized that I wasn't alone—the yard was full of people. Someone had lit a bonfire, which beckoned with its warmth. Beyond it, beside the stone wall, a small crowd had gathered and a meeting was in progress.

My curiosity piqued, I went over to investigate.

Only then did I realize what a truly unusual group of people had come to Derek's farewell party. There were all sorts of unexpected faces: Mr. Jefferson, Daniel Weaver, some graduate students I knew from the anthropology and art departments, Gineeva and several of her friends—and even Myrna!

Surely, no one would object if I joined them.

It soon became apparent that I had walked in on a strategy session to plan a Commencement Day protest rally. The ugly rumors had turned out to be true: for that year's commencement ceremony, Indiana University's administration and the Young Republicans had joined forces to invite as their honored guest speaker that obnoxious proponent of "White Supremacy," Alabama's notorious Governor George Wallace!

This was a cause for which I was more than willing to sacrifice whatever remnants of standing I might still have at school. That Indiana University could do something so vile, so insensitive to the feelings of any segment, however small, of the student population, was infuriating—though it shouldn't, I reminded myself as I settled onto the grass beside Myrna, be surprising. Having lived in Indiana for the better part of a year, I should know to expect this sort of thing.

". . . And we'll be carrying signs," Daniel was saying—I got the distinct impression that he was leading the discussion. "The Steering Committee has decided that our message should be that we're not protesting Wallace's right to speak, but that we despise what he stands for."

There was an appreciative stirring in the audience and a smattering of applause.

Mr. Jefferson caught my eye and nodded, smiling across the circle. Then he turned and said something to Daniel that I couldn't quite make out, although I thought I heard my name mentioned.

"Good idea!" Daniel replied, glancing over at me. "Thanks for joining us, Meri. Randolph Jefferson has just volunteered to get us a supply of poster materials, and he's suggesting that, since you're in his department, you might be willing to help distribute them to the various poster-making teams."

"Gladly."

"Can I help, Meri?"

I turned. It was Myrna asking.

My suitemate was certainly full of surprises! I wondered how she could have reacted to Kennedy's assassination as she had, yet feel sympathy for this particular cause. Perhaps this time it was more personal, knowing Caralene, Pixie, and their friends as she now did. In any case, this obviously wasn't an appropriate time to question her.

"Please do!" I told her. "Maybe we can organize a poster-painting session of our own in the dorm."

"Excellent, ladies." Daniel was obviously enjoying his

prominent position. "Now for other business: we should discuss the rally itself. That's going to be a bit trickier to organize."

"We should have ushers," someone suggested. "You know, people who'll keep things orderly."

"Sounds like a good idea," one of the graduate students seconded.

"Sounds like a necessity!" someone else said. "This could be dangerous."

The talk continued. It felt good to be with them, all of us focused on the same goal.

Now, if only I can work things out with Derek, so we feel better about what happened, I thought, *I'll be satisfied.*

For two people who had been so honest with each other, ours had not been an honest parting. Derek had taught me to believe that we both deserved better—and I intended to try to do something about it.

But tonight was definitely not the right time.

I was grateful to be able to join a carload of people who were returning to campus early. As we drove off, I looked back at Derek's little house, full of longing and regret, certain that I would never see it again.

The first thing next morning, after giving myself a stern pep talk about all of this being for the best, I picked up the telephone and dialed Derek's number. Standing in the washroom, listening to the phone ring, I realized that I was hoping he wouldn't answer.

"Hello?"

Somehow, I forced myself to go on—one of the most difficult things I had ever done. "Hi, Derek."

"Oh, it's you, Meri." He sounded wary.

"Don't hang up," I blurted out. "Just talk to me for a couple of minutes. I promise I didn't call to make things worse. I'm trying to help both of us feel better."

"Sure, I'll listen. But what's there to say?"

"I hated the way we acted last night. It's stupid to pretend we don't know each other. We were truthful about our feelings before, so we should be able to talk about this now."

"I guess you're right. But I felt awful about the way we ended things. I didn't know what to say when I saw you."

"It *was* hard, wasn't it?"

"Yes. But I still think we did the right thing when we stopped seeing each other."

It was like another slash of the knife.

He sighed. "If we'd had more time, I promise you, it would have been different."

"It hurts to hear you say that."

"It certainly does!"

"You make me think about what might have been . . ."

"Which is why I've been avoiding you."

"Well, pretending to be strangers feels a heck of a lot worse."

"You have a point." He hesitated. "What bothers me the most is thinking about how much this whole business must have upset you."

"I'm disappointed"—I chose my words with care—"but remember: I told you at the beginning that I wasn't afraid. In spite of what happened, I enjoyed every moment we spent together."

"I feel good about that, too."

Now that we were finally talking, life didn't seem quite so bad. For several minutes more, we discussed the events of the past few weeks, but Derek was right: there really wasn't anything to say that hadn't already been said.

And now our futures awaited us.

"I heard from Betsy that you might not be back next year," he said. "Is that definite?"

"Pretty much. You know how I feel about a lot of the stuff that goes on around here. And now this Wallace crap! The school may be offering us the world's finest education, but politically it stinks. And I know I'll never be able to close my eyes to prejudice the way everyone in the music department seems to be able to . . . Besides, I just found out that I've definitely been blacklisted. My advisor called to give me the happy news. My grades are excellent, but the school has classified me as a subversive." My laugh was ironic. "And we both know they're not about to give scholarships to subversives. Anyway, this Wallace protest should really finish me off. I couldn't afford to come back, even if I wanted to—which I don't."

"I'm sorry."

"Don't be. It's just as well: it forces the issue."

"Do you know what you're going to do next year?"

"I'm not sure. I've been looking into several schools, especially in New York, since that would be the cheapest alternative. But that's not really where I want to go."

"Aren't there other possibilities? Have you given any thought to Berkeley?"

"Well, yes . . . I have." I hadn't intended to tell him—I was afraid he'd think that I was trying to chase him all the way to California. But since he was the one who'd brought it up . . .

"Actually, I've written to them," I admitted. "It looks like I'd have to work my way through school, but there are worse fates than that. And my parents probably won't make too much of a fuss since I have those relatives in San Francisco."

"That's great! I hope it works out. My family could help you get settled—maybe even help you find a place to live."

"Gee, I'd really appreciate that."

"Okay, I'll tell them to expect to hear from you . . . Wait. I have a better idea. Give me your address in New York, and I'll write to you this summer. That way you can keep me posted about your plans."

We talked a bit longer. Derek seemed very excited by the possibility that I might actually be at Berkeley in the fall. After giving me his address in Los Angeles, he told me that his thesis had finally been accepted.

"Oh, Derek, I'm so glad!"

"Me, too! Believe me, I can't get out of here fast enough, although it means I'll miss the protest rally. I'm packing even as we speak."

"I wish I could leave right now, too. But I have to stay until after finals next week."

For a moment, he didn't say anything, and when he spoke at last, his voice was carefully neutral. "So that means you've got some free time right now, doesn't it?"

"Well, yes . . ."

"So do I . . ."

I waited, holding my breath.

"But we'd better not." I could hear the finality in his voice. "We'd better leave things as they are. If we saw each other right now, there's no telling what we might be tempted to do."

Please tempt me! I almost blurted out. But what I actually said was, "I guess you're right."

That troublesome inner voice of mine did not agree. If he'd asked me just then, I would gladly have jumped in his car and driven all the way to California with him—and to hell with my finals!

"Promise me you'll write," he said, "no matter what you decide about Berkeley. I promise I'll write back."

"Okay."

"And I'll make you another promise: if you come to California, I'll be there to welcome you."

"It's a deal!"

Just before we hung up, he said, "Gee, Meri, thanks for calling. I feel so much better now."

And I was certain that he meant it.

So we ended our conversation. At least now, even if I never saw or heard from him again, we had mostly good feelings to remember each other by.

For I knew that whatever happened, I would never forget him.

chapter 25: hoosier hysteria

Commencement Day began as a warm, sunny morning that threatened to become quite hot as time went on. I awoke very early, as soon as the birds started singing.

So did Pixie.

Both of us were too nervous to sleep in.

Pixie, Caralene, Myrna, and I had breakfast with Rachel and Gineeva in the dorm cafeteria. My friends, even those who had already finished their finals, as well as many graduate students who ordinarily would have left school before finals week had even begun, had stayed on to participate in the protest.

That morning, as we sat around the breakfast table, no one, not even Pixie, ate much, and no one mentioned what all of us were thinking: that we were about to take an unpopular and conspicuous stand on an extremely controversial issue. How much actual physical danger we might face was an unknown quantity that didn't make the equation any easier to assess—or our nerves any less jittery.

Pixie, at the far end of our table, was nursing a spectacular black eye, and her left arm was in a sling. Both were souvenirs of her most recent automobile adventure.

The previous week, on a rainy afternoon, she had unintentionally turned the wrong way into a one-way street. While looking backwards over her shoulder, trying to figure out what was wrong, she had driven at slow speed, head-on, into a parked truck. Her car had been pretty badly smashed up, but fortunately no one had been seriously injured.

Gineeva, who had been involved in several other driving mishaps with Pixie over the years, had somehow managed to avoid this one. She was still gloating over her good fortune at breakfast that morning—although I suspected her teasing had more to do with distracting herself from thinking about the protest rally than either malice or pleasure.

I, for one, was grateful for the diversion.

"Girl, remember last winter when we almost crashed on that big hill south of town?" she asked Pixie.

"Sure, I remember. So what? Nothing bad happened."

"Yeah, well let me tell you, you sure had me praying!" She turned to address the rest of us. "You should have seen it. There we were, racing down that icy hill like a bat out of hell, when all of a sudden I saw that another car was going to cross the intersection at the bottom, same time as we were. I almost pissed in my pants! 'Watch out, Pixie!' I shouted, but she just kept on a-goin'! And all of a sudden, our car hits this icy patch, and next thing I know we're skidding down sideways, slithering and sliding all over the place, like this." Her moving hand described an erratic downward arc through the air. "I was sure we were goners. And fool that I am, I kept on yelling, 'Stop, Pixie! Stop!' at the top of my lungs." She snorted in disgust. "As if that was gonna make any difference."

"I *told* you not to jump," Pixie said.

Rachel giggled, but I could tell that her heart really wasn't in it.

"So what happened next?" I demanded.

"Gineeva jumped." Pixie gave her friend a pitying look.

"Yeah, and I had a sprained ankle and a mashed-up shoulder for a month afterwards. And what about Pixie, you ask? Why, she sailed right on through that intersection, going sideways, just as slick as you please. She even missed the other car."

"That just goes to show you, Gineeva," Pixie said primly. "You ought to have more faith in my driving."

Everyone laughed.

"So as you see it, Gineeva," Rachel summarized, "Pixie got her comeuppance with this accident?"

"Amen to that! Girl, you look like something the cat drug in!"

As the laughter tapered off, my attention returned to Rachel. Despite her attempted humor, she looked tired and disheveled. She admitted she'd been up all the previous night writing—a frantic effort to complete her term papers on time. This atypical behavior was due to the fact that, as Pixie had mentioned months earlier, she had volunteered to participate in a voter education campaign in the South that summer—which meant she had to finish her work before leaving town. Today's ordeal, she said, would simply be a trial run: a small sample of what she could expect to encounter in the Deep South in the coming months.

Caralene sat quietly beside Pixie with her usual self-contained dignity. I wondered what thoughts were going through that beautiful head, and I wished I could have gotten to know her better during the past year. But Caralene, although not unfriendly, had always kept very much to herself. I respected her. As I had said to Pixie, she was a lady.

Myrna picked at her food. Of all of us, she had changed the most in the year I had known her. Gone was the brash, bouncy young lady who had so repelled Pixie, Caralene, Rachel, and myself that first day. Now she was more self-confident and quiet, more settled and sure. I liked her, and I still felt ashamed that Rachel and I had teased her so.

Also to her credit, she had taken on the thankless job of assisting Daniel in organizing our protest rally. Later that morning, she would accompany him to the university president's office, where they would officially inform the administration of our intention to picket commencement exercises. This news was bound to be poorly received. Myrna had placed herself in a highly visible and therefore vulnerable position, and she was understandably nervous.

I had to leave the cafeteria before the others had finished

eating; I had an anthropology final to take. But I had trouble concentrating on my exam, haunted by visions of my friends sitting in their places, stoically awaiting whatever fate had in store for all of us.

I couldn't help wondering about the following morning: Would we all still be here, safe and unhurt, eating breakfast together as usual? How would we feel about whatever had happened at today's rally?

After my exam, I returned to the dorm for a quick snack—yet another carton of milk—and then it was time to go. Pixie, Caralene, Gineeva, Rachel, and I met Shennandoah and several of her friends in our downstairs lobby, and together we left Morrison Hall.

Commencement exercises were scheduled to take place in the main auditorium, not far from the art building. Our silent protest was to occur across the plaza, in front of the fountain where Karen Chandler had so daringly danced in the nude earlier that spring. Daniel had asked us all to check in two hours before the ceremony so we would be well organized and in our positions before the Wallace supporters arrived. And there was no doubt in anyone's mind: there would be Wallace supporters. We just didn't know how many.

My friends and I were among the first to reach the fountain, but before long we were joined by others. As each newcomer appeared, I noticed that he or she carried his or her sign a bit awkwardly, almost like a protective shield—which only served to emphasize how vulnerable and exposed all of us felt. Yet, glancing around the empty plaza, I detected no outward signs of hostility—no uniformed campus police, no spying eyes. We were alone with our signs and each other. It seemed impossible that the situation would alter noticeably in the next two hours.

Why, then, this gut-spasming nervousness?

The cool shadow of the auditorium was beginning to slide

across the plaza, while the building itself, with its pure white classical facade, loomed huge, dominating the view. From the sidewalk, wide steps led upward past marble columns to oversized front doors where, in a scant two hours, George Wallace himself, Prejudice Incarnate, would enter.

Standing there, I thought back over the school year, recalling other events that had taken place in that same auditorium: a dazzling Van Cliburn piano recital, my unfortunate and embarrassing "dream date" with Mr. Jefferson, and the memorial services for President Kennedy. And today, a contemptible man from Alabama would disgrace our school by appearing there, where other, more honorable men had stood.

What a sad commentary on Indiana University!

A breath of hot wind ruffled my hair, returning me to the present. A short distance away, Pixie and Rachel seemed to be having an argument while Caralene, Gineeva, and Shennandoah looked on with interest. I moved closer to listen.

"Sure, silent protests are effective—up to a point," Rachel was saying, "but it's too easy for the administration to ignore them. Sometimes violence is the only way to get their attention."

"I don't believe in that kind of attention." Pixie's face was stern. "Violence is wrong. It will never accomplish anything. We have a duty to protest, but we should do it with quiet dignity. Like Dr. King or Gandhi."

"Well, that's certainly a change, coming from you!" Rachel suddenly grinned. "If George Wallace had come here last year, you wouldn't have been caught dead doing this. Remember: you didn't believe in protests, period. So I guess some of my radical ideas must have rubbed off on you after all—even if you won't admit it."

"'Course I admit it, Rae," Pixie said with real affection. "You're absolutely right. If this was last year, I wouldn't be here. But like I was telling Meri yesterday: keeping in my place doesn't seem quite as important as it used to. There comes a time when you have to stand up and be counted."

"Amen to that!" Gineeva chimed in. "Indiana University

has some nerve inviting that bastard Wallace! And we're not gonna to take it lying down."

"Pixie and I talked it over when we first heard the rumors," Caralene said quietly. "And we agreed we'd have to take part in whatever protest happened. Because if we don't take a stand this time, we never will—and that would be doing his supporters a favor."

"It surely would," Gineeva seconded.

"But what about violence?" Shennandoah persisted. The huge diamond on Toshio's engagement ring glittered as she encompassed us all with a wave of her hand. "Does everyone agree with Rachel?"

"How can they disagree?" Rachel demanded. "The Negroes in this country have an obligation to protest the way they've been treated—are still being treated. They're second-class citizens, and the only way to put a stop to that, is to show they're a force to be reckoned with—even if they have to resort to violence to get the point across."

I shuddered. "Gosh, Rachel, I'd hate to see it come to that. I'd rather have peaceful demonstrations, like today's."

"Who says today's demonstration is going to be peaceful?" she said. "Where's your guarantee? Oh, sure, we'll behave ourselves, but what about the Wallace gang? Who speaks for them?"

We glanced at each other nervously out of the corners of our eyes. Rachel had dared to voice our deepest, unspoken fears.

"Well, I'm sure they'll behave," I began rather weakly, "because . . ."

But we were interrupted by the arrival of a group of graduate students from Derek's farewell party. And they were followed by Derek's friends, Cassie and Terry, who greeted me with hugs and good-luck wishes from Derek, who was already back in California. Mr. Jefferson and several other professors followed close on the Stevenses heels. I realized that it must have taken tremendous courage for them to come. After all, their jobs were on the line. They would have to answer directly to the administration for their actions today.

Now we were a respectable, if modest sized, group. Several people had brought children. The youngest sat on her father's shoulders, laughing and waving at the adults, while the older ones wasted no time in commandeering some of our signs. Soon they were marching back and forth in front of the fountain, pretending they were in a parade.

A chill went through me, despite the oppressive heat.

Overhead, thunderheads massed, scudding across the sky.

Meanwhile, the Wallace supporters had begun to arrive. Some stood talking at the foot of the steps leading up to the auditorium, while others made their way inside, casting occasional, suspicious glances in our direction.

Daniel came rushing up, out of breath, trailed by an even more breathless Myrna. His face showed signs of the strain of the past few weeks: there were dark circles under his eyes and tired lines pinched his mouth. His expression was grim.

"What happened with President Stahr?" several voices asked at once.

We all quieted as Daniel began his report.

"The University has been duly notified, in person and in writing, of our intention to demonstrate here today. We also told them that there were going to be young children present, and we asked for police protection."

"Good," one of the fathers said.

"Our request has been denied."

Although this was not entirely unexpected news, it was disheartening. Several people groaned.

Daniel held up his hands for silence. "The official position is that since we haven't been given permission to demonstrate, we do so at our own risk . . . So now it's up to us. Anyone with children should feel to free to leave right now if they're uncomfortable with the situation. There'll be no hard feelings." He paused, but no one moved. "Fine. Then let's get ready. Is everyone here? Is anyone you know of missing?" His eyes scanned the thirty-five or so people who had gathered around him.

"A couple of my friends haven't come yet," someone said.

"Well, it's getting late, so we'll go on without them for now. And when they arrive you can catch them up on our plans . . . Okay, here are our guidelines: This demonstration will be orderly and dignified. You will stand in your assigned places. Those with children will be stationed toward the back, in case things get nasty. Hold your posters up as high as you can, and remain quiet. Remember, this is a silent protest, to show the intensity of our feelings. Don't allow yourselves to be dragged down to the level of the hecklers. Don't respond to them, and no matter what they say, no name-calling. And if they"—he gestured toward the exponentially increasing throng on the opposite side of the plaza—"get out of hand, we'll attempt to make a calm and dignified exit from this area. Whatever you do, don't panic—and don't run! That might only make things worse. And if we do have to leave, it's important that we leave together, as a group. We'll all be much safer that way," he concluded. "Any questions?"

Several people wanted him to clarify the escape procedures, and it was a while before everyone understood the plan.

I shifted uncomfortably from foot to foot, fingering the edges of my sign, wondering how a person could be both bored and nervous at the same time. Sweat trickled down my sides, leaving wet patches on my blouse. I propped my poster against my hip, clenching and unclenching my sweaty hands.

Thunder rumbled in the distance.

I wished I'd worn a hat.

Now Daniel and Myrna were moving among us, assigning places. By this point, several more demonstrators had joined us, and there was a buzz of conversation as they were brought up to date.

Pixie stood on my right, Rachel on my left, and beyond her were Caralene and Shennandoah. Gineeva was next to Pixie, and she kept up a running, muttered conversation with herself the whole time we were there.

By now the plaza was packed, and more people kept coming.

Across the way, the latest arrivals carried confederate flags, which they waved enthusiastically in commemoration of this historic event. One young man—I thought it might be Larry, my troublesome former English classmate, though in the milling crowd I couldn't be certain—had pinned a confederate flag on the back of his shirt and was making his way through the gathering, shaking hands and slapping shoulders in greeting.

The sounds of excited talk and laughter drifted over us. Soon the crowd had taken over the entire plaza, and there was little room left in which to move around. People were standing shoulder to shoulder, yet there remained a narrow margin of pavement around our group, an empty sort of no man's land. It was becoming difficult for me to see all the way over to the auditorium steps. Nevertheless, I held my poster as high as I could, hoping its message would be visible: "GEORGE WALLACE GO HOME!! You do NOT belong at Indiana University!"

Individuals in the crowd soon became aware of our protest. Several people made rude comments, but we ignored them. And all the time, beneath the excited hum in the air, I could hear Gineeva, growling to herself like an angry bear.

The shadow of the auditorium was fully upon us now.

Suddenly there was a stirring on the far side of the plaza, and seconds later a motorcade came into view, complete with a siren-wailing motorcycle escort. Slowly, a passage was cleared, and the cars inched forward. Bright red, white, and blue confederate flags shimmered like mirages in the sizzling heat, and people began chanting: "Wal-lace! Wal-lace! We want Wallace!"

"Here comes the governor!" voices cried.

The car reached the auditorium steps and glided to a halt. Simultaneously, all four doors flew open, and black-suited security men erupted from the interior. Assisted by policemen, they began pushing and shoving people out of the way, clearing a path across the sidewalk. This accomplished, one of the security guards leaned into the open door and spoke to someone within the car.

A tall, dapper man stepped out: Indiana University's own president, Elvis Stahr. Even from a distance, the proud way he carried himself and the practiced ease with which he greeted the crowd convinced me that local gossip was true: he had high political aspirations.

He was immediately joined by the officers of the Young Republicans. Then a hush fell over the crowd as everyone waited for the guest of honor to appear.

At last, a heavyset, dark-haired man emerged from the car, dwarfed by President Stahr, the Young Republicans, and the cluster of bodyguards. For a moment, he was nearly swallowed up by the surge of cheering onlookers who crowded closer, eager for a word or touch.

Disappointment knifed through me. What an insignificant little person! Could this unprepossessing fellow really be such a potent symbol of segregation and racial intolerance, of all that was vicious and evil?

But the moment passed, and my emotions swung the other way as hundreds of voices thundered in unison—a single, adoring voice—"Wal-lace! Wal-lace!" . . . and then burst into a spontaneous rendition of "Dixie."

I shuddered.

What was evil, I decided, was the crowd mentality, especially when manipulated by a demagogue. George Wallace was the crowd's prejudice in human form, the embodiment of all of those ugly beliefs that were, to me, so morally repugnant.

As the last note of "Dixie" echoed into silence, Wallace raised both hands above his head in a triumphant gesture. When he began speaking, I could just make out the movement of his lips, but I was too far away to hear his actual words.

The monster that was the crowd roared again, thousands strong, as Wallace, with a jaunty wave, turned and started up the auditorium steps, accompanied by his hosts. Together, they entered the building and vanished, followed by the bodyguards, a phalanx of police officers, and a small group of spectators who managed to squeeze in after them.

For several moments, there wasn't a sound in the plaza— but then conversation swelled to fill the anticlimactic vacuum that followed. The show was over. George Wallace had come and gone—at least for the time being. There was no more room in the auditorium for a single additional spectator and nothing more to see.

Beneath a patchwork sky that was at once a brilliant blue and leaden with heavy, gray-bottomed clouds—a study in contrasts between light and dark, heat and chill—our silent vigil continued.

But the crowd was already beginning to grow restless, shifting in place without diminishing in numbers. The mood seemed uncertain. People were tired of waiting but unwilling to go home, unsure whether or not it was worth staying around for the next hour or so in hopes of catching a final, fleeting glimpse of Wallace as he left the auditorium.

Inevitably, their attention turned to us.

Someone nearby made a remark about "that lousy bunch of nigger-lovers with the signs" and I heard Gineeva growl in response, although she didn't otherwise respond.

The epithet was taken up by others further away.

Before long, everyone knew we were there.

Without any conscious organization, the crowd began hemming us in, drifting closer and closer to the fountain's rim, as the people farthest away pressed forward to get a better look at us.

Our precious no man's land was rapidly shrinking. Instinctively, our little group drew together. Parents of the smallest children picked them up, while the older ones crept closer to their parents, who enfolded them against their sides in an age-old protective gesture.

Gineeva kept muttering.

Only then, with so many hostile eyes focused on us, did I fully realize that we were outnumbered by many hundreds to one.

Suddenly, from somewhere in the milling throng, a voice called out, "What the hell are those nigger-lovers doing here? No one invited them!"

"Yeah!" several voices agreed. "Why are they here?"

"Those nigger-lovers oughta go home!" someone yelled.

Several others took up the chant.

"Nigger-lovers! Nigger-lovers!"

More voices joined in.

"Nigger-lovers, go home!"

A rock sailed past us in a magnificent, slow-motion arc and landed in the fountain with a heavy splash. For the moment it had little or no significance for me, but the crowd laughed—a gigantic, booming, impersonal, nightmare voice with several thousand heads.

Ominously, the monster pressed closer. The campus police, who had been all over the plaza until minutes ago, were suddenly nowhere to be seen.

Another rock flew by. Apparently the crowd liked the idea, for several more followed.

"Nigger-lovers, go home! Nigger-lovers, go home!" the monster chanted. "Nigger-lovers, go home!"

"All right, let's get out of here!" Daniel yelled over the commotion. "Follow emergency procedures!"

"GET THOSE NIGGER-LOVERS!!!" an insane voice shrieked, sending a chill down my spine.

Cheering, jeering, howling broke out all around us like a cresting tidal wave.

"Walk slowly and stay together!" Daniel's familiar voice cut through the roaring in my ears.

"NIGGER-LOVERS!!!"

I was drowning in sound.

Buffeted and jostled from all sides by threatening bystanders, we began inching away from the fountain. A rock came hurtling out of nowhere and struck the man with the smallest child. She screamed as blood flowered on her father's forehead. He staggered, and friends on either side caught his elbows to keep him from going down.

Hatred transformed the surrounding faces into grotesque, inhuman masks, nightmare creatures howling unspeakable epithets.

Step by step, our group began to move faster and faster. The crowd flowed into the space created by our passing, shoving us forward at an ever-accelerating rate.

A heavy boot crashed into the legs of the girl in front of me. She stumbled, and I saw a fist smash into Daniel's shoulder.

But somehow we kept moving.

And then, miraculously, through a rift in the crowd, I caught a glimpse of green grass and sunlight up ahead—the edge of the plaza!

With a final burst of energy, we cleared the last of the hecklers. There, as if by an unspoken agreement, we all hesitated for the barest instant to take a deep gulp of fresh air.

At our backs, the crowd-monster howled, crying for blood.

We threw down our signs and ran for our lives.

The next afternoon, I hurried through my French final. I had to walk out early so as not to miss my train.

Norman was helping Pixie move her things out of the dorm, and they offered to drive me to the station. Racing across town in Pixie's beat-up car, I couldn't think of a thing to say to them, and when we arrived, the train had already pulled in. My luggage was whisked efficiently aboard by an eager porter almost before Norman had a chance to lift it out of the trunk.

There was barely time for a quick hug for each of them.

"Take care, Pixie."

"You, too."

We stood there for a moment, holding each other at arm's length. I wasn't sure what she was doing, but I knew that I was memorizing her face.

"So what are you going to do this summer?" she finally asked.

I shrugged. "Help my parents move into their new house. Rest up. Keep hoping that I get accepted at Berkeley . . ."

"You won't be coming back here, then?" Although she already knew the answer, her eyes were intense.

"BOOARD!!" the conductor called out.

I felt an overwhelming sense of urgency as I started to lose my grip on her. "Wait, Pixie!" I clutched her arms. "Before you go, there's something I need to tell you."

"What's that?"

"A promise I made—to myself—and I want to make it to you, too." I took a deep breath. "As soon as I can tell it right—when I get myself untangled from all of this emotional mess—I'm going to write about this year: you, me, our friends, and everything that's happened to us. And I'll get it published . . . no matter how long it takes. I swear I will!"

She grinned. "I don't doubt it."

We hugged each other again, hard.

"Be good, Pixie—but not too good. I know we'll see each other again."

Her earthy chuckle sounded in my ears, and tears blurred my vision as I stumbled onto the train.

And then, in a sudden, surreal change of environment, I found myself sitting in a comfortably padded seat, in an air-conditioned car, looking out at them, framed in the window, almost as if they were actors in a movie.

And the train was moving, carrying me into my future . . .

Pixie and Norman stood together on the platform, waving good-bye.

Pixie blew a kiss.

The station was whisked away, sliding out of view. Off in the distance, I glimpsed the campus clock tower and several of the older buildings, gray limestone architectural wonders swathed in ivy and partially hidden by trees—a shifting kaleidoscope of impressions that rapidly accelerated into history.

Idly, I glanced down at a newspaper that had been discarded on the seat beside me. A bold headline, "INDY 500 TODAY!" dominated the page, but it was another item that caught my eye: an article about the previous day's commencement rally.

I skimmed through, following the story to the back page, where a large aerial photograph seemed to jump off the page at me.

Almost the entire field of the picture was taken up by a mass of humanity, so densely packed that it looked like a swarm of ants. I kept looking, and . . . *there*. Somewhat off-center there was another, far smaller, black spot, quarantined from the main body by a neat white ring—a circle that encapsulated my friends and me. It was truly a miracle that we had nothing worse to show for it than a few minor cuts and bruises, considering what might have . . .

With a shudder, I put down the paper.

Best not to think about what might have happened.

Seated on the speeding train, I stared sightlessly out of the window, oblivious to the green Indiana countryside flickering past. Bitterness welled up inside of me like bile.

One whole year of my life gone—totally wasted! And what do I have to show for it?

In my mind's eye the past year unfolded: the events, trivial and dramatic; the classes; the faces; the conversations. In a single year, I had learned a great deal about other people, and much about myself, something about love, and a lot about hate. I could never, ever go back, but I would always remember, and not all of the memories were bad.

And now the future awaited. What would it bring, I wondered?

Berkeley, I hoped. Derek had made it sound like a good place to be, a welcome change from the past year's turmoil. California seemed to whisper siren promises of peace and a fresh start—and perhaps a chance to continue my adventure with Derek.

Thinking of him reminded me of my other friends: Rachel and Shennandoah, Daniel and Myrna, Caralene and Gineeva. And, of course, Pixie.

Especially Pixie. She sprang to life in my mind: the mischievous face with its pointy chin and surprised-looking eyebrows, the reddish-brown hair and turned-up nose, the impish grin lurking behind a pose of assumed dignity, and that hearty, life-affirming, contagious chuckle.

I knew I would never forget her.

She—and all of my friends—had enriched me, cared for me, given shape and meaning to my daily existence. Without their love and support, Indiana would have been intolerable.

With a sigh, I glanced once again at the aerial photograph and the small circle that encompassed my world.

Well, was it really a waste of time? I asked myself.

In my heart, I knew the answer.

epilogue

Hoosier Hysteria is a true story: all of these events actually did take place, although not necessarily in the exact order given. With the aid of my admittedly sketchy diary, conversations have been recreated to the best of my ability, faithful in content if not in precise words. The names of the innocent—as well as most of the guilty—have been changed to protect their privacy.

I admit to having exercised some artistic license, yet reality is often stranger than fiction. The passage of time may blur our memories, but our hearts really do know the truth.

—Meri Henriques Vahl

acknowledgments

After trying unsuccessfully for many years to convince any editor, agent, or publisher to so much as take a look at *Hoosier Hysteria*, I would like to express my heartfelt gratitude to Brooke Warner and her terrific team at She Writes Press for helping me turn my manuscript into the reality of a published book. Thanks also go to my friends and family for their enthusiastic support, and a special thank you to Isabel R. Feldman for not only taking, but also preserving and then sharing, her wonderful photo of me and some of my Indiana University friends, which appears on the cover of this book.

about the author

After leaving Indiana University, Meri Henriques Vahl arrived at the University of California, Berkeley just in time to witness the Free Speech Movement. Since earning her bachelor's degree in Fine Art at Berkeley, she has worked as a graphic artist and musician, and is currently an award-winning art quilter who teaches at various venues in the US and overseas. Vahl has two adult children and lives in central California with her husband and two rowdy felines.

Author photo © Jim Vahl

SELECTED TITLES FROM SHE WRITES PRESS

She Writes Press is an independent publishing company founded to serve women writers everywhere. Visit us at www.shewritespress.com.

The Outskirts of Hope: A Memoir by Jo Ivester. $16.95, 978-1-63152-964-1. A moving, inspirational memoir about how living and working in an all-black town during the height of the civil rights movement profoundly affected the author's entire family—and how they in turn impacted the community.

All the Ghosts Dance Free: A Memoir by Terry Cameron Baldwin. $16.95, 978-1-63152-822-4. A poetic memoir that explores the legacy of alcoholism and teen suicide in one woman's life—and her efforts to create an authentic existence in the face of that legacy.

The Butterfly Groove: A Mother's Mystery, A Daughter's Journey by Jessica Barraco. $16.95, 978-1-63152-800-2. In an attempt to solve the mystery of her deceased mother's life, Jessica Barraco retraces the older woman's steps nearly forty years earlier—and finds herself along the way.

The Sportscaster's Daughter: A Memoir by Cindi Michael. $16.95, 978-1-63152-107-2. Despite being disowned by her father—sportscaster George Michael, said to be the man who inspired ESPN's *SportsCenter*—Cindi Michael manages financially and heals emotionally, ultimately finding confidence from within.

The S Word by Paolina Milana. $16.95, 978-1-63152-927-6. An insider's account of growing up with a schizophrenic mother, and the disastrous toll the illness—and her Sicilian Catholic family's code of secrecy—takes upon her young life.

Catching Homelessness: A Nurse's Story of Falling Through the Safety Net by Josephine Ensign. $16.95, 978-1-63152-117-1. The compelling true story of a nurse's work with—and young adult passage through—homelessness.